MARSH, MEADOW, MOUNTAIN
Natural Places of the Delaware Valley

NATURAL PLACES OF THE DELAWARE VALLEY

Meadow, Mountain

Edited by John J. Harding

Illustrations by Carol Decker

TEMPLE UNIVERSITY PRESS   Philadelphia

Temple University Press, Philadelphia 19122
Copyright © 1986 by Temple University. All rights reserved
Drawings copyright © Carol Decker
First published 1986
Printed in the United States of America

Library of Congress Cataloging-in-Publication Data
Main entry under title:

Marsh, meadow, mountain.

  Bibliography
  Includes index.
  1. Natural history—Delaware River Valley
(N.Y.–Del. and N.J.)—Guide-books. 2. Delaware
River Valley (N.Y.–Del. and N.J.)—Description
and travel—Guide-books. 3. Natural history—
Pennsylvania—Guide-books. I. Harding, John J.
QH104.5.D44M37 1986   508.749   85-17297
ISBN 0-87722-391-2
ISBN 0-87722-401-3 (pbk.)

To the contributing authors,
whose knowledge and enthusiasm have
made these pages come to life

To Eleanor,
whose constant support and invaluable research
assistance made this guide possible

To my children, John and Kathryn,
whose curiosity and companionship have
added extra joy to our weekend treks

Fred C. Arnold received his M.S. in environmental education from Cornell University in 1976 and has written a number of articles on local natural history as well as *The Painter Trees* (Special Publication no. 1 of the Tyler Arboretum). He was Education Coordinator at the Tyler Arboretum from 1977 to 1983 and is currently Director of the Irvine Natural Science Center near Baltimore.

D. W. Bennett received his A.B. in geology from Amherst College in 1952 and has written books and articles on the natural history of New Jersey (including *New Jersey Coastwalks*). He is Executive Director of the American Littoral Society, Sandy Hook, New Jersey.

Alan Brady has been a birder and bird photographer for many years, lately with an affinity for the ocean. His photographs and articles on nature topics have appeared in numerous periodicals and bird books, both locally and nationally.

Gregory Breese received his B.A. in biology from Rutgers University in 1975 and has worked for the U.S. Fish and Wildlife Service since 1978 at the Tinicum National Environmental Center in Philadelphia.

Carol Decker, naturalist and wildlife artist, has spent countless hours studying, sketching, and painting all of nature over the past thirty-five years. Her work appears regularly in *New Jersey Outdoors* magazine and many other regional and national publications and books, including more recently *Wood Notes* and *Memories from a Naturalist's Notebook*.

Anne Galli holds an M.S. in ecology from Rutgers University and has authored numerous articles on the natural history of New Jersey. She has been an environmental educator for fifteen years, was formerly the Assistant Director of the Wetlands Institute, and is presently Director of Environmental Operations for the Hackensack Meadowlands Development Commission, New Jersey.

LIST OF CONTRIBUTORS

John J. Harding, M.D. has been an avid naturalist since childhood and has co-authored *Birding the Delaware Valley Region*. Professionally, he is the Director of the Consultation-Liaison Psychiatry Service at Temple University Hospital and a recent recipient of the Lindback Foundation Award for Distinguished Teaching at Temple University School of Medicine.

Louis Harris, M.D. is a physician whose interest in the Pine Barrens developed over two decades of walking its roads and trails and canoeing its rivers. He is presently Associate Professor of Psychiatry at Temple University School of Medicine and the Director of the Psychiatric Inpatient Unit at Temple University Hospital.

Jacquelyn L. Katzmire is currently working toward a B.S. in both environmental studies and biology at East Stroudsburg University, Pennsylvania. She is Project Coordinator and Principal Investigator for the Delaware Water Gap National Recreation Area Wintering Bald Eagle Study, now in its second year.

Larry M. Rymon received his Ph.D. from Oregon State University in 1968. At present, Dr. Rymon is Professor of Biology and Coordinator of the Environmental Studies Program at East Stroudsburg University. He serves as the Director of Research for both the Pennsylvania River Otter Reintroduction Program and the Pennsylvania Osprey Reintroduction Program.

The Mountains 83
Delaware Water Gap
National Recreation Area,
Pennsylvania
BY LARRY M. RYMON AND JACQUELYN L. KATZMIRE

The Eastern Deciduous Forest 3
Ridley Creek State Park and
Tyler Arboretum, Pennsylvania
BY JOHN J. HARDING AND FRED C. ARNOLD

The Fresh-Water Marsh 49
Tinicum National
Environmental Center, Pennsylvania
BY GREGORY BREESE

CONTENTS

PREFACE xi
INDEX 243

The Atlantic Ocean 221
Pelagic Boat Trip
from the New Jersey Coast
BY ALAN BRADY

The Pine Barrens 125
Wharton State Forest, New Jersey
BY LOUIS HARRIS

The Salt-Water Marsh 157
Wetlands Institute, New Jersey
BY ANNE GALLI

The Barrier Beach and Island 193
Stone Harbor Point, New Jersey
BY D. W. BENNETT

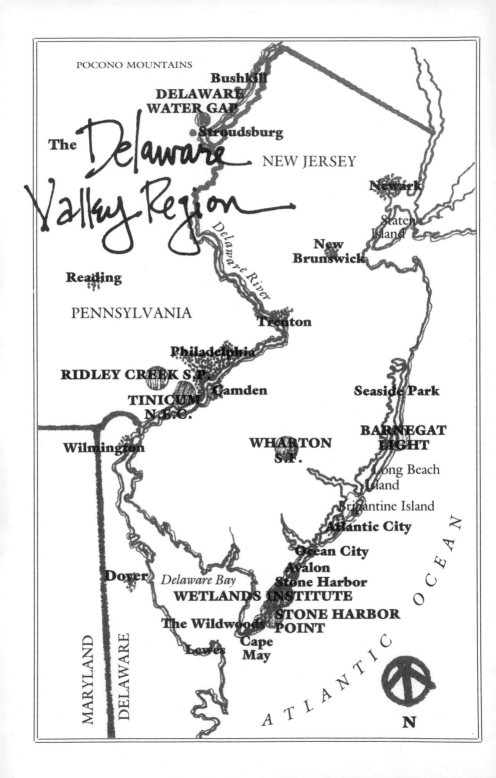

PREFACE

The Delaware Valley Region is a land of rich historical, cultural, and environmental diversity. Stretching eastward from the rolling farmlands of Lancaster County, in southeastern Pennsylvania, across the Delaware River and the New Jersey coastal plain to the Atlantic Ocean, this expanse is bounded on the north by the Pocono Mountains, an extension of the Appalachian system, and on the south by Delaware Bay. Few other locales in the United States contain as many varied habitats—each with its distinctive vegetation and wildlife.

This book will help the reader begin to explore the many ecosystems between the ocean and the mountains. These include salt- and fresh-water marshes, barrier beaches, "pine barrens," deciduous woodlands, Canadian-zone or boreal forests, meadows, and successional fields, among others. Chapters on seven prime habitats have been written by expert naturalists—each with a long-standing knowledge of his or her chosen area. Some are professionals who have served as biologists and educators for nature centers, while others are weekend hobbyists. All share a love for the special places they describe.

Each site has been chosen because it is both representative of the habitat and accessible to visitors. Because other sites may be equally worthy, a list of these is included at the end of each chapter. Each chapter also includes detailed maps, traveler's directions, and a suggested reading list.

The focus throughout the book centers on the interrelationships among living things in the biological community. Each naturalist discusses those birds, trees, shrubs, wildflowers, mammals, reptiles, amphibians, butterflies, insects, fish, and invertebrates that are most likely to be encountered in that ecosystem. Species names generally conform to the most recent field guide terminology; former or alternate names are included in parentheses for first usage in each chapter. The authors also take note of the increasing and often disruptive role of man in the system. The accent is on spring and summer walks when the greatest variety of species are present and when the amateur naturalist is most likely to be afield. An exception is the salt-water marsh, which is best visited during the early fall when there are fewer marauding insects. However, there is also reference to species present during other seasons because, in fact, a trip to these areas is worthwhile any time of the year. Of course, not all the species mentioned will be seen on any one trip. The reader is taken on a guided excursion—either walking or driving (or boating, in one instance)—that best samples the habitat. Occasionally two or more walks replace a single extended tour, especially when the site (Ridley Creek State Park or the Pine Barrens, for example) includes more than one type of ecosystem.

Within a two-hour drive from Philadelphia, one can find virtually every habitat from ocean to mountains. Proximity to several other metropolitan areas in the "northeast corridor" (New York City, Baltimore, Washington, D.C., etc.) make these fragile wilds even more attractive. Why does the Delaware Valley Region possess such diversity? Part of the answer lies in the area's geological history. The quality of the soil (moisture, porosity, mineral content, etc.), as influenced by its underlying geology, largely determines the characteristic vegetation, and the vegetation largely determines the associated wildlife.

The region is composed of five physiographic provinces or zones (physiography is the study of the land's physical features above and below the surface). The first province, the Atlantic Coastal Plain, stretches westward from the Atlantic Ocean across central and southern New Jersey and coastal Delaware to the "fall line." The "fall line," where Atlantic-bound rivers and streams become unnavigable due to rapids and falls, runs on a diagonal roughly drawn through Trenton, New Jersey, Philadelphia, Pennsylvania, and Wilmington, Delaware. This "fall line," which generally runs in a northeast to southwest direction as do the physiographic provinces, transects the Delaware River Valley several times. West and northwest of here is the second province—the Piedmont, with its rolling hills, farmlands, deciduous woodlands, and successional fields. The Piedmont encompasses much of central New Jersey, most of southeastern Pennsylvania, and the northern tip of Delaware. Working northwestward, one next encounters the Reading Prong, a thin sliver of ancient, eroded mountains that are part of the New England Upland Province. Known as the Highlands as they cut across northern New Jersey, they barely dip into Pennsylvania at Reading. Further northwestward one encounters the Ridge and Valley Province with its Kittatinny Ridge (part of the Appalachians), which includes such important locales for the naturalist as the Delaware Water Gap National Recreation Area and Hawk Mountain Sanctuary. The Delaware Valley Region's northernmost limit is the Appalachian Plateau Province, which contains much of what we call the Pocono Mountains; Canadian-zone forests can still be found here. Remnants of these boreal forests also exist along the Kittatinny Ridge.

Readers interested in a more detailed description of our area's geological underpinnings (such as plate tectonics or volcanic eruptions) and the effect of our climatic history (such as ice ages or glacial retreats) are referred to several excellent texts in the reading list following the Preface. In addition, each chapter includes a brief geological-historical description of "how the area came to be." Of special note is an excellent summary found in "The Mountains."

This book is intended for readers interested in the natural world; it assumes there is a desire to learn something more about common indigenous birds, trees, wildflowers, mammals, butterflies, and so forth. Those looking for novel recreational opportunities are also welcome, and this book suggests where to go and what to see, hear, smell, and touch. Readers should be aware of the excellent Peterson Field Guide Series, which offers an identification guide for everything from birds to stars, from wildflowers to animal tracks. The Golden Field Guide Series is also very good, although to date it lacks a guide for some major subjects. Similarly, the reader should possess some basic equipment. Binoculars, for example, are invaluable. The standard 7×35 power is probably the most versatile, although eight, nine, and ten power are often preferred by those interested in birding. A hand-held magnifying lens is helpful for examining the more diminutive members of the flower, moss, insect, and invertebrate families. A compass and topographical maps are good investments, especially in the wilderness areas of the Pine Barrens and the Poconos.

Many of the parks, refuges, and nature centers mentioned in this book serve a potpourri of guided nature walks, identification seminars, and educational classes that appeal to the beginner and experienced naturalist alike. A seasonal calendar of events is usually available at their headquarters. Various organizations, including bird clubs, local Audubon Society chapters, horticultural groups, and even shell and herpetology (reptiles and amphibians) clubs have a full schedule of activities catering to the wants of those hobbyists. Becoming a member of the Academy of Natural Sciences of Philadelphia at 19th and the Parkway is highly recommended—not only for the use of its museum facilities but also for its wealth of periodic exhibits, nature tours, ecology workshops, lectures, and just for contact with others akin in mind and spirit.

Since practically all the locations in this book lie within a two-hour drive of Philadelphia, there is little worry about overnight accommodations. The weather is generally cooperative, with daytime temperatures in the summer averaging 80°–92° F while the winter norms range between 25° and 45°. Spring (mid-April through May) is probably the best time to be afield and is absolutely glorious with temperatures in the sixties and seventies. However, one should remember that the Pocono Mountains are approximately five to ten degrees cooler than other areas; also, although the coast is often a few degrees warmer in the winter, gusty winds create a bracing wind-chill factor. Most of the refuges have excellent foot trails, so walking shoes are usually adequate. Rubber boots are useful for those addicted to sloshing through marshes. Serious hazards are rare indeed, but nuisances such as Poison-ivy, biting flies, ticks, and mosquitos can be expected June through September, depending on the locale. Simple precautions and insect repellent can minimize these drawbacks.

Above all else, this guide is intended to whet the appetite for experiencing the dynamic interactions between a living habitat and its inhabitants. I hope that this introduction will encourage readers to discover and explore their own favorite beaches, marshes, and forests—their own "special place" to be.

John J. Harding

General Suggested Readings

A suggested reading list specific to each habitat follows each subsequent chapter. The following list is composed of books, articles, and other materials that cover special geographical sections or combinations of several habitats in the Delaware Valley Region. Also included are texts of general interest spanning such topics as the geology of the area, ecology, animal behavior, and regional vegetation and wildlife.

Some of the following books are available in local bookstores. The more specialized or dated material may only be found in reference libraries. Much of this list, however, is stocked in the bookstores associated with various nature centers (for example, Schuylkill Valley Nature Center, Tyler Arboretum, and Rancocas Nature Center). Most are also available from the publisher. Particular mention should be made of Dover Publications, which specializes in republication of rare books and scholarly natural history classics. Many of their works are available through the National Audubon Society, 950 Third Avenue, New York, N.Y. 10022. Phone: (212) 832-3200.

Akers, James F. *All Year Birding in Southern New Jersey*. Pomona, N.J.: Center for Environmental Research, Stockton State College, 1981.

Anderson, Karl. "Turtles, the Reptiles of New Jersey." *New Jersey Outdoors*, March/April 1984, pp. 17–20.

Andrews, William A., ed. *A Guide to the Study of Terrestrial Ecology*. Englewood Cliffs, N.J.: Prentice-Hall, 1974.

Bates, M. *The Forest and the Sea*. New York: Random House, 1960.

Berger, Andrew J. *Bird Study*. New York: Dover Publications, 1961.

Boyle, William J., Jr., ed. *New Jersey Field Trip Guide*. Summit, N.J.: Summit Nature Club, 1979.

Brady, Alan, et al. *A Field List of Birds of the Delaware Valley Region*. Philadelphia: Delaware Valley Ornithological Club. In Press.

Brown, Vinson. *The Amateur Naturalist's Handbook*. Englewood Cliffs, N.J.: Prentice-Hall, 1980.

Claibourne, Robert. *Climate, Man and History*. New York: W. W. Norton, 1970.

Clapham, W. B., Jr. *Natural Ecosystems*. New York: Macmillan, 1973.

Cruickshank, Alan D., and Helen G. Cruickshank. *1001 Questions Answered about Birds*. New York: Dover Publications, 1976.

Curtis, Brian. *The Life Story of the Fish: His Manners and Morals*. New York: Dover Publications, 1961.

Dann, Kevin T. *25 Walks in New Jersey*. New Brunswick, N.J.: Rutgers University Press, 1982.

Dennis, John V. *A Complete Guide to Bird Feeding*. New York: Alfred A. Knopf, 1975.

Durrell, Gerald, and Lee Durrell. *The Amateur Naturalist*. New York: Alfred A. Knopf, 1984.

Eibl-Eibesfeldt, I. *Ethology: The Biology of Behavior*. New York: Holt, Rinehart and Winston, 1970.

Fables, David. *Annotated List of New Jersey Birds*. Newark, N.J.: Urner Ornithological Club, 1955.

Farb, Peter. *Ecology*. New York: Life Nature Library, Time-Life Books, 1964.

———. *The Living Soil*. New York: Harper & Row, 1959.

Felt, Ephraim Porter. *Plant Galls and Gall Makers*. Ithaca, N.Y.: Comstock, 1940.

Fenneman, N. M. *Physiography of the Eastern United States*. New York: McGraw-Hill, 1938.

Fleming, Lorraine M. *Delaware's Outstanding Natural Areas and Their Preservation*. Hockessin, Del.: Delaware Nature Education Society, 1978.

Freethy, Ron. *How Birds Work: A Guide to Bird Biology*. London: Blandford Press, 1982; distributed by Sterling Publishing, New York.

Frost, Stuart W. *Insect Life and Insect Natural History*. New York: Dover Publications, 1959.

Geyer, Alan R., and William H. Bolles. *Outstanding Scenic Geological Features of Pennsylvania*. Harrisburg, Pa.: Bureau of Topographic and Geologic Survey, 1979.

Gibbons, Euell. *Stalking the Wild Asparagus*. New York: David McKay, 1962.

Godfrey, Michael A. *A Sierra Club Naturalist's Guide: The Piedmont*. San Francisco: Sierra Club Books, 1980. (Excellent.)

Goodwin, Bruce K. *Guidebook to the Geology of the Philadelphia Area*. Harrisburg, Pa.: Pennsylvania Geological Survey, Bulletin G 41, 1964.

Griffin, Donald R. *Bird Migration*. New York: Dover Publications, 1974.

Hall, Alan. *The Wild Food Trailguide*. New York: Holt, Rinehart and Winston, 1973.

Harding, John J., and Justin J. Harding. *Birding the Delaware Valley Region: A Comprehensive Guide to Birdwatching in Southeastern Pennsylvania, Central and Southern New Jersey, and Northcentral Delaware*. Philadelphia: Temple University Press, 1980.

Headstrom, Richard. *Adventures with Insects*. New York: Dover Publications, 1982.

———. *Nature Discoveries with a Hand Lens*. New York: Dover Publications, 1981.

Hoffman, Carolyn. *Fifty Hikes in Eastern Pennsylvania*. Woodstock, Vt.: Backcountry Publications, 1982.

Keehn, Sally M., and David C. Keehn. *Hexcursions: Daytripping in and around Pennsylvania's Dutch Country, the Delaware Valley and Poconos*. New York: Hastings House, 1982.

Kilham, Lawrence. *A Naturalist's Field Guide*. Harrisburg, Pa.: Stackpole Books, 1981.

Klots, Alexander B., and Elsie B. Klots. *1001 Questions Answered about Insects*. New York: Dover Publications, 1977.

Krieger, Louis C. C. *The Mushroom Handbook*. New York: Dover Publications, 1967.

Lawrence, Susannah. *The Audubon Society Field Guide to the Natural Places of the Mid-Atlantic States: Coastal*. New York: Pantheon Books, 1984.

——— and Barbara Gross. *The Audubon Society Field Guide to the Natural Places of the Mid-Atlantic States: Inland*. New York: Pantheon Books, 1984.

Laycock, George. *The Bird Watcher's Bible*. Garden City, N.Y.: Doubleday, 1976.

Leahy, Christopher. *The Birdwatcher's Companion: An Encyclopedic Handbook of North American Birdlife*. New York: Hill and Wang, 1982.

Leck, Charles F. *Birds of New Jersey: Their Habits and Habitats*. New Brunswick, N.J.: Rutgers University Press, 1975.

————. *The Status and Distribution of New Jersey's Birds*. New Brunswick, N.J.: Rutgers University Press, 1984.

Lomax, Joseph L., Joan M. Galli, and Anne E. Galli. *The Wildlife of Cape May County, New Jersey*. Pomona, N.J.: Center for Environmental Research, Stockton State College, 1980.

Marshall, Norman B. *The Life of Fishes*. Cleveland, Ohio: World, 1966.

Martin, A. C., H. S. Zim, and A. L. Nelson. *American Wildlife and Plants: A Guide to Wildlife Food Habits*. New York: Dover Publications, 1961.

McPhee, John. *In Suspect Terrain*. New York: Farrar, Straus & Giroux, 1983.

Mead, Chris. *Bird Migration*. New York: Facts on File, 1983.

Morgan, Ann Haven. *Field Book of Animals in Winter*. New York: G. P. Putnam & Sons, 1939.

New Jersey Audubon. Published monthly by New Jersey Audubon Society, 790 Ewing Avenue, Franklin Lakes, N.J. 07417.

New Jersey Outdoors. Published bimonthly by New Jersey Outdoors, P.O. Box 1390, Trenton, N.J. 08625.

Palmer, E. Laurence, and H. Seymour Fowler. *Fieldbook of Natural History*. New York: McGraw-Hill, 1975.

Parker, Hampton W. *Snakes of the World*. New York: Dover Publications, 1977.

Perrone, Steve, ed. *Guide to New Jersey's Wildlife Management Areas*. 5th ed. Trenton, N.J.: Department of Environmental Protection, Division of Fish, Game and Shellfisheries, 1984.

Perry, John, and Jane G. Perry. *The Random House Guide to Natural Areas of the Eastern United States*. New York: Random House, 1980.

Pettingill, Olin S., Jr. *A Guide to Bird Finding East of the Mississippi.* 2nd ed. New York: Oxford University Press, 1977.

Poole, Earl L. *Pennsylvania Birds: An Annotated List.* Philadelphia: Delaware Valley Ornithological Club, 1964.

Pyle, Michael. *The Audubon Society Handbook for Butterfly Watchers.* New York: Charles Scribner & Sons, 1984.

Quinn, John R. *The Winter Woods.* Old Greenwich, Conn.: Chatham Press, 1976.

Ricklets, Robert. *The Economy of Nature: A Textbook in Basic Ecology.* Portland, Ore.: Chiron Press, 1976.

Riley, Laura, and William Riley. *Guide to the National Wildlife Refuges.* Garden City, N.Y.: Doubleday, Anchor Press, 1979.

Robichaud, Beryl, and Murray F. Buell. *Vegetation of New Jersey: A Study of Landscape Diversity.* New Brunswick, N.J.: Rutgers University Press, 1973.

Ruffner, James A. *Climates of the United States.* Detroit, Mich.: Gale Research, 1978.

Saunders, Charles F. *Edible and Useful Wild Plants of the United States and Canada.* New York: Dover Publications, 1976.

Smith, Howard. *A Naturalist's Guide to the Year.* New York: E. P. Dutton, 1985.

Smith, Richard P. *Animal Tracks and Signs of North America.* Harrisburg, Pa.: Stackpole Books, 1982.

Smith, Robert Leo. *Ecology and Field Biology.* 3rd ed. New York: Harper & Row, 1980. (The "definitive" text.)

Stearn, Colin W., Thomas H. Clark, and Robert L. Carroll. *Geological Evolution of North America.* New York: John Wiley & Sons, 1979.

Stokes, Donald W. *A Guide to Bird Behavior,* vol. 1. Boston: Little, Brown, 1979.

———. *A Guide to Observing Insect Lives.* Boston: Little, Brown, 1983.

——— and Lillian Q. Stokes. *A Guide to Bird Behavior,* vol. 2. Boston: Little, Brown, 1983.

——— and Lillian Q. Stokes. *A Guide to Enjoying Wildflowers.* Boston: Little, Brown, 1985.

Tinbergen, N. *Animal Behavior.* New York: Life Nature Library, Time-Life Books, 1965.

U.S. Department of Agriculture. *Common Weeds of the United States*. New York: Dover Publications, 1971.

Von Frisch, Karl. *Animal Architecture*. New York: Harcourt Brace Jovanovich, 1974.

Wakeley, James S., and Lillian D. Wakeley. *Birds of Pennsylvania: Natural History and Conservation*. Harrisburg, Pa.: Pennsylvania Game Commission, 1984.

Willard, Bradford. *Pennsylvania Geology Summarized*. Pennsylvania Topographic and Geologic Service, Educational Series no. 4. Harrisburg, Pa.: Pennsylvania Department of Environmental Resources, 1962.

Wolfe, Peter E. *The Geology and Landscapes of New Jersey*. New York: Crane, Russak, 1977.

Wood, Merrill. *Birds of Pennsylvania: When and Where to Find Them*. Rev. ed. University Park, Pa.: Pennsylvania State University, Agricultural Experiment Station, 1973.

Woodbury, David O. *The Great White Mantle*. New York: Viking Press, 1962.

MARSH, MEADOW, MOUNTAIN
Natural Places of the Delaware Valley

the Eastern Deciduous Forest

JOHN J. HARDING
FRED C. ARNOLD

A collage of assorted broad-leaved hardwood trees with their accompanying vegetation and wildlife once dominated much of the eastern United States. They formed vast tracts of "deciduous" woodlands, that is, forests of trees that shed their leaves each year after the growing season. Hardly any virgin woodlands remain in our area; most of the deciduous trees we see today are second-, third-, or even fourth-generation descendants.

Since colonial times trees have been razed for lumber and the creation of agricultural lands, or ravaged by fires and disease. The American Chestnut, for example, was "king" of the eastern deciduous forest until dethroned by a blight introduced from

3

the Orient in the early 1900s. Through a process called "succession," which will be discussed later in this chapter, these laid-bare areas have regenerated into mature forests again. Scientists also call a mature woodland a "climax" forest, which means an ecosystem in which the plant community is able to perpetuate itself.

The mature forest, while stable, is not static. For example, when wind or the axe or the Gypsy Moth fells a large oak, a skylight in the canopy is created allowing sunlight to bathe the forest floor. In this new light, young upstarts of the same species and other trees and plants compete for eventual dominance as they head for the sky.

Trees and plants, with their leaves converting water and carbon dioxide into food via the process of photosynthesis, are the primary *producers* found in this habitat. Everything else depends on them. *Consumers*, including other forms of vegetation (decomposers like fungi) and wildlife, rely on them for food. Multiple food chains and webs form—many of which lead to man. Just as important, oxygen is released during the food production process; also, plants "scrub" the air and soil, removing various harmful toxins from our environment. Our forests are truly the givers of life.

A variety of other habitats—fresh-water streams, open meadows, and successional fields (meadows gradually developing into woods)—are often intimately associated with the eastern deciduous forest. We will explore two such natural areas in southeastern Pennsylvania.

Although these are not virgin forests, large parts have been untouched by man for many decades. These forests grow on the clayey but surprisingly fertile soils of the Piedmont, whose many productive farms testify to the eons of accumulated organic material. The terrain is a vast plain of gently rolling hills which are but remnants of a very ancient mountain system worn down over the ages by erosion.

RIDLEY CREEK STATE PARK

Ridley Creek State Park, a 2,600-acre tract in Delaware County, Pennsylvania, acquired during the 1960s and opened to public use in 1972, was part of the former Jeffords estate.

WORKINGS OF AN ECOSYSTEM

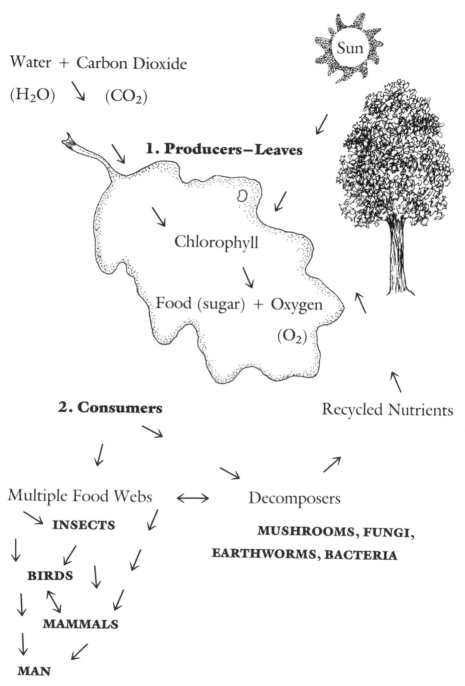

Water + Carbon Dioxide

(H_2O) (CO_2)

Sun

1. Producers–Leaves

Chlorophyll

Food (sugar) + Oxygen

(O_2)

Recycled Nutrients

2. Consumers

Multiple Food Webs ⟷ Decomposers

INSECTS

MUSHROOMS, FUNGI,
EARTHWORMS, BACTERIA

BIRDS

MAMMALS

MAN

The Jeffords' Hunting Hill mansion, constructed in 1914, now serves as the park office and reception center. In addition to several historic colonial buildings on the grounds, the park provides facilities for hiking, horseback riding, biking, cross-country skiing, trout fishing, and picnicking. The Colonial Pennsylvania Plantation within the state park is a living museum of a 1776 Delaware County farm. For an admission fee, the public may observe and participate in authentic colonial farming scenes, including the making of farm tools, clothing, furniture, and colonial meals. Other colonial chores include spinning, crop harvesting, butter churning, salting and smoking of meat, and food preservation. The Plantation is closed during the winter months.

Nearby, the Tyler (Painter) Arboretum, over 700 acres of both formal and informal plant collections, has extensive hiking trails and is famous for its rhododendron collection, dogwood and holly plantings, and a 120-year-old Giant Sequoia. This acreage was originally granted by William Penn of Philadelphia fame to Thomas Minshall and remained in the possession of his descendants—Minshalls, Painters, and Tylers—until it was bequeathed as a public arboretum in 1945. Several historic buildings—for example, Lachford Hall—grace the grounds and provide a glimpse of gentry life during the mid-1800s. Tyler Arboretum sponsors various nature-oriented activities for members and nonmembers alike, including birdwatching rambles, wildflower walks, "owl prowls," and supervised courses dealing with everything from flower arranging to children's programs on insect and pond study. A seasonal schedule of activities is available at the historic old barn which has been developed as an educational center and bookstore.

One of the more exciting walks in Ridley Creek State Park is along Sycamore Mills Road adjoining Ridley Creek itself, with a short excursion up Forge Road. This area, located in the extreme southeastern portion of the park, is worth a visit throughout the year, with each season providing its own delights. Spring, especially the month of May, is perhaps the best time, as a wealth of both migrating and nesting birds, deciduous trees, wildflowers, reptiles, amphibians, and butterflies are in full display.

Begin at the Sycamore Mills Bridge at the junction of Bishop Hollow Road (Ridley Creek Road) and Chapel Hill Road; you can park immediately to the right of the bridge in an eighteen-car paved lot, or go seventy yards to the left along Barren Road to a smaller six-car earthen lot. Check the roadside bank between these lots for an enormous bed of the lovely wildflower Dutchman's-breeches which will be described in more detail shortly. After passing around the gate by the first parking lot next to the bridge, check the vine-draped Eastern White Pines beside the old house for migrating warblers and vireos. Well over twenty species of warblers pass through Ridley Creek State Park during their spring migration, while at least fourteen kinds remain to breed along Sycamore Mills and Forge Roads.

Scan the sparsely leaved Black Walnut trees bordering the parking lot for the Ruby-throated Hummingbird in May and early June. Later in the summer, these diminutive birds flit from resting perches to savor the nectar of the orange Trumpet-creeper flowers that encircle the upper reaches of the huge Black Walnut near the old springhouse. Since the Black Walnut, a favorite of the early settlers, was often planted around their dwellings, their presence makes it worthwhile to search for ruins in even the thickest of woods.

Across from the springhouse, American Sycamore trees with their mottled bark and late-emerging leaves loom over Ridley Creek and its trout fishermen. The more open canopy of the streamside provides good nesting for brightly ornamented Northern (Baltimore) Orioles, while overhead Chimney Swifts engage in aerial acrobatics. Throughout May, you will notice birdwatchers by the gate searching for the Cerulean Warbler. This handsome blue and white warbler—first heard, then seen—gleans insects from the canopy leaves shading Sycamore Mills Road.

Continue to walk north (upstream) along Sycamore Mills Road, which has been closed to auto traffic since it became part of the state park in the 1970s. For the next 150 yards American Sycamores line the creek and shade several colonial buildings, remnants of a small eighteenth-century village which grew up around the site of a mill. Now known as Sycamore Mills, the area was once variously named Bishop's Mill and Upper

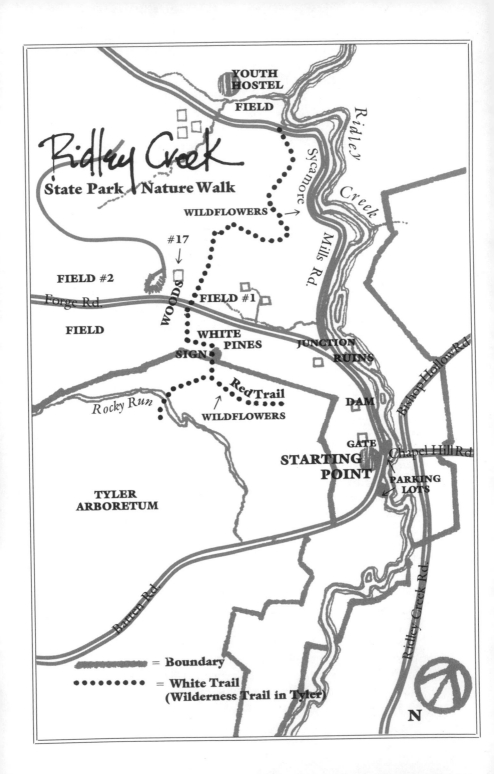

Providence Corn Mill, and has been designated as the "Ridley Creek Historic District" on the National Register of Historic Places. To the left is a typical eastern deciduous woodland (which will be described shortly). A large boulder dam and waterfall soon interrupt Ridley Creek; Cedar Waxwings sometimes mob this area during their fall migration (late August through September) and snatch insects that hatch from the stream. Immediately above the dam and across from an old house is a small stand of Common Sunflowers; these attract American Goldfinches during the late summer and early fall when the flowerheads go to seed. During the warmer months, Eastern Painted Turtles, Northern Water Snakes, and Green and Pickerel Frogs bask on the partially submerged logs ringing the small island above the dam. Check the exposed creek edges above the dam for the Black, Spicebush, and Eastern Tiger Swallowtail butterflies; they often alight on the mineral-rich mud mid-April through May. Black Willow trees border the creek here and are a favorite haunt for the Yellow Warbler. In May, look for the Brown-headed Cowbird awaiting a chance to lay its own egg in the Yellow Warbler's nest. In some years, a pair of Canada Geese nest in the vicinity and loudly chase fishermen who approach too closely.

Continue to walk north (upstream) along Sycamore Mills Road for another seventy yards until Forge Road leads to the left up a wooded hillside. As you pass the burned-out colonial house on your right look for the yellow Pale Touch-me-not (Jewelweed), which blooms during the summer (late July through September). Another nice stand guards the parking lot back by the gate. The more abundant orange Spotted Touch-me-not can be found in many moist locations along Ridley Creek. Touch-me-not is somewhat of a misnomer, since the plant is benign; its seed pods pop open when brushed against by a passerby during the early fall. Earlier to blossom, Celandine, a member of the poppy family with four-petaled, yellow flowers, also stands nearby. Scolding chatter reveals the Red Squirrel, which is usually more at home in evergreen forests. You may also glimpse the secretive Eastern Chipmunk as it scurries about the rocky stubble of the foundation.

At the junction with Forge Road, check the bank between Sycamore Mills Road and the creek for a small, wild planting of Dutchman's-breeches, a member of the bleeding-heart family which blooms in late April and early May. Its fernlike leaves guard the delicate spray of creamy, upside-down pantaloons that gives this wildflower its name. Here, too, look for Cutleaved Toothwort, Spring-beauty, and Trout-lily (Adder's-tongue). The Acadian Flycatcher, with its distinctive *ka-zeek'* or *piz-za'* call, nests on the low-hanging branches of the American Beech. The smooth gray bark of these trees is scarred with the graffiti of generations. In May, listen for the loud rattle of the Belted Kingfisher as it patrols the creek searching for fish. Over a month before, even as early as the first mild days in mid-March and before the songbirds have returned, the loud chirping of the Northern Spring Peepers fills the air. Hundreds of these small frogs breed in the brushy pools lining Ridley Creek, yet are rarely seen. By mid-April, the chorus of peepers is joined by the long trilling calls of American Toads.

The lush wet woodlands along Ridley Creek are preferred by flora and fauna that can tolerate the frequent flooding inherent to such streams. In addition to trees like the Black Willow, American Sycamore, American Beech, and an occasional Black Walnut, the following may also be found: Green Ash, Red and Silver Maples, Box Elder (Ashleaf Maple), Shagbark Hickory, River Birch, Swamp White and Pin Oaks, Sweetgum and Sour-gum (Black Gum or Black Tupelo), Honey Locust, American Elm, Eastern (Common) Cottonwood, American Hornbeam (Blue Beech), Hazel (Smooth) Alder, and Hackberry, among others.

This wet or "hydric" zone blends almost imperceptibly into the well-drained or "mesic" woodlands bordering Forge Road. Many tree species occur in both zones as long as sufficient moisture is available. Forge Road's moderately sloping hillsides exemplify the "classic" eastern deciduous forest that accounts for the largest percentage of woodlands in the Piedmont Region of the Delaware Valley. Most of the remainder of this chapter will concentrate on the mesic environment.

The third and last subtype of eastern deciduous forest—dry or "xeric"—tends to occur on steeper slopes with poor, thin soils that rapidly drain water. Although more common in the mountainous regions of the tristate area, a few stands occur in the more hilly sections of Tyler Arboretum's East Woods. Such dry woodlands are often populated by a less diverse oak-hickory community (with Chestnut Oak often predominating). Similar habitats can also be found along the Atlantic Coastal Plain, whose sandy, porous soils prove equally inept at retaining water despite a much gentler slope. It is important to remember that in many locales these three zones are but arbitrary divisions that gradually mix and blend.

The trees of these deciduous woodlands shed their leaves every autumn, usually after a spectacular riot of colors. This results from adaptation to avoid excessive water loss through the leaves (which normally give off water vapor through a process called transpiration) during a time when water is much less available because of winter's freezing. On some cue, perhaps the onset of cooler, drier weather, perhaps the decreasing length of daylight—but not frost as is commonly believed—a band of cells forms at the base of the stem, gradually cutting off the water supply to the leaf. This causes the die-off of the water-sensitive green chlorophyll pigment that is responsible for photosynthesis and food production. As this pigment disappears and the green color fades, the other natural pigments present in the leaf (the reds, oranges, yellows, purples, and so on) get a chance to show off their finery, however briefly, before the leaf falls. Thereafter is the best time to spot evergreens, including pines, spruces, firs, and hemlocks, which are generally absent in such an environment and often reflect plantings by man. The most common of the uncommon evergreens in the mature deciduous forest are the Eastern White Pine and the Eastern Hemlock, the latter favoring steep, north-facing ravines.

The deciduous woodland is a complex plant community with four distinct layers of vegetation: the canopy of the tallest trees, the understory (subcanopy) made up of younger trees of the same species and other species which mature to a shorter height, the shrub layer, and the herbaceous layer of ferns and wildflowers. Each layer provides wildlife different opportunities for food and shelter. The casual walker must pay attention to all these layers in order to discover the richness of the forest.

Approximately ten yards up Forge Road, a Shagbark Hickory greets the visitor; its shaggy, gray, disheveled bark is especially noticeable during winter. Further up the incline, where the soil tends to be a bit drier, Mockernut and Pignut Hickories are occasionally found. American Beech, Tuliptree, White and Green Ashes, and various oaks and maples abound in the canopy. The highest trees are the Tuliptrees or Yellow-poplars, the tallest species in eastern North America, with distinctive greenish-yellow, tulip-shaped flowers that crown their extensive foliage.

The oak family is strongly represented and can be split into two general groups: the White Oaks and the Black (or Red) Oaks. Members of the Black group, including the Black, Northern Red, and Scarlet Oaks (these oaks frequently hybridize making exact identification difficult), are by far the most common here. They can be told from the White Oak group, including the White and the Chestnut Oaks, by the shape of their leaves, bark color, and acorns. Leaves of the Black Oak group have sharp, pointed lobes with bristle-tipped teeth compared to the smooth, rounded lobes of the White Oak group. The Black Oak group generally has darker bark and bitter-tasting acorns which take two years to mature. The sweeter White Oak acorns take only one season for maturation. Watch for Gray Squirrels, especially during early fall, when they gather various nuts for winter storage.

The commonest maple is the Red Maple, a sometimes canopy participant, especially when teamed with American Beech, but most of the time serving as "king of the understory." Its leaves have triangular, finely toothed lobes compared to the five-lobed, prominently toothed leaves of the less common Sugar and Norway Maples. Flowering Dogwood, Sour-gum, American Hornbeam (Blue Beech), and Eastern Hophornbeam (Ironwood) are also popular inhabitants of the understory. Mapleleaf Viburnum, Witch-hazel, and Spicebush are the most common species in the shrub layer, thriving on the light filtered through the dense canopy. The latter two favor the moister regions towards the bottom of slopes.

These woods host many species of native wildflowers growing in the herbaceous layer—plants that either bloom before the trees have leafed-out or are especially adapted to shade. As you walk up Forge Road during early May, you will see Dutchman's-breeches along with Wild Geranium, Wild Ginger, Common Blue and Smooth Yellow Violets, False Solomon's-seal, Solomon's-seal, May-apple, Jack-in-the-pulpit, and various ferns. A few weeks earlier, before the trees have leafed-out, Cut-leaved Toothwort, Spring-beauty, Trout-lily, and Bloodroot blossom; the latter two are all but done by May 1. Although both Solomon's-seals have oval, green leaves alternating along their stems, the False Solomon's-seal is graced with a terminal cluster of airy, white flowers leading some to call it Solomon's Plume, while the Solomon's-seal ("true") has paired greenish-yellow flowers along the length of the stalk.

Halfway up the incline, to the right and immediately bordering the macadam road, look for the spectacular Showy Orchis poking out from the leaf litter during mid-May. One or two specimens of this lovely member of the orchid family, with purple and white blooms spiraling around its central spike, can sometimes be seen if not trampled underfoot by a passerby. Loose colonies of May-apples are scattered along the hillsides, especially the moister sections. Their single, large, white flower, peeking out from under umbrella-like leaves, soon turns into an oblong, green fruit (the "apple" that is reportedly edible in the fall), but beware of the root, stem, and leaves, which are poisonous. Despite its toxic qualities for humans, May-apple leaves are a favored food of deer during the spring and early summer, leaving many "umbrella-less" stalks to be found by the observant walker.

Approximately four-fifths up the incline and situated at the base of a huge Black Oak (about twenty feet up over the road-bank and to the left of the paved road) is a small patch of Wood Anemone that can just be spotted from the road during early May. Upon closer inspection, notice the simple white blossom surrounded by a whorl of deeply toothed green leaves. Later in the summer, when things have quieted down, search the hillside between the first third of Forge Road and Sycamore Mills Road just below for Indian Cucumber-root (early June), Spotted Wintergreen (late June to early July), Enchanter's Nightshade (July), and Maidenhair Fern. Starting in July, especially during wet summers, look for waxy-white Indian-pipes poking through the leaf litter. This saprophyte, lacking green chlorophyll to manufacture food, obtains its sustenance from decomposing leaves and other material, and in this way is similar to the unrelated, numerous fungi also found here. It's a nice arrangement: since little sunlight reaches the forest floor, the presence of chlorophyll is less helpful and decomposers are greatly needed to help recycle nutrients and add humus to the system.

Please do not pick or otherwise disturb any plants, no matter how seductive. Save them for the next visitor. Transplanting wildflowers to the home garden is often a death sentence as the critical habitat requirements can't be duplicated. Such collecting has been a major cause for several of our native plants' being on the endangered list.

Walking up Forge Road, look and listen for the common nesting songbirds of the eastern deciduous forest: Red-bellied, Hairy, and Downy Woodpeckers, Great Crested Flycatcher, Eastern Wood-Pewee, Carolina Chickadee, Tufted Titmouse, White-breasted Nuthatch, Carolina Wren, Blue-gray Gnatcatcher, Scarlet Tanager, Red-eyed Vireo, Black-and-white Warbler, Ovenbird, Kentucky Warbler, and American Redstart. The loud, rising *teach'-er, teach'-er, teach'-er* . . . song of the Ovenbird is constantly heard May through early July, yet this handsome warbler is rarely seen as it searches the forest floor for insects. Almost as vocal but more pleasing to the ear, the nesting thrushes—American Robin, Wood Thrush, and Veery—abound here. Several of the above species, including the woodpeckers, Great Crested Flycatcher, Carolina Chickadee, Tufted Titmouse, White-breasted Nuthatch, and Carolina Wren, nest in tree cavities excavated from dead or dying hardwoods. With the recent firewood-cutting craze, these species will have fewer nesting sites, making the preservation of areas like Ridley Creek State Park even more pressing.

Among the reptiles and amphibians, the Eastern Box Turtle, Eastern Garter Snake, American Toad, and two color phases of the Red-backed Salamander (red-backed and lead-backed) are the common inhabitants of Ridley Creek State Park's well-drained (mesic) deciduous woodlands. An occasional Spotted Salamander is also encountered, particularly in the spring, when they venture out to visit breeding pools. During April, great numbers of American Toads gather by the creek to breed, and it is not unusual to see the vocal male riding piggy-back on the larger, gravid female as she hugs the muddy edges of the stream and its adjacent pools. Look for other species known to occur in the eastern deciduous forest, including Northern Brown (DeKay's) Snake, Northern Ringneck Snake, and Wood Turtle. Although I have never seen them at Ridley Creek State Park, as a youngster I chanced upon them occasionally in woodland tracts to the west and north (in French Creek State Park and Delmont Boy Scout Reservation, for example). They like to hide under and about rocks and decaying logs and are rarely seen.

After climbing several hundred yards along Forge Road, the visitor begins to leave the dark woodland and crosses a running spring which courses down to Ridley Creek. Several varieties of salamanders, including Northern Two-lined, Northern Dusky, and Northern Red Salamanders, can be found here and at other cooler, spring-fed streams throughout the park and nearby Tyler Arboretum. Skunk Cabbage favors the damper areas to the right of the road. Its mottled, brownish-green hood protecting the delicate blossoms within can be seen pushing through barely thawed March mud. On warm March days, the Mourning Cloak butterfly with yellow-trimmed, dark chocolate wings interrupts the relatively dormant landscape. Along with the raspy call of the newly arrived Eastern Phoebe and the now distinct chorus of Northern Spring Peepers, this handsome butterfly promises that spring is soon to follow. Check the muddy areas along the small creek to the right of the road for animal tracks, especially those of the White-tailed Deer, Raccoon, Striped Skunk, and Opossum. Tracks are often the only sign of these largely nocturnal denizens of the woodlands. A large stand of mature Eastern White Pines borders the left side of the road for the next one-quarter mile or so. Be on the lookout for deer!

An interesting side-trip beckons from the other side of these pines. At the top of Forge Road take the white-blazed trail to the left, loop around the top of the pine stand, and walk downhill along the trail paralleling Forge Road. Shortly, at the sign for the Tyler Barn, take the red-blazed trail (Painter Brothers Trail) and walk downhill and east for about fifty yards. Here a heavily wooded hillside descends to Rocky Run Stream below (you are now in Tyler Arboretum). One May, when chasing down the elusive Worm-eating Warbler known mostly by its insect-like trill, I came upon a glorious display of wildflowers on this slope. Wild Geranium, Showy Orchis, and Rue-anemone are plentiful here, in addition to many of the more common wildflowers already described.

Now back to Forge Road! Approximately 150 yards beyond where Forge Road crosses the spring, a narrow road lined by Northern (Common) Catalpa trees leads off to the right toward a group of colonial buildings that serve as a residence for park personnel. Now the habitat begins to change dramatically.

White-tailed Deer

Immediately beyond this road and to the right of Forge Road (opposite the pine stand) is a prime example of a successional field—a scrubby meadow overgrown with saplings and dense thickets of Multiflora Rose, Staghorn and Smooth Sumacs, Japanese Honeysuckle, Virginia Creeper, and wild grapes. This meadow is on its way, slowly but surely, to becoming a deciduous woodland. One-hundred yards farther up Forge Road is another successional field (just beyond picnic area 17); it is generally drier and more open than the first and even earlier in its transition to a woodland. Other fields in the park (along Sandy Flash Drive, for example, which bisects Ridley Creek State Park) are more open and meadowlike. Indeed, the full spectrum of successional changes—from newly mowed fields to climax forest—can be found somewhere in the park at any given time.

There are two types of succession, primary and secondary. Primary succession in our region is infrequent and basically entails the building of soil on barren surfaces such as sand or rocky outcroppings. Primitive plants such as lichens and mosses begin this laborious process. Secondary succession is quicker (though often taking a century or more), much more common in our area, and has allowed the historical cycle of forest-to-farm-to-forest to repeat itself since early European colonization. The soil is already there; only the landscape alters. It is a restorative process of vegetational changes in which certain plant communities replace one another until a self-perpetuating climax community (such as a forest) is attained—that is, barring interference from man or natural catastrophes. Each step of the process, each vanguard of plants and trees is accompanied by wildlife especially adapted to that stage.

The Clement's model has traditionally been used to explain secondary succession. It suggests that succession is predictable, with each plant community changing its local environment to its own detriment, thus preparing the way for the next wave of vegetation and wildlife. Eventually, a stable, self-sustaining ecosystem is established. This view is somewhat oversimplified, and several alternative theories are presently vying for the right to explain the process. The reading list following both the Preface and this chapter will help those who want to pursue this complex topic.

Similarly, the various stages of secondary succession can be either exhaustively defined and split into multiple, complex gradations, or kept simple. The earliest stage is the herbaceous, when various grasses, wildflowers, and small shrubs dominate for approximately a decade. Most of the remaining description of Ridley Creek State Park will showcase the flora and fauna of this fascinating and beautiful stage. Next comes the woody successional phase, when both conifers and hardwoods begin to assert their authority. The Delaware Valley Region is particularly interesting in that a mixture of conifers (Red Cedar [Eastern], Virginia Pine, and so forth) and hardwoods begin to dominate the fields south of a diagonal drawn from Trenton, New Jersey, through the northern part of Philadelphia, to the Maryland-Pennsylvania border. North of this arbitrary line hardwood pioneers tend to dominate during this phase (Black Locust, Red Maple, Green and White Ashes, Black Cherry, American Elm, Flowering Dogwood, Tuliptree, and Ailanthus [Tree-of-Heaven] being among the more common). The final phase is a lengthy, complicated affair with the various trees mentioned above both coexisting and competing among themselves and with newcomers such as American Beech, oaks, and hickories. This latter group will eventually dominate the mature forest. Many pioneers disappear. Some become relegated to the understory, but a few species eventually make it to the top.

Let us return to the walk. The birds, wildflowers, mammals, reptiles, amphibians, and insects found in these fields differ markedly from those inhabiting the deciduous forest. Incidentally, avoid entering all but the periphery of the first two fields. First, most of the representative plants and wildlife can be clearly observed from the edges; the field above picnic area 17 probably offers the better vantage of the two. Second, a combination of briers, ticks, and Poison-ivy makes entry into the thicker sections of these fields unpleasant. Other, more open fields in the park are crisscrossed with paths that provide for easier exploring.

Four brightly colored members of the warbler clan favor these fields for nesting and feeding during May. The Common Yellowthroat, the male with his characteristic "lone ranger" mask, hides in the thickets but often can be lured to view by "psshing" or "squeaking"—a technique of making kissinglike sounds against the back of one's hand. The Yellow-breasted Chat, also a skulker, serves up such a bizarre repertoire of calls, honks, and whistles on early May mornings that the budding naturalist sometimes feels the butt of some practical joke. The Prairie Warbler is also common here, singing its upscale *zee-zee-zee-zee-zee* . . . from the branches of a Sweet (American) Crab Apple or Black Locust sapling. Lastly, the dapper Blue-winged Warbler gives its sneezy *bee'-bzzz* call from the lower branches of the White Ash trees that line Forge Road. Other nesting birds that prefer these brushy meadows and their wooded edges include Ring-necked Pheasant, American Woodcock (look for its dramatic nuptial flights on March evenings), Mourning Dove, Northern (Yellow-shafted) Flicker, Eastern Kingbird, Eastern Phoebe, Willow (Traill's) Flycatcher, Tree and Barn Swallows, American (Common) Crow, House Wren, Northern Mockingbird, Gray Catbird, Brown Thrasher, Eastern Bluebird, Northern Cardinal, Indigo Bunting, American Goldfinch, Rufous-sided Towhee, and Field, Chipping, and Song Sparrows.

The most common mammal is the Eastern Meadow Vole, a stocky, short-tailed, mouselike creature whose runways criss-cross these successional fields just beneath the protecting grasses. With populations of hundreds per acre the vole is a vital food source for hawks, owls, snakes, and other predators. In addition, the Eastern Cottontail (Rabbit), Woodchuck (Groundhog), Long-tailed Weasel, and Striped Skunk inhabit these fields, although the latter two are infrequently seen. Be on the lookout for the Red Fox, which has recently increased its numbers in nearby Chester County. A vixen with four pups was seen in the brushy field next to picnic area 17 during the spring of 1985. In winter, its neat, four-toed tracks cross the open country in a direct, purposeful manner. Slender, hair-filled scats or droppings provide further signs that this wary animal is around.

Besides the Eastern Garter Snake and the Eastern Milk Snake, both of which are common although secretive, the Northern Black Racer is the other reptile most often favoring this habitat. This large snake has a sweet tooth for fledglings in the nest. Its presence in the unmowed portions of nearby Tyler Arboretum's Pinetum has prompted the fastening of concave snake guards around some of the poles supporting bluebird nesting boxes. Since most amphibians are obligated to spend their lives in or near water, or at least near moist environs, there are few representatives of this group in brushy meadows. The American Toad, an exception, does its share to keep marauding insects in check.

These successional fields host a colorful array of wildflowers throughout the warmer months. Although May is the peak period for many woodland wildflowers, very little blooms in the fields at this time. Common Dandelion, Common Cinquefoil, Common Chickweed, Common Blue Violet, Field Pussytoes, and White and Red Clovers blossom in early May, while Oxeye (Field) Daisy, hawkweeds, and Common Buttercup begin to show their colors around Memorial Day. Most of the other field wildflowers prefer summer. Not all indigenous wildflowers will be found in any one field, and each variety has its own blooming time. The following discussion is a composite, but a thorough canvassing of the fields throughout the park, and indeed other similar habitats in our region, should produce all the species mentioned—plus more.

One of the more interesting relationships in nature lies between flowers and butterflies. While most butterflies will feed on the nectar of a variety of flowers, the caterpillar or larval stage will often feed on only one family or even one species of flower, shrub, or tree. This association generally limits the nature of the butterfly population at any given location.

Despite the sacrifice of some foliage to voracious caterpillars, most plants benefit from this mutual association. Adult butterflies help pollinate wildflowers, many of which have evolved butterfly-attracting adaptations such as deeply set nectaries and bright colors. White and Red Clovers, members of the pea (legume) family, attract legions of bees and butterflies May through September. Larvae of the Common (Clouded) Sulphur butterfly—adults with their bright yellow wings neatly trimmed with black—favor clover, as do the larvae of the Eastern Tailed Blue butterfly.

Two of the commonest wildflowers of these brushy meadows are the Yarrow, with aromatic fernlike leaves and flat head of small, white flowers, and the superficially similar Wild Carrot or Queen Anne's Lace, with lacy, white flower clusters often with a tiny, purple floret in the center. For some reason, although it blooms elsewhere throughout July, Queen Anne's Lace in the field above picnic area 17 comes into its own only at month's end, just as the Yarrow begins to fade. Queen Anne's Lace, which curls up in the fall to form a brown, cuplike "bird's-nest," is a member of the parsley family and attracts the larvae of the Black Swallowtail butterfly. This striking butterfly, with a double row of yellow spots along its wings, closely resembles the Spicebush Swallowtail, which has only a single row of yellow spots plus a splash of greenish-blue on the hindwings. The Spicebush Swallowtail caterpillar favors the greenery of its namesake, the Spicebush, which is one of the most abundant shrubs in the deciduous forest.

Several species of thistles—the Bull Thistle and Canada Thistle are among the most common—allure hordes of American Goldfinches during the late summer and early fall when their flowerheads go to seed. Earlier in the summer, their bright pinkish-purple flowers seduce many kinds of butterflies; the plants themselves serve as hosts for the caterpillars of the Painted Lady butterfly. Larvae of the closely related American Painted Lady favor the Common Burdock, whose thistle-like burs, or flowerheads, attach themselves to the clothing or fur of any passerby, a very successful adaptation resulting in seed dispersal. Ridding oneself of these ubiquitous, brown burs is often the unwelcome finale after an autumn walk through thickets.

Another troublesome plant, the Stinging Nettle, hosts the larvae of the Red Admiral, a striking, red-banded, black butterfly closely related to the Painted Ladies. Stinging Nettles also provide forage for the caterpillars of the Compton and Milbert's Tortoise Shells, Painted Lady, and two members of the angle wings family—the Question Mark and the Comma.

The Common Milkweed (abundant) and the orange-colored Butterfly-weed (uncommon here, but several nice specimens occur along the road between picnic areas 17 and 16) have a special attraction for adult butterflies. The Common Milkweed can be told by calamine-lotion pink flower clusters that bloom late June through early August and turn into greenish-brown seedpods that eventually spew forth "parachute" seeds to ride the autumn breezes. Not only do adult Monarch butterflies prefer milkweed; their larvae demand it. Substances in milkweed leaves supposedly impart a flavor to these insects that makes them disagreeable to birds and other predators. The nearly identical adult Viceroy butterfly, whose larvae feed on the Black Willows and Tuliptrees lining Ridley Creek, benefits from visual mimicry—tricking the would-be predator into believing it is the distasteful Monarch.

Two other handsome butterflies, the Red-spotted Purple and the Eastern Tiger Swallowtail (the latter perhaps the most frequently seen of all the butterflies here), are regular visitors to these brushy meadows. Their caterpillars feast on the Black Cherry trees that dot the wooded edges of the fields. Other common butterflies include the Cabbage Butterfly (European), Greater and Lesser Fritillaries (several species of each), Little Wood Satyr, Common Wood Nymph, and various members of the skipper, hairstreak, copper, and blue families.

Most of the field wildflowers already mentioned, save the Common Milkweed, its cousin the Butterfly-weed, Common Cinquefoil, and Common Blue Violet, are aliens introduced long ago from Europe. The following two representatives of the snapdragon family are also naturalized citizens. Patches of Butter-and-eggs (Toadflax) are easily recognized by their spikes of dainty yellow and orange flowers that bloom throughout the summer, while the Common Mullein, with large, wooly leaves spiraling around its towering flower stalk, stands alone or in groups of twos or threes throughout the meadow, especially in areas with poorer soils.

Many meadow wildflowers are also found along the greenbelts that border highways throughout the tristate region (especially Queen Anne's Lace, Chicory, Common Mullein, Common Milkweed, and various thistles). Other common plants of successional fields include the native Common Evening-primrose (August through September), Deptford Pink, various members of the buttercup, hawkweed, Joe-Pye-weed, and ironweed groups (the last two favor moist areas), and

Chicory, whose blue (sometimes white) flowers grace the roadside during the late summer. Also keep an eye open for Moth Mullein, Common St. Johnswort, and White and Yellow Sweet Clovers. Several colorful species of the daisy or composite family, the largest family of flowering plants and including the Ox-eye Daisy, Daisy Fleabane, Black-eyed Susan, Thin-leaved Coneflower, and various purple and white asters, can also be found in the more open and drier sections of these brushy meadows through the warmer months.

It is best to consult a flower guide to distinguish the different types of the late-blooming asters, and the same is true for the goldenrods that take over these fields during the late summer and early fall. These native members of the daisy family, with their showy, yellow flower clusters (unjustly accused of causing hayfever—usually ragweeds are the culprit), can be identified by the shape and silhouette of their flower clusters and by the veining on their leaves. But again, check the guide since there are over sixty species in our general area.

Scan the goldenrods' stems for the greenish-brown galls which are noticeable during the colder months. These one-inch hard spheres develop after the Goldenrod Gallfly, a relative of the notorious Mediterranean Fruitfly, lays its single egg on the goldenrod's stem in the early summer. The newly hatched larva secretes a growth-inducing substance that causes the plant's tissue to form a pithy swelling, the gall, which serves as a protective chamber for the developing larva during the winter. In early spring the adult fly emerges from the side of the gall leaving a barely visible exit hole. Other insects, including certain species of wasps, beetles, and moths, can also be the culprits. Sometimes, their offspring even parasitize an already present gallfly larva. Some galls sport a larger, more visible hole towards the center of the sphere—the work of a Downy Woodpecker drilling into the gall for larvae. In late September check the goldenrod flowers for Locust Borers, Soldier Beetles, Polistes Wasps, Tarnished Plant Bugs, Honeybees, and other insects seeking late-season pollen and nectar before the onset of the killing frosts of fall.

One can continue southwest along Forge Road with its alternating patches of woodlots and successional fields, or return to Sycamore Mills Road and walk upstream along Ridley

Creek for another mile or so to a large field situated below the park's youth hostel. Along the way, a mixture of mesic deciduous woodland and streamside (hydric) habitats greets the visitor. About one hundred yards upstream past the junction with Forge Road is a partially open area favored by fishermen. Jacob's-ladder (May) and Common Sunflower (mid-July through September) are common to the left of Sycamore Mills Road while Spotted Joe-Pye-weed and several related species favor the stream's edge to the right and generally are in full bloom during mid-August. Legend has it that an Indian, Joe Pye, used this plant to cure typhus. Flanking the creek, look for Dwarf Ginseng (May), Fringed Loosestrife (late June through early July), Tall Meadow-rue (July), and Boneset (August).

Further along, about one-half mile past Forge Road, is a high loop overlooking the creek below. The moist, shaded roadbank immediately to your left is alive with wildflowers mid-April through May. Bloodroot, Spring-beauty, Common Blue and Smooth Yellow Violets, Dutchman's-breeches, Solomon's-seals ("true" and False), May-apple, Jack-in-the-pulpit, various species of ferns, and Wild Ginger all take their respective turns. Wild Ginger is a peculiar wildflower: its large heart-shaped leaves give it away, but you must gently displace the leaf litter to find its brown, cup-shaped flower hiding at ground level where it is pollinated by ground beetles.

Save time to visit the nearby Tyler Arboretum for its spring display of rhododendrons, azaleas, and dogwoods—and especially for its great variety of native American wildflowers.

TYLER ARBORETUM

The Tyler Arboretum can be entered daily throughout the year from 8 A.M. to dusk via the main entrance on Painter Road. A parking lot and bicycle rack are located there, along with posted regulations regarding visits to this 720-acre natural area famous for its horticultural collections. Naturalists visiting the Arboretum do well to visit the Education Center, open 9 A.M. until 4 P.M. seven days a week, to obtain trail maps and to check on bird sightings and wildflower displays in the Arboretum. Walking trails start in the valley below the Barn.

For a fine introduction to some of the best natural areas within the Arboretum, start at the wooden bridge which carries the gravel roadway below the Barn across the small stream called Rocky Run. Just upstream from the bridge are a number of Turtlehead plants in flower from August to October. Both the blossoms and the winter seed capsules resemble the head of its reptilian namesake. The leaves of this plant are the food for the caterpillar of the Baltimore (Checkerspot) butterfly, state insect of Maryland.

Walk downstream along the blue-blazed Rocky Run Trail. The small valley to the left is the principle site of the trees which survive from the plant collections of Jacob and Minshall Painter, whose ubiquitous interest in the intellectual pursuits of the mid-nineteenth century included collecting interesting flora. Within the valley are specimens of Baldcypress, Cedar-of-Lebanon, Franklintree, River Birch, and Yulan Magnolia, to name a few, which are one hundred and fifty years old.

The small pond to the left of the trail just before the woods is an excellent American Toad breeding pond in mid-April. The pond was built around 1950 to provide irrigation water for the rhododendron collection then being planted uphill from Rocky Run. This collection of native, Asian, and hybrid rhododendrons and azaleas has become the premier of its kind in the East, well worth a visit during its peak blossoming in mid-May and a good birding spot much of the year.

Just 150 yards downstream from the pond, where a small erosion gully crosses the trail, is a small pool that serves as a breeding site for Wood Frogs in early March. Listen for their quacklike calls and then proceed quietly to the pool on your left to see these black-masked frogs during the short breeding season. While at the pool, look upstream for a bizarrely shaped tree. This Red Maple started as a seedling on a tree stump. When the stump rotted away it left the maple standing on two large roots which had grown down the sides of the stump.

Back on the main trail take the left-hand fork to stay at the bottom of the hill parallel to the stream. Both the Great Horned Owl and the Eastern Screech-Owl are known to frequent this area. The varied habitat for hunting and the mature trees with cavities and occasional broken tops prove perfect for these night-shift predators. Old maps of the Arboretum prop-

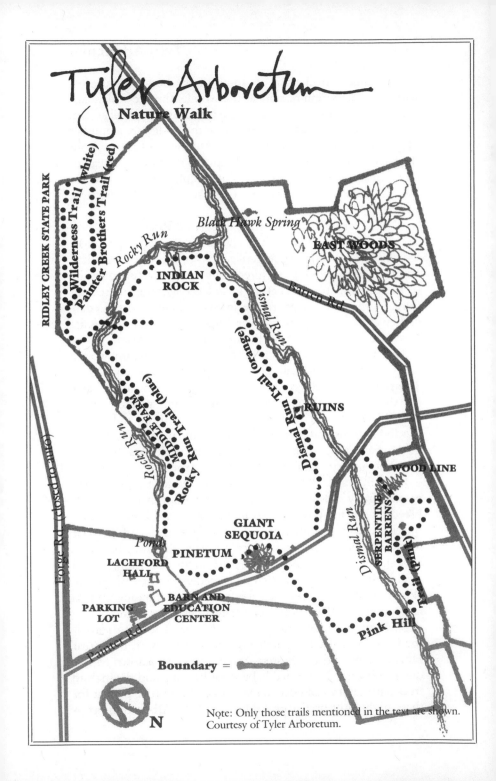

Tyler Arboretum
Nature Walk

RIDLEY CREEK STATE PARK

Wilderness Trail (white)

Painter Brothers Trail (red)

Rocky Run

Black Hawk Spring

EAST WOODS

INDIAN ROCK

Dismal Run Trail (orange)

Barren Rd

MIDDLE FARM Trail (blue)

Rocky Run

Rocky Run Trail

RUINS

Dismal Run

WOOD LINE

SERPENTINE BARRENS

Forge Rd. (closed to auto.)

GIANT SEQUOIA

Dismal Run

Pink Hill Trail (pink)

Pond

LACHFORD HALL

PINETUM

PARKING LOT

BARN AND EDUCATION CENTER

Painter Rd.

Pink Hill

Boundary = ━━━

N

Note: Only those trails mentioned in the text are shown.
Courtesy of Tyler Arboretum.

erty suggest that this area has been wooded since at least the 1860s. Look for the low hummock and ditch of a water ram; one of the Painter brothers set up the ram to provide water for a farmhouse once located at the edge of the open area ahead. This and the occasional stump of a tree cut long ago provide the only evidence of disturbance aside from the trails themselves.

In early June, watch for a pale, slender stalk with a single, gracefully downturned blossom, the One-flowered Cancerroot. This 6-inch-tall wildflower bears no leaves, obtaining all its needed food from the many kinds of plants it parasitizes. Two other nongreen wildflowers can be found in the wooded areas along this trail. In mid to late summer Indian-pipes appear, thicker-stalked and white, resembling a fungus. By September, maroon and yellow Beechdrops ring the soil surrounding the American Beech trees from which they obtain their food.

Tree species here are mostly American Beech, Tuliptree, White Oak, and Northern Red Oak. Understory trees include Sour-gum (Black Gum or Black Tupelo) and Red Maple; shrubs are mainly Spicebush, Mapleleaf Viburnum, Witchhazel, and a few scattered Pink Azaleas (Pinxter-flower). A Louisiana Waterthrush usually nests close to the pond, and Acadian Flycatchers, Veeries, Wood Thrushes, and Ovenbirds can usually be found here. As you approach the brushy edge of Middle Farm, about one-half mile from the Education Center, watch for an abundance of birds almost year-round. Here an ecotone, the boundary between two plant communities with abundant food and shelter resources, plays host to a variety of species. In the winter, look for berry-eating Eastern Bluebirds and American Robins as well as various sparrows, Northern Cardinals, and the occasional Rufous-sided Towhee or Gray Catbird. In spring and summer look for Indigo Buntings, White-eyed Vireos, and Common Yellowthroats.

This meadow is one of several in the Arboretum being managed to demonstrate the early stages of succession. The area to the right of the trail is divided into three sections, one of which is mowed each fall. The other two remain unmowed through the winter to provide food and cover for wildlife. No portion of the field goes more than three years without being cut, which keeps woody plants whose seeds have been borne by wind or birds to a mowable diameter. A census of fleshy-fruited trees and shrubs in the meadow hints at the preferred foods of local songbirds—Flowering Dogwood, blackberry and raspberry species, and Multiflora Rose are the most common.

The meadow is a good place in the fall to identify goldenrod and aster species. Also look for flat-topped Yarrow and the curious narrow pods of Intermediate Dogbane. Its close relative Indian Hemp was used by Native Americans to make cordage.

As you enter the woods at the far side of the field, continue along the same elevation, paralleling Rocky Run as it begins to curve east towards its eventual confluence with Dismal Run in the next valley. In spring, watch for patches of low-growing Wood Anemone with its white blossoms and five-part leaves. As you come to a sharp turn in the blue-blazed Rocky Run Trail, about 250 yards into the woods, ignore the turn back and continue east along the valley. Look uphill to the right at the straight line of trees marking an old field or woodlot boundary. Broad spreading branches on the beeches and other trees show they grew in open sun or light shade, unlike the straight-trunked, few-limbed shape of a forest-grown tree.

Witch-hazels along the trail display two interesting galls, the Cone Gall visible on leaves as a dunce-cap-like protrusion, and the Spiny Gall, a small prickly growth on twigs which is visible year-round. Both are made by the plant when irritated by aphids, which then continue their development within the protective gall.

As the trail starts downhill watch for several branches to the left. The first of these, marked with red and white blazes, leads to a crossing of Rocky Run. If you proceed 35 yards downstream, without crossing, you will find Indian Rock, located at the base of a large old Tuliptree alongside the "falls" area of Rocky Run. This low round rock with its "X" groove aligned to the cardinal compass points (based on true rather than magnetic north) has been explained in a number of ways: an Indian grinding stone, a sacred marker, a landmark for the Underground Railroad, an ancient Phoenician artifact. Each story has its appeal.

Watch for two orchids in this area: Puttyroot with its single white-striped leaf visible all winter, and the Showy Orchis with its purple and white flowers appearing in May.

Return to the main trail and go downhill into Dismal Run Valley. You have now traveled over a mile from the Barn. Despite the name, this is one of the best areas in the Arboretum for spring wildflowers. The rich alluvial soils and shaded woodlands grow Nodding Trillium, Goldenseal, Wild Geranium, Jacob's-ladder, Jack-in-the-pulpit, Wild Ginger, Dwarf Ginseng, False Hellebore, Trout-lily (Adder's-tongue), violets, May-apple, and Blue Cohosh, among others. Check near the streams and to the right of the trail as you enter Dismal Run Valley.

Showy Orchis

As you walk south through the valley, several trails branch to the right up the hillside. Deer often spend their days resting on these slopes where warm air rising from the valley can warn them of approaching danger. In about half a mile you will encounter the ruins of a building on the right of Dismal Run Trail called Valley Cottage, a former tenant farm. The wet slopes of the valley provided the watered meadows needed for growing colonial era crops (see the Colonial Pennsylvania Plantation, page 6). A Box Elder (Ashleaf Maple) and Virginia Creeper grow on the ruined building, demonstrating how nature's constant successions undo the works of man. A large broken oak to the right of the trail past the ruin has been the nest site of Great Horned Owls. The southeast slopes of this section produce a mild microclimate good for winter birds and birdwatching.

The trail eventually reaches a fire gate on Painter Road 375 yards past Valley Cottage. Turn right to return to the Education Center or extend your walk with a visit to an unusual natural area, Pink Hill. This serpentine barren possesses soil, low in calcium and high in magnesium, that inhibits the growth of most plant life typical of the nonserpentine soils of the surrounding area. The mineral serpentine is found along the edges of the tectonic plates of the earth's crust that make up the continents. As you cross Dismal Run to the barren, you in effect (according to many geologists) cross the ancient boundary between the North American and African continents before their massive plates drifted apart some 200 million years ago.

To reach the barren, turn left at the gate and proceed 100 yards along Painter Road. Cross a bridge over Dismal Run to the first fire gate on the south side of the road, then take the trail behind the fire gate straight uphill towards a woodline at the hilltop. Notice how shallow the soil is. Derived from bedrock that is high in the mineral serpentine, these soils have created the open prairielike vegetation that early settlers called barrens. Scattered through Pennsylvania, Maryland, and Virginia, many of these barrens have been quarried for stone or developed for housing. Few retain their original vegetation. Yet except for a few tree species alien to the region, this barren is much as it was three or four hundred years ago.

Spring wildflowers here include Moss-pink, for which the hill is named, Field Chickweed, Lyre-leaved Rock Cress and Northern Downy Violet. The Moss-pinks or Moss Phlox reach their peak just before Mother's Day. As spring progresses into summer and summer to fall, a steady progression of interesting wildflowers can be found, including Small's Ragwort, Sundrops, Devil's-bit, Pale-spike Lobelia, Wood Lily, Rose-pink, Narrow-leaved Mountain-mint, Slender Ladies'-tresses, Silver-rod, and the Barren's Aster. Unusual woody plants include the Blackjack Oak (found also in the Pine Barrens), Virginia Pine (Scrub Pine), American Hazel, tangles of greenbrier, and New Jersey Tea.

Slightly better soils at the top of the hill give rise to a scrubby forest of Black, Scarlet, and Blackjack Oaks. Watch for chestnut sprouts as the trail curves toward the right and heads downhill. The American Chestnut was one of the most valuable trees in the eastern deciduous forest, prized for its strong, decay-resistant wood and edible nuts. In 1904 a fungus common to the Chinese Chestnut appeared on trees in the New York Zoological Park and within decades swept through the woodlands of America. With no resistance to the fungus, the American Chestnut dies back to the root system as the fungus spreads beneath the bark, girding the tree. Little remains but scattered stumps and doomed sprouts from persistent old root systems. A salvage cut was conducted soon after the blight first swept the area, similar to recent salvage cuts of oaks killed by the Gypsy Moth.

Following the pink blazes another 0.8 miles will return you to the Education Center. Springs at the bottom of the hill make for damp walking much of the year, but remind one of the important role natural areas play in allowing water tables to be recharged. In early spring, watch for the Round-leaved Yellow Violet in these moist spots.

The trail jogs right and then crosses Dismal Run. Watch for a large Butternut tree to the left of the trail just past the stream. Its compound leaves, light-colored broken bark, and monkey-face-shaped leaf scars make it identifiable all year round. The nuthusks of the Butternut provided the dye for Confederate uniforms during the Civil War. The forest on this side of the stream is much younger, the gneissic bedrock beneath having produced soils suitable for farming at one time. Gneiss, a banded metamorphic rock formed by intense heat and pressure within the earth's crust, lacks serpentine's relatively inhospitable properties for most plantlife.

The trail goes up a steep hill, rewarding the hiker with a view of the ruins of a magnificent stone barn. A little prowling reveals a farmhouse and springhouse hidden in a jungle of Japanese Honeysuckle and Kentucky Coffeetrees (native to western Pennsylvania). You might wish to look for Northern Dusky Salamanders in the springhouse waters before following the pink trail through old field areas of Tuliptree, grapevines, Multiflora Rose, Box Elder, and Smooth Sumac.

The trail bears right, passing backyards that remind one that encroaching development threatens all natural areas. A huge White Oak is a "good neighbor tree," allowed to live at the edge of property lines because neighbors were loathe to infringe on what might belong to the next landowner. As you enter an open area that the Arboretum is planting with shade trees, the trail proceeds across the road and then turns left to the Education Center by route of the Pinetum. This collection of conifer specimens includes the largest Giant Sequoia east of the Mississippi. Watch for Eastern Bluebirds and finches here in the winter.

The Arboretum's East Woods, some of whose hillier sections are representative of dry (xeric) deciduous woodlands, has been actively managed in recent years according to modern forestry techniques. Consequently, tree cutting has occurred, in part fueled by the defoliation by Gypsy Moth caterpillars. Gypsy Moths favor oaks, the predominant canopy trees here. Forest ecologists generally agree that chemical sprays (often indiscriminately toxic to many forms of wildlife) are inappropriate for controlling this pest, except in dense oak woodlands around homes where the deleterious effects of a major outbreak can be considerable. However, most healthy trees will survive one or two defoliations, unless further weakened by drought or secondary invading organisms. A guide to the East Woods is available at the Arboretum's Education Center.

The walks outlined in this chapter touch both the usual and the unique. The Arboretum contains over twenty miles of trails winding through several different habitats. Coupled with the extensive bridle, bicycling, and hiking trails of adjacent Ridley Creek State Park, the naturalist has almost limitless opportunities for exploration. Try them all!

Pileated Woodpecker

For more information contact:

Ridley Creek State Park
Sycamore Mills Road
Route 36
Media, Pennsylvania 19063
Phone: (215) 566-4800

The Tyler Arboretum
Box 216
515 Painter Road
Lima, Pennsylvania 19037
Phone: (215) 566-5431, (215) 566-9133

Directions to Ridley Creek State Park and Tyler Arboretum, Pennsylvania

From the City Line Avenue Exit of the Schuylkill Expressway (Interstate 76), continue for 5.3 miles along U.S. 1 South to the intersection with Route 3 (West Chester Pike). Make a right on Route 3 West and drive 5.8 miles to the intersection with Route 252 in Newtown Square. Proceed past this light on Route 3 West to the next light (0.1 miles further). Turn left on Bishop Hollow Road and travel 3.3 miles to Chapel Hill Road (passing the intersections with Gradyville and Providence Roads). Make a right on Chapel Hill Road across the narrow Sycamore Mills Bridge. An eighteen-car paved parking lot and the start of the nature walk are to your immediate right. To the left is Barren Road (to Tyler Arboretum). A one-way trip takes approximately forty minutes from the Schuylkill Expressway.

If the parking lots next to the Sycamore Mills Bridge are full, proceed to picnic area 17 in the state park proper. Then walk down Forge Road to Sycamore Mills Road. The main entrance to Ridley Creek State Park is reached by driving 3.3 miles along Route 3 West past the intersection with Route 252. Turn left on the main park road (Sandy Flash Drive) and travel 3 miles to the park office. To reach picnic area 17, take the second left after the park office along Sandy Flash Drive South (0.5 miles past the headquarters). Drive 0.9 miles along this winding road to the large parking lot abutting Forge Road. This winding road is closed during the colder months.

To reach Tyler Arboretum, after crossing Sycamore Mills Bridge turn left on Barren Road and drive 1.2 miles to Painter Road. Turn right on Painter Road and drive another 1 mile to the Arboretum's parking lot on your right. There is now a two-dollar parking fee for nonmembers. Follow the signs for the short walk to the Education Center and the start of the nature walk.

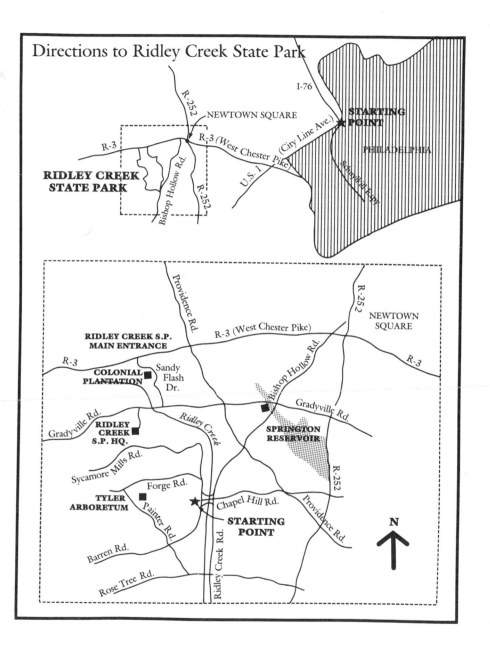

Directions to Ridley Creek State Park

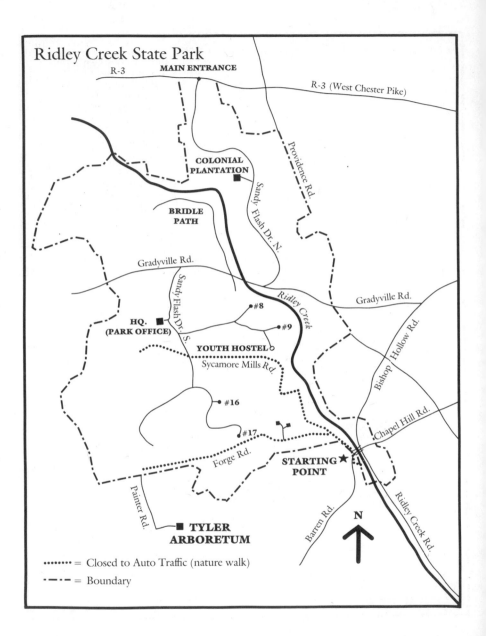

Ridley Creek State Park

R-3 MAIN ENTRANCE

R-3 (West Chester Pike)

Providence Rd.

COLONIAL PLANTATION

Sandy Flash Dr. N.

BRIDLE PATH

Gradyville Rd.

Ridley Creek

Gradyville Rd.

#8

Sandy Flash Dr. S.

HQ. (PARK OFFICE)

#9

YOUTH HOSTEL

Sycamore Mills Rd.

Bishop Hollow Rd.

#16

Chapel Hill Rd.

#17

Forge Rd.

STARTING POINT ★

Painter Rd.

TYLER ARBORETUM

Barren Rd.

N

Ridley Creek Rd.

•••••••• = Closed to Auto Traffic (nature walk)

—·—·— = Boundary

Deciduous Forests of the Delaware Valley Region

PENNSYLVANIA

These forested areas listed below have been selected because they are both representative and open to the public. Most are characteristic of the Piedmont Physiographic Province. Examples of deciduous woodlands in the more mountainous regions will be covered in "The Mountains."

Audubon Wildlife Sanctuary, Montgomery County, Audubon, Pennsylvania, off Route 363 (near Valley Forge National Historic Park). Visit historic Mill Grove on the grounds (John James Audubon's first American home). Visitor center and museum. Phone: (215) 666-5593.

Bowman's Hill State Wildflower Preserve, Bucks County, near New Hope, Pennsylvania, off Route 32 (within Washington Crossing Historic Park). Famous for its native wildflower collections. Nature center. Phone: (215) 862-2924.

Brandywine Battlefield State Park, Delaware County, near Chadds Ford, Pennsylvania, off U.S. 1 (west of U.S. 202). Museum. Phone: (215) 459-3342. Visit nearby famous Longwood Gardens, Kennett Square, off U.S. 1. Phone: (215) 388-6741. Also visit nearby Brandywine River Museum, Chadds Ford, off U.S. 1 (grounds incorporate trails along Brandywine River and fresh-water marshes). Phone: (215) 459-1900.

Churchville Nature Center, Bucks County, Churchville, Pennsylvania, near Holland and Newtown off Route 532. Also contains fresh-water lake. Nature center. Phone: (215) 357-4005.

Delaware Canal (Theodore Roosevelt State Park), Bucks County, between Morrisville and Lumberville, Pennsylvania, along the Delaware River off Route 32. Many access points along this extensive canal and towpath. Visit Washington Crossing Historic Park and the quaint village of New Hope along the way. Phone: (215) 982-5560.

Evansburg State Park, Montgomery County, near Skippack and Collegeville, Pennsylvania, off Route 73. Skippack Creek with its fresh-water environs runs through the park. Phone: (215) 489-3729.

Fairmount Park, western Philadelphia, Pennsylvania, scenic loop from Belmont Mansion to Chamounix along the Schuylkill River Valley. Phone (Fairmount Park Commission): (215) 686-2176 or 686-2177.

Five-Mile Woods Preserve, Bucks County, near Yardley, Pennsylvania, off I-95. This deciduous woodland is in the Atlantic Coastal Plain Physiographic Province, which barely touches southeastern Pennsylvania. Phone: (215) 493-0697.

French Creek State Park, Berks and Chester Counties, near Elverson, Pennsylvania, off Routes 23 and 345. One of the most unique and diverse locales in our region with good examples of all three subtypes of eastern deciduous woodlands: dry (xeric), well-drained (mesic), and wet (hydric). Also contains fresh-water lakes and marshes. Part of Horse Shoe Trail goes through park. Phone: (215) 582-1514. Visit nearby famous Hopewell Village National Historic Site (a restored early American iron-making community), near Elverson, Pennsylvania, off Routes 23 and 345. Phone: (215) 582-8773.

Glen Providence Park, Delaware County, near Media, Pennsylvania, off U.S. 1. Phone: (215) 565-4564.

Hay Creek, Berks County, near Birdsboro, Pennsylvania, southeast of Reading and northwest of French Creek State Park off Route 82. Good birding.

Neshaminy State Park, Bucks County, Cornwells Heights,

Pennsylvania, off U.S. 13. Borders the fresh-water environs of Neshaminy Creek and the Delaware River. Phone: (215) 639-4538.

Nockamixon State Park, Bucks County, near Quakertown, Pennsylvania, off Routes 412 or 313. Also contains large fresh-water impoundment. Phone: (215) 257-3646.

Nolde Forest State Park, Berks County, near Reading, Pennsylvania, off Route 625. Contains some fresh-water marsh habitat also. Designated as Environmental Education Center.

Nottingham Park, Chester County, near Nottingham, Pennsylvania, off U.S. 1 and Route 272. Extensive serpentine barrens (see Tyler Arboretum section) with great variety of unusual flora and fauna (Pitch Pine, Aleutian Maidenhair Fern, various western prairie grasses, Northern Copperhead, Whippoor-will, Pine Warbler, and so forth). Phone: (215) 932-9195. Visit nearby Goat Hill Serpentine Barrens on Red Pump Road off U.S. 1S, west of Nottingham Park. Only location of Hairy Field Chickweed.

Octoraro Area, Chester and Lancaster Counties, between Quarryville and Oxford, Pennsylvania, off Route 472. Also contains extensive fresh-water streams, impoundments, and marshes. Good for certain nesting birds uncommon elsewhere in southeastern Pennsylvania (Barred Owl, Whip-poor-will, Yellow-throated, Prothonotary, and Worm-eating Warblers, and so forth).

Peace Valley Nature Center, Bucks County, near Doylestown, Pennsylvania, off Route 313. Part of the much larger Peace Valley (County) Park and also abuts a fresh-water lake. Nature center. Phone: (215) 345-7860.

Pennypack Park and Environmental Center, northeastern Philadelphia, Pennsylvania, bisected by U.S. 1 (Roosevelt Boulevard). Also contains fresh-water stream. Nature center. Phone: (215) 671-0440.

Schuylkill Valley Nature Center, Roxborough, Philadelphia, Pennsylvania, off Hagy's Mill Rd. Also contains a small fresh-water pond. Nature center, bookstore, and excellent reference library. Phone: (215) 482-7300.

Smedley Park, Delaware County, between Springfield Mall and Media, Pennsylvania, off U.S. 1. Contains section of the Springfield Trail and also access to Crum Creek Valley with its deciduous woods, fresh-water stream and marshes, and so forth. Contact the Delaware County Park Headquarters: (215) 565-4564.

Tyler State Park, Bucks County, near Newtown, Pennsylvania, off Route 332. Also contains fresh-water stream (Neshaminy Creek). Phone: (215) 968-2021.

Valley Forge National Historic Park, Montgomery and Chester Counties, Valley Forge, Pennsylvania, near King of Prussia off Routes 23 and 363. Can be reached via I-76 or Pennsylvania Turnpike. Horse Shoe Trail begins here. Famous historical landmark (General Washington's 1777–78 winter headquarters). Visitor center. Phone: (215) 783-7700. Museum. Phone: (215) 783-0535.

Washington Crossing Historic Park, Bucks County, near New Hope, Pennsylvania, off Routes 532 and 32. Site of historic river crossing by American Revolutionary Army, 1776. Also contains Bowman's Hill State Wildflower Preserve. Visitor center and museum. Phone: (215) 493-4076.

Wissahickon Valley, northwestern Philadelphia, Pennsylvania. From Bells Mill Road (off U.S. 422) the Wissahickon Creek section of Fairmount Park stretches for approximately seven miles southwestward to the creek's confluence with the Schuylkill River. Similar to Ridley Creek State Park in many aspects, this "wilderness within the city" is famous for its complex geological formations. Contact Fairmount Park Commission. Phone: (215) 686-2176 or 686-2177. Visit nearby Morris Arboretum in the Chestnut Hill section of Philadelphia.

Phone: (215) 247-5777. Also visit the adjacent Andorra Natural Area with its visitor center to obtain more information on the Wissahickon Valley. Phone: (215) 242-5610.

NEW JERSEY

The deciduous woodlands in the Piedmont of central New Jersey and along the inner Atlantic Coastal Plain bordering the Delaware Bay are similar to those of Pennsylvania. The outer Atlantic Coastal Plain adjacent to the ocean and the southern tip of the state (Cape May County) frequently hosts the less diverse oak-hickory forest community, which seems better adapted to the sandy, porous (xeric or dry) soil. Deciduous woodlands in more mountainous regions will be covered in "The Mountains."

Assunpink Wildlife Management Area, Mercer and Monmouth Counties, near Hightstown, New Jersey, off Route 539. Also contains fresh-water lake and marshes. Phone: (609) 259-7954.

Atlantic County Park, Atlantic County, Estell Manor, New Jersey, near Mays Landing off Route 50. Nature center. Phone: (609) 625-1897.

Bull's Island (section of **Delaware and Raritan Canal State Park**), Hunterdon County, near Lambertville, New Jersey, off Route 29 between the Delaware River and the Raritan Canal. Also contains fresh-water environs. Famous birding area with breeding Cliff Swallow, Acadian Flycatcher, Yellow-throated, Cerulean, and Prothonotary Warblers. Phone: (201) 873-3050.

Cape May County Park, Cape May County, Cape May County Court House, New Jersey, near Stone Harbor off Garden State Parkway or U.S. 9. Classic oak-hickory community. Local breeding colony of Red-headed Woodpeckers. Phone:

(609) 465-5271. Also visit nearby Wetlands Institute (see "The Salt-Water Marsh").

Glassboro Wildlife Management Area (Glassboro Woods), Gloucester County, near Glassboro, New Jersey, off Route 47 and U.S. 322. Also contains fresh-water environs. Phone: (609) 785-0455.

Herrontown Woods, Mercer County, near Princeton, New Jersey, off U.S. 1, Route 571, and Route 27 (Nassau Street). Also contains fresh-water stream and lowlands. Contact Mercer County Park Commission. Phone: (609) 989-6530.

Higbee Beach Wildlife Management Area, Cape May County, near Cape May Point State Park, New Jersey, but on the Delaware Bay side, south of the Cape May Canal. From Sunset Boulevard in Cape May Point take Bayshore Road and after 1.8 miles make a left on New England Road to the parking lot 1.2 miles further. A truly unique area of multiple habitats (deciduous woods, successional fields, fresh- and some salt-water marshes, barrier dunes, beaches) long famous for fall birding. Oak-hickory forest surrounds parts of the fresh-water Pond Creek Meadow. Phone: (609) 628-3221.

Parvin State Park, Salem County, near Vineland, New Jersey, off Route 540. Mixture of flora and fauna native to the Pine Barrens, the Piedmont, and the inner Atlantic Coastal Plain. Phone: (609) 692-7039.

Princeton Institute Woods, Mercer County, near Princeton, New Jersey, off U.S. 1 and Routes 571 and 27. Also contains fresh-water stream and marshes (especially adjacent Charles Rogers Sanctuary, formerly called the Princeton Wildlife Refuge). Famous birding area: spring migration, breeding Prothonotary Warbler, and wintering owls.

Rancocas State Park and Nature Center, Burlington County, near Mount Holly, New Jersey, off I-295. Also contains fresh-water creek and marshes. Nature center, great bookstore, and library. Phone: (609) 261-2495.

Washington Crossing State Park, Mercer County, near Titusville, New Jersey, off Routes 29 and 546. Site of historic river crossing by American Revolutionary Army, 1776. Visitor center, museum, and nature center. Phone: (609) 737-0623 for the state park and (609) 737-0609 for the nature center.

DELAWARE

The deciduous forests of northern Delaware are part of the Piedmont and similar to those in nearby southeastern Pennsylvania. North-central and coastal Delaware (especially that part bordering the Delaware Bay) are part of the inner Atlantic Coastal Plain and so too are similar to areas described in the Pennsylvania section. Parcels of wet (hydric) woodlands are often found bordering the extensive marshes of the refuges along the Delaware Bay.

Alapocas Woods, New Castle County, near Wilmington, Delaware, off Route 141. Also contains fresh-water streams and borders Brandywine River. Famous birding locale especially during spring migration and also interesting from a geological perspective (bisected by a fault).

Bellevue State Park, New Castle County, near Wilmington, Delaware, off I-95 (along the Delaware River). Contains freshwater pond. Phone: (302) 571-3390.

Blackbird State Forest, New Castle County, near Blackbird, Delaware, off U.S. 13 and then Route 471. Also known for the presence of "Carolina Bays," shallow fresh-water depressions or ponds of mysterious origin found along the Atlantic Coastal Plain. Contains good examples of wet woodlands.

Brandywine Creek State Park, New Castle County, near Greenville, Delaware, off Route 100 (south of Chadds Ford, Pa.). Also contains fresh-water creek, floodplain, and marshes where the endangered Bog Turtle has been reported. Famous for its Tuliptree Trail with a fine collection of old, tall Tuliptrees as well as other deciduous trees. Nature center. Phone: (302) 571-3534.

Iron Hill Hardwoods, New Castle County, near Newark, Delaware, at junction of I-95 and Route 896.

Lums Pond State Park, New Castle County, near Kirkwood, Delaware, off Route 71 (along Chesapeake-Delaware Canal). Also contains fresh-water environs and features fossil hunting. Nature center. Phone: (302) 368-6989.

Norman G. Wilder Wildlife Area, Kent County, near Dover, Delaware, off Routes 10 and 246 (from U.S. 13). Contact Delaware Division of Fish and Wildlife. Phone: (302) 736-4431.

Eastern Tiger Swallowtail

Rockford Park, New Castle County, near Wilmington, Delaware, off Route 52. Located across the Brandywine Creek from Alapocas Woods. Contact New Castle County Department of Recreation. Phone: (302) 995-7610.

Walter S. Carpenter, Jr. State Park, New Castle County, near Newark, Delaware, off Route 896. Phone: (302) 731-1310.

White Clay Creek Valley, New Castle County, near Newark, Delaware, off Routes 72 and 896. Also contains fresh-water environs with both well-drained and wet woodland habitats. Good birding area.

Winterthur Museum and Gardens, New Castle County, Winterthur, Delaware, south of Longwood Gardens, Pennsylvania, and off Route 52. Famous for its Americana and contains a fifteen-acre deciduous woodland on the grounds. Visitor center and museum. Phone: (302) 654-1548.

Suggested Readings on the Eastern Deciduous Forest and the Woodlands of the Delaware Valley Region

Arnold, Fred. *The Painter Trees* (Special Publication no. 1). Lima, Pa.: John J. Tyler Arboretum, 1977.

Ballard, Francis, and Marion Rivinus. *Guide to the Wissahickon Valley*. Philadelphia: Friends of the Wissahickon, 1965.

Barbour, Michael G., Jack H. Bork, and Wanna D. Pitts. *Terrestrial Plant Ecology*. Menlo Park, Cal.: Benjamin/Cummings, 1980.

Birr, Lisa, and Douglas Walter. *The Woodland Management Demonstration Trail* (Special Publication no. 2). Lima, Pa.: John J. Tyler Arboretum, 1982.

Braun, E. Lucy. *Deciduous Forests of Eastern North America*. New York: Hafner Press, 1950.

Daubenmire, D. *Plant Communities: A Textbook of Synecology*. New York: Harper & Row, 1968. (Strong on succession.)

Delcourt, Hazel R. "The Virtue of Forests, Virgin and Otherwise." *Natural History*, June 1981.

Executive Committee for Bowman's Hill State Wildflower Preserve. *Native Plants of Pennsylvania: A Trail Guide to Bowman's Hill State Wild Flower Preserve, Washington Crossing State Park, Bucks County, Pennsylvania*. Wynnewood, Pa.: Livingston, 1963.

Eyre, F. H., ed. *Forest Cover Types of the United States and Canada*. Washington, D.C.: Society of American Foresters, 1980.

Farb, Peter, and The Editors of Time-Life Books. *The Forest*. New York: Life Nature Library, Time-Life Books, 1980.

Fisher, Alan. *Country Walks Near Philadelphia*. Boston: Appalachian Mountain Club, 1983.

Godfrey, Michael A. *A Sierra Club Naturalist's Guide: The Piedmont*. San Francisco: Sierra Club Books, 1980. (Excellent.)

Haas, Franklin C. "The Birds of Ridley Creek State Park." *Cassinia* 60 (1984): 23–33.

Horn, Henry S. "Forest Succession." *Scientific American*, May 1975.

Ketchum, Richard M. *The Secret Life of the Forest*. New York: American Heritage Press, 1970.

Klein, Esther M. *Fairmount Park: A History and a Guidebook*. Bryn Mawr, Pa.: Harcum Junior College Press, 1974.

Knapp, R., ed. *Vegetation Dynamics: Handbook of Vegetation Science*, vol. 8. The Hague: W. Junk, 1974.

Korling, Torkel, and Robert O. Petty. *Wild Plants in Flower: The Eastern Deciduous Forest*. Chicago: Chicago Review, 1978.

List, Albert, Jr., and Ilka List. *A Walk in the Forest*. New York: Thomas Y. Crowell, 1977.

McCormick, Jack. *The Life of the Forest*. New York: McGraw-Hill, 1966.

McGinley, Anthony J. *A Thumbnail Sketch of Sycamore Mills.* Pennsylvania Bureau of State Parks, 1978.

McNeill, John T. *Rambling Along the Pennypack.* Philadelphia: Reliable Reproduction, 1963.

Miller, Gary. "Secondary Succession Following Fire on a Serpentine Barren." *Proceedings of the Pennsylvania Academy of Sciences* 55 (1981): 62–64.

Minckler, Leon S. *Woodland Ecology: Environmental Forestry for the Small Owner.* 2nd ed. Syracuse, N.Y.: Syracuse University Press, 1975.

Neal, Ernest G. *Woodland Ecology.* Cambridge, Mass.: Harvard University Press, 1958.

Page, Jake, and The Editors of Time-Life Books. *Forest.* Alexandria, Va.: Planet Earth, Time-Life Books, 1983.

Peattie, Donald C. *A Natural History of Trees of Eastern and Central North America.* Boston: Houghton Mifflin, 1950.

Platt, Rutherford. *The Great American Forest.* Englewood Cliffs, N.J.: Prentice-Hall, 1965.

Rivinus, Willis M. *A Wayfarers Guide to the Delaware Canal.* Philadelphia: Dorrance, 1964.

Selsam, Millicent E. *Birth of a Forest.* New York: Harper & Row, 1964.

Spurr, Stephen H., and Burton V. Barnes. *Forest Ecology.* 3rd ed. New York: John Wiley & Sons, 1980.

Stokes, Donald W. *A Guide to Nature in Winter.* Boston: Little, Brown, 1976.

The Homeowner and the Gypsy Moth: Guidelines for Control. USDA Home and Garden Bulletin no. 227, 1979.

Watts, May. *Reading the Landscape of America.* Rev. ed. New York: Macmillan, 1975.

White, Theo B. *Fairmount, Philadelphia's Park.* Philadelphia: The Art Alliance Press, 1975.

Whittaker, R. H., et al. "The Ecology of Serpentine Soils." *Ecology* 35 (1954): 258–66.

Wissahickon Valley: Roads and Paths. Philadelphia: Friends of the Wissahickon, 1974. (Map with commentary.)

Yoder, C. P. "Bill." *Delaware Canal Journal.* Bethlehem, Pa.: Canal Press, 1972.

the Fresh-Water Marsh

GREGORY BREESE

The term **"fresh-water marsh"** refers to any community of plants and animals that live in an area containing wet soils and lacking trees. From a geological perspective, all marshes are young and rapidly changing landforms, an intermediate step in the successional process that transforms open water into dry, forested land. Because marshes form a buffer or transitional zone between open water and dry land, they vary greatly in size, from narrow strips and pockets measured in square yards to large expanses measured in hundreds of acres.

Probably the least known type of marsh is found in fresh-water tidal areas. Seemingly a contradiction in terms, this ecosystem occurs where wide, slow-moving streams are close enough to the ocean to be influenced by the tides and yet far enough away so that salt is either not present or found in very small amounts. The last significant example of this ecosystem in Pennsylvania survives in the southwest corner of Philadelphia, near the Philadelphia International Airport, at the Tinicum National Environmental Center. The center also hosts several other wetland habitats as well as old fields and small woodlands.

The Tinicum National Environmental Center was established by Congress in 1972 as a unit of the U.S. Fish and Wildlife Service's National Wildlife Refuge System. The U.S. Fish and Wildlife Service manages the center in order to protect the plants and animals, provide an area for environmental education, and provide an area for outdoor recreation—as long as this last objective does not interfere with the first two. Currently the center contains approximately 900 acres, about 300 of which are fresh-water tidal marsh. When land acquisition is completed the center will be about 1,200 acres in size.

Admission is free and visitors are welcome between the hours of 8 A.M. and sunset. Activities include nature observation, photography, hiking, bicycling, fishing (with a Pennsylvania license), and canoeing (you must bring your own). Dogs must be kept on a leash. No collecting of plants or animals is permitted, except for fish. Travel directions can be found at the end of this chapter and other information can be obtained by calling the visitor center: (215) 365-3118, located at 86th and Lindbergh Boulevard, and staffed from 8:00 A.M. until 4:30 P.M. every day, including holidays.

One of the best walks at Tinicum begins at the visitor center and proceeds along the main dike trail to the observation blind that overlooks Darby Creek's tidal mud flats, a distance of 1.3 miles. This becomes a 2.6-mile round trip if you backtrack to the visitor center, longer if you continue on other trails. The dike trail displays open fields, lowland woods, tidal creeks, swamps, ponds, fresh-water marshes, and fresh-water tidal marshes. This diversity provides opportunities to view a wide variety of plants and animals during any season.

For instance, midwinter (January and early February) is a bleak time of year with cold temperatures and strong winds, but a perfect time to look for insect galls. Goldenrod Bunch Galls, Goldenrod Ball Galls, Blackberry Knot Galls, and Horned Oak Galls are the most common, but new ones are still being found. This time of year also provides good viewing of Red-tailed Hawks, Northern Harriers (Marsh Hawks), American Kestrels (Sparrow Hawks), and an occasional Rough-legged Hawk or Short-eared Owl. And if conditions are just right, turtles might be seen swimming under the ice.

As winter ends things start happening fast. At the end of February or early March, Wood Frogs and Northern Spring Peepers begin their distinctive choruses. Mourning Cloak butterflies come out of hibernation and can be seen on warm days. And one of the first wildflowers of the season can be seen— Pennsylvania Bittercress, with its dainty white flowers. April is the time for migrating waterfowl and hawks. Turtles and snakes come out of hibernation and are most easily seen at this time of year. Wildflowers such as Lesser Celandine and Garlic Mustard are abundant.

The first three weeks of May bring superlative birding as the warblers and shorebirds migrate through. Late May is the best time to view waterfowl broods. By early June all the migratory birds have passed through, the resident species are busy nesting, and all the emergent wetland plants are visible although not always identifiable.

June is mulberry time with both Red and White Mulberry trees present. Ring-necked Pheasant chicks and young Eastern Cottontails (Rabbits) have left their nests and can sometimes be seen. This is also the start of the butterfly season; more than 50 species have been identified at Tinicum. July provides tasty blackberries almost everywhere you look. This is a good time to spot one of Tinicum's "specialties"—the Least Bittern. Botanists can find over 50 species of wildflowers blooming at one time and entomologists can observe insect behavior in one of the most fascinating orders of insects—*Odonata*, the dragonflies and damselflies. During August immature Little Blue Herons move into the area, along with an occasional adult Little Blue Heron and Tricolored (Louisiana) Heron. Shorebirds start their southbound migration and appear on the mudflats. Wild Rice flowers and produces seeds that are devoured by large flocks of Bobolinks and Red-winged Blackbirds.

September brings the southbound warblers and the peak of the shorebird migration. Early waterfowl such as the Blue-winged Teal arrive to feed on the Wild Rice seed. The water-fowl migration peaks in October, along with sparrows and hawks. Muskrats become more active than usual, cutting cat-tails for their winter homes, and Monarch butterflies migrate south. As winter begins the last of the migrants pass through and the winter residents (Red-tailed Hawks, American Black Ducks, Northern Pintails, Black-crowned Night-Herons, etc.) settle in for the cold weather. Tinicum is one of the best loca-tions in the tristate area for wintering sparrows, with at least 10 species usually present.

The description that follows represents a typical walk be-tween May and June. The best place to begin is inside the visi-tor center, where a staff member can provide information, the tide table can be consulted, and the latest bird sightings can be checked on the visitor's checklist. Then walk behind the visitor center toward the canoe launch parking lot. Be sure to check the Northern Bayberry bushes in the visitor center yard for Yellow-rumped (Myrtle) Warblers and American Goldfinches. The Yellow-rumped Warbler used to be called the Myrtle War-bler because of its fondness for bayberries, also known as Wax-myrtle berries, which are still used for making candles and soap. Continue to the canoe launch and check the tide in Darby Creek. The difference between high and low tide at the launch is approximately 5 feet. The influence of the tide is so strong that the creek flows upstream as the tide comes in and flows downstream as it goes out. The depth of the creek at this point ranges from less than 2 feet at low tide to over 6 feet at high tide. During storm tides the creek has been over 8 feet, al-most as high as the canoe launch pilings! Keep an eye out for Belted Kingfishers; the unobstructed view makes this one of the better areas for seeing them.

Across the creek are oil storage tanks of the Gulf Oil Com-pany. Gulf maintains an underground pipeline through the Tinicum National Environmental Center, very close to the ca-noe launch. Their tankers unload on the Delaware River side of the Philadelphia International Airport. The oil is pumped

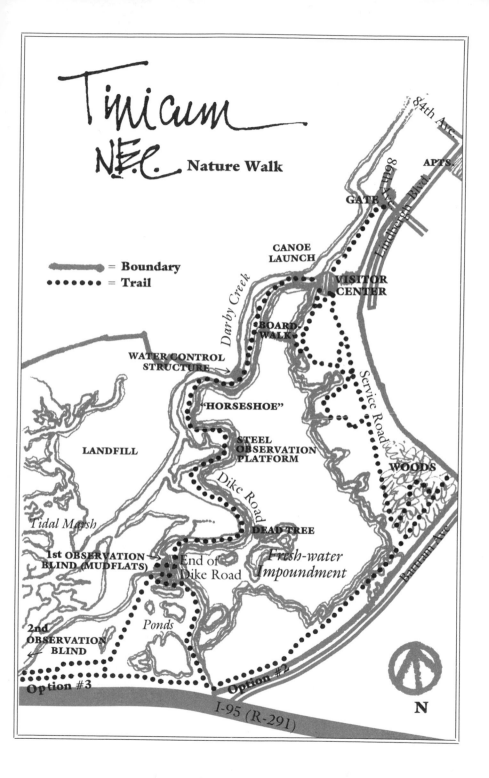

Tinicum N.E.C. Nature Walk

84th Ave

APTS.

GATE

86th Ave

Lindbergh Blvd.

CANOE
LAUNCH

VISITOR
CENTER

= Boundary
••••••• = Trail

Darby Creek

BOARD-
WALK

WATER CONTROL
STRUCTURE →

Service Road

"HORSESHOE"

STEEL
OBSERVATION
PLATFORM

LANDFILL

WOODS

Dike Road

Tidal Marsh

DEAD TREE

Fresh-water
Impoundment

1st OBSERVATION →
BLIND (MUDFLATS)

End of
Dike Road

Bartram Ave

2nd
OBSERVATION
BLIND ←

Ponds

Option #3

Option #2

I-95 (R-291)

N

through the pipeline to these tanks, from which it is later distributed to refineries in the surrounding area. As you face the creek, at the beginning of the ramp to the canoe launch, look to your left at a lush stand of Stinging Nettles. Although they are painful if touched, nettles have more protein than any other leafy green plant yet analyzed, and they make a tasty cooked vegetable or addition to soups and stews.

Moving past the regulation sign and toward the bar gate, check the Green Ash trees on the other side of the parking lot for warblers. About 30 species of warblers can be seen at Tinicum during a good year (the peak of the warbler migration occurs during the first three weeks of May). The trail that goes down the wooden steps, just beyond the bar gate, passes through a mixture of old fields and clumps of trees and shrubs and is particularly suited for warblers. As you pass the bar gate note a dead willow tree on your left, just at the edge of the impoundment. For the past few years Northern (Yellow-shafted) Flickers have made nesting cavities in this tree and then have been evicted by European Starlings. Starlings have also taken over most of Tinicum's Wood Duck and Purple Martin nesting boxes. Starlings were introduced to this country in the mid-1800s and have reduced the numbers of several of our native cavity nesters.

The dike you are walking on may have been built in part during colonial times by the first Swedish settlers. Since then people have been building and modifying dikes and filling in the original 6,000 acres of tidal marsh to such an extent that it is hard to tell what is original and what is recent. Originally undertaken for agricultural purposes, the dikes have more recently facilitated the dumping of dredged material from nearby rivers which provided more dry land for development. Written records indicate that this dike, in its present form, was built for flood control during the 1930s. The theory was that when Darby Creek, on your right, reached flood stage, the water control structures could be opened to let water from the creek flow into the impoundment on your left, thus protecting downstream homes from flooding.

In the 1950s Gulf Oil Company, the owner, intended to use the impoundment as a settling basin for dredge spoil from the

Schuylkill River. At this point, local birders and the Philadelphia Conservationists began a campaign to protect this valuable wetland. Eventually the Philadelphia Conservationists persuaded Gulf Oil to donate the 145-acre impoundment to Philadelphia as the Tinicum Marsh Wildlife Preserve. This protected the impoundment and, through the city's efforts, gave many people a chance to observe plants and animals in a marsh habitat. Unfortunately, it left the adjacent tidal marsh, which was vital as a feeding and nesting area, vulnerable to development.

In the 1960s two roads were planned that would probably have destroyed the tidal marsh—I-95 and a local road that would have passed through the center of the marsh, perpendicular to I-95. Eventually, in 1972, through the efforts of local citizens coordinated by the Philadelphia Conservationists, the Concerned Area Residents for the Preservation of Tinicum Marsh (CARP), and the League of Women Voters, Congress authorized the U.S. Fish and Wildlife Service to take over the Tinicum Marsh Wildlife Preserve and purchase the land needed to protect the last remaining fresh-water tidal marsh in Pennsylvania.

Walking along the first section of the dike, toward the first bend, the edge of the impoundment on your left looks more swamplike because of the thick stand of Black and Sandbar Willows, which are common wetland trees. This is a good area to observe Song Sparrows and Yellow Warblers singing during the morning hours. The Yellow Warbler as well as the Common Yellowthroat (another warbler) are very common at Tinicum, as might be expected since both are intimately associated with shrubby wetlands. Just after the main stand of willows is one of the few European Alder trees in Tinicum, easily recognized by the miniature "pinecones" (called strobiles) on the twigs. A Long-tailed Weasel has its den along this section of the trail and can sometimes be seen carrying unlucky mice to its young.

Just beyond the first bench is an old Honey Locust tree, a member of the legume family that prefers moist soils. Note the long sharp thorns (with thorns on its thorns!) and the small oval leaflets on the compound leaves (a leaf composed of many separate leaflets). During the early fall the bean-like, twisted seedpods form and the pulp of the green, unripe pods makes a sweet trailside nibble for hikers. On the Darby Creek side of the dike stands a grove of Green Ash trees and willows, growing on a mudbar. This mudbar formed because the creek water tries to move in a straight line while the dike curves to the left, thus allowing sediment to be deposited along the dike. At the base of the trees is a lush carpet of Lesser Celandine, very similar in appearance and habitat requirements to Marsh-marigold (Cowslip), but differentiated from the latter by yellow flowers that have both sepals and petals, while Marsh-marigold's flowers have only petal-like sepals.

The impoundment edge to your left along the next section of dike is more typical of a fresh-water marsh, with dense non-woody vegetation growing in shallow water. Listen for the insectlike trill of the Swamp Sparrow, which is common in both swamps and marshes (after all, a swamp is simply a marsh with trees). The dominant plant here is Purple (Spiked) Loosestrife, originally imported from Europe as an ornamental. Purple Loosestrife has spread quickly and efficiently, taking over many marshes in the northeast. Its beautiful, bright purple flowers reach their peak in July and produce a nectar flow during the summer that is appreciated by beekeepers; the stems provide cover for animals such as Muskrats, waterfowl, and Common Moorhens (Common Gallinules). Unfortunately, it prevents the growth of native marsh plants such as cattails, sedges, rushes, and pond weeds that would provide a better food source as well as cover for our native wildlife. This plant is now a serious problem throughout the northeastern United States.

As you reach the Purple Loosestrife keep a sharp eye out for turtles. Both the Midland Painted and the Eastern Painted Turtles occur here and interbreeding between these two sub-species creates hybrids with all possible intermediate characteristics. In addition to Painted Turtles, Snapping Turtles, Red-eared Turtles (the common "pet store" variety, originally from the Mississippi River Valley, that were released when their owners became bored), Stinkpots (Musk Turtles), Spotted Turtles, Red-bellied Turtles (endangered in Pennsylvania), Eastern Box Turtles, Wood Turtles, and perhaps the Eastern

Mud Turtle (also endangered in Pennsylvania, but no recent sightings have been made) can be found at Tinicum. Tinicum is the only known location for the Eastern Mud Turtle in Pennsylvania and one of only three Pennsylvania haunts of the largest of the basking turtles—the Red-bellied. Other reptiles that occur at Tinicum are the Eastern Garter Snake, the Northern Water Snake, and the Northern Brown (DeKay's) Snake. Unconfirmed sightings of the Eastern Ribbon Snake and the Northern Black Racer have been reported.

Painted Turtle

Amphibians are also common at Tinicum but are very hard to find due to the thick vegetation. Northern Spring Peepers and Wood Frogs are the most abundant judging from their spring choruses in March. Also found are Pickerel Frogs, American Toads, Fowler's Toads, Green Frogs, Southern Leopard Frogs (very rare, endangered in Pennsylvania), and Bullfrogs. This is roughly the order in which their mating choruses can be heard, with the tardy Bullfrogs sounding off in early June.

This section of the dike also provides one of the best spots for observing Red-winged Blackbird behavior. During spring mornings there are usually three or four males singing and displaying as they divide up territory for breeding purposes. If you watch for a while you will be able to draw a map outlining each one's "property." Each polygamous male will attract several females who will then subdivide his territory, competing among themselves. While observing the blackbirds you will also have a good chance to observe Common Moorhens as they call and move through openings in the Purple Loosestrife. Watch for the Sora and the Virginia Rail as well!

The band of Purple Loosestrife narrows and becomes restricted to the very edge of the impoundment as you reach the wooden boardwalk. Growing along the edge of the impoundment at the boardwalk is Great Bur-reed, an emergent plant that looks a lot like cattail. It can be identified by the prominent midrib in the leaves and, during the summer season, by its unique round flowers and the ball-like, spiked fruit. Another emergent fresh-water plant in this location is Yellow Iris, identified by its distinctive yellow flowers in May. The boardwalk crosses the impoundment and connects to the trail that began with the wooden steps back at the bar gate.

This end of the boardwalk is also a good place to watch dragonflies and damselflies. Although very little has been written about these insects, they are large, easy to approach, and superb fliers. Dragonflies hold their wings out horizontally when perched, while damselflies hold theirs vertically and together. Midday is the best time for observing them. The males patrol their territory (much as male songbirds do) while waiting for females to arrive. The males will posture and attack other males that enter their territory. When a female arrives, they mate and she then lays her eggs at the water's surface. The hatched nymphs are voracious predators that feed on anything they can catch. The following spring the nymphs climb out of the water, shed their skin, and become adults. After feeding on flying insects in the fields and woods they return to the water to mate and repeat the cycle.

As you may have noticed, there are several small nesting boxes in the water and a larger nesting box by the middle of the boardwalk. The larger is a Wood Duck nesting box, although it has only been used by European Starlings recently, and the smaller ones are for Tree Swallows. The Tree Swallow boxes are practically the same as Eastern Bluebird nesting boxes, and Tree Swallows fill more or less the same niche that Eastern Bluebirds do. Both feed on flying insects such as mosquitoes, except that Tree Swallows do so in the marsh. Tinicum's Tree Swallow population is so large and successful that competition among the swallows for the boxes is fierce.

Tree Swallow

The next section of dike, from the boardwalk to the following bend in the trail, is the most popular fishing area at Tinicum. The fish found here are typical of the warm, muddy conditions found in a fresh-water marsh—Mummichog, Banded Killifish, *Gambusia* (nicknamed "mosquito fish" because they feed on mosquito larvae), Carp, Brown Bullhead, Channel Catfish (found only in the creek), American Eel, Black and White Crappies, Pumpkinseed Sunfish, Yellow Perch, Gizzard Shad, and an occasional White Bass and Spot. During times of drought Blue Crabs can be found in the creek, perhaps indicating a change to brackish (more salty) conditions resulting from the reduced stream flow. Carp, like European Starlings and Purple Loosestrife, are another alien that have done well at the expense of native plants and animals. Their large, uncontrolled population coupled with omnivorous habits has reduced the available food supply, and their constant stirring of bottom sediments has prevented emergent plants from growing. Thus Carp have diminished the food and cover available to native wildlife. In the summer of 1985 a Carp control program was begun by temporarily draining the impoundment; it will be refilled by rain and Darby Creek.

Across the creek is a sewage treatment plant, and behind it an abandoned incinerator (the smokestack). The incinerator has been abandoned for many years, but there are people around who tell stories about paddling near it and being unable to touch the bottom of their metal canoe because of the fiercely hot water being discharged. The sewage treatment plant was converted to a pumping station a few years ago as part of a program to regionalize waste-water treatment. It now pumps raw sewage to the Southwest Philadelphia Sewage Treatment Plant near the airport.

As the trail curves to the right, the creek side of the dike becomes very steep. The steepness is just the opposite result of the conditions that form a mudbar—the creek water tries to continue in a straight line but hits the dike, which curves to the right. As the water is forced to the right it scours or erodes the dike, thereby creating a steep bank. Across the creek, at low tide, is a smaller mudbar that commonly has shorebirds such as Greater and Lesser Yellowlegs feeding on it. On your left, in

FRESH-WATER MARSH FOOD WEB

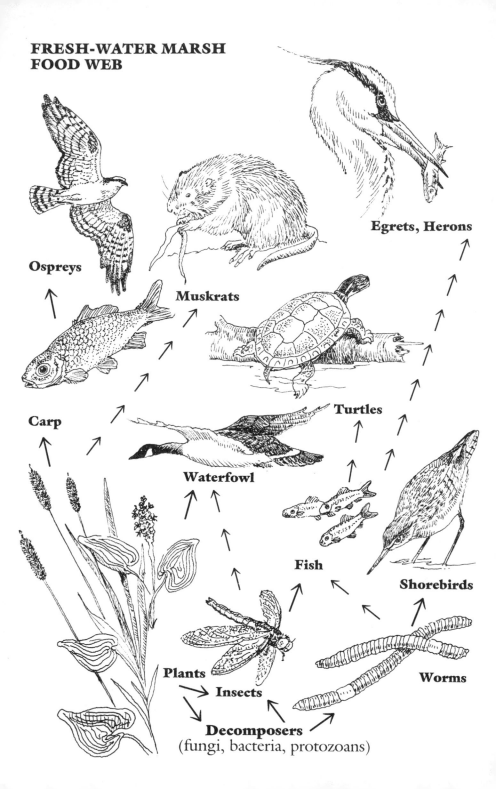

Ospreys

Muskrats

Egrets, Herons

Carp

Turtles

Waterfowl

Fish

Shorebirds

Plants

Insects

Worms

Decomposers
(fungi, bacteria, protozoans)

the impoundment, just past a few willows, dense vegetation stretches across what is known as the "horseshoe" area of the dike. This is another good area for observing Red-winged Blackbirds as well as Marsh (Long-billed Marsh) Wrens, Common Moorhens, Canada Geese, Mallards, American Black Ducks, and an occasional Blue-winged or Green-winged Teal. This dense vegetation is a very important nesting area for Tinicum's waterfowl and each year several pairs of Canada Geese, American Black Ducks, and Mallards build their nests in this spot.

Beyond the dense vegetation, in the open water at the "top" of the horseshoe, the impoundment becomes very shallow, making it an ideal spot for viewing migratory shorebirds such as Greater and Lesser Yellowlegs, Least Sandpipers, and Solitary Sandpipers. It is also a likely area for herons and egrets; in fact, it is probably the most promising area for seeing the somewhat elusive Least Bittern. Least Bitterns, smallest members of the heron family, are only a foot long and 2–4 ounces in weight. Thanks to their small size, their drab coloration of browns and tans, and their habit of standing motionless, they are commonly overlooked by visitors. When alarmed, Least Bitterns point their bills straight up, a sign of their close relationship to the much larger American Bittern (an even more difficult bird to find). Other commonly seen members of the heron family are the Great Blue Heron, Black-crowned Night-Heron, Green-backed (Green) Heron, Great (Common) Egret, and Snowy Egret. This shallow area is also heavily used by spawning Carp.

Moving along the dike, around the "top" of the horseshoe bend, the creek side of the dike again widens as a mudbar forms. This mudbar has a mixture of trees, shrubs, and wetland plants such as Spatterdock (Yellow Pond-lily), Pickerelweed, and cattails. Under the first clump of willows, by the Purple Martin house, is a good place to see the difference between Wood Nettles, which have rounded, alternating leaves and very few stinging hairs, and Stinging Nettles, which have opposite, narrow leaves and abundant stinging hairs. Beyond the trees is a stand of Common Reed Grass (*Phragmites*). Also known as Plume Grass and Cane Grass, this tall picturesque plant with the feathery plumes has little food value for wildlife and prevents other more valuable plants from growing. It is a serious pest.

Tinicum has two different cattails—Common (Broad-leaved) Cattail and Narrow-leaved Cattail. Both can be seen where the trail turns to the left again, and they can be differentiated by the width of their leaves and by the fact that Narrow-leaved Cattail flower spikes have a separation between the pollen head and the seed head. Cattails are sometimes referred to as the "supermarket of the swamps," and with good reason. During every season a part of the cattail can be used to prepare a tasty food. For instance, in the spring young cattail stalks can be eaten raw or cooked like asparagus. During late spring or early summer the immature flower spikes can be cooked and eaten like corn-on-the-cob. In early summer the pollen can be gathered and used for flour. From late summer through early spring the sprouts at the leading ends of the roots can be eaten raw or cooked like new potatoes. And during the winter the rootstocks can be crushed to produce a good quality flour. In addition to its use as food, cattails are used ornamentally in dried flower arrangements. The fluffy seeds can also be used for insulation and the leaves woven into rush seating in furniture construction.

Many fresh-water marsh animals depend heavily on cattails. Muskrats, for example, eat cattails (a major part of their diet) as well as use them to build their houses and feeding platforms. Marsh Wrens, Red-winged Blackbirds, Least Bitterns, American Bitterns, Common Moorhens, Virginia Rails, and Soras all use cattails for nesting and feeding. And the Cattail Moth lives only in cattail marshes, overwintering (hibernating) as larvae in the seed head of the cattail. In fact, most of the fluffy cattail seed heads that can be seen in the late winter are inhabited by the moth larvae, which bind the seeds to the stalk with their silk.

Across the creek is a large, sparsely vegetated, eroding hill, the infamous Folcroft Landfill. Although closed for over ten years, Folcroft Landfill remains a potential threat to the marsh because of toxic chemicals that may have been dumped there and that could insidiously leak into the marsh. To the left of the landfill and across the creek you can see the fresh-water tidal marsh for the first time. It is a broad, flat area where

Darby Creek spreads into a network of interconnecting water-ways surrounding vast "islands" of dense marsh vegetation.

Continuing along the dike, just before you reach an old water control structure, look to your left for several small, scrubby-looking trees with compound leaves and short thorns. These are Hercules-club trees, particularly interesting for their unusual twice compound leaf (sometimes this species even has thrice compound leaves!). The water control structure no longer functions due to silting and sediment buildup on the creek side, but the mudbars are used by shorebirds. Listen also for the *fitz-bew* call of the Willow (Traill's) Flycatcher, a common bird in swampy areas and a favorite with Tinicum's birders.

As you continue toward the observation platform, be on the lookout for the Barn Swallow, with its rusty-brown breast and a strongly forked tail. These swallows nest on ledges under the observation platform. In addition to Barn Swallows and Tree Swallows, which are classic denizens of marshes and open fields, Bank and Northern Rough-winged Swallows appear at Tinicum during migration, along with an occasional Cliff Swallow and Purple Martin. Incidentally, the electrical wires and utility poles, while no longer hooked up, were left in place as perching areas and are often used by the immature swallows in late summer. During the late summer beginning birders should be wary—immature Tree Swallows are brown-backed and sometimes have a smudgy breast band that makes it easy to confuse them with Bank Swallows.

The observation platform is all that remains of the original visitor center. The old wood structure was burned by vandals, rebuilt with concrete and steel, burned again with the aid of flammable liquids (note the heat-warped steel beams below the upper deck), and finally abandoned. It now serves as a destination and resting spot, with a small interpretive display. During the early spring and fall it offers a good vantage point from which to observe waterfowl and terns. These include Canada Geese, Mallards, American Black Ducks, Northern Pintails, Blue-winged and Green-winged Teals, Northern Shovelers, Ruddy Ducks, American Coots, and an occasional Gadwall, American Wigeon, Canvasback, Ring-necked Duck, Bufflehead, Greater and Lesser Scaup, Pied-billed Grebe, and Common and Hooded Mergansers. Among the terns, Forster's Tern is by far the most common, especially in early fall, but occasionally Common, Black, and Caspian Terns also turn up.

As the trail curves to the right, shortly after leaving the observation platform, look for Hackberry trees (members of the elm family) on the creek side of the dike. They come just after the Box Elders, also known as Ashleaf Maples because of their compound leaves (the Box Elder and the Red Maple are the two maples typical of wetland areas). During the summer the leaves of the Hackberry become covered with Hackberry Nipple Galls. Insect galls are chambers made by the plant in response to a chemical that certain insects (such as gallflies, gallwasps, and aphids) produce when they inject an egg into the leaf or when they are in larval form within the chamber. The larval insect eats the inside of the chamber and grows until it enters the pupal stage. After pupating it emerges in adult form, mates, and repeats the process. This is a highly specialized relationship between a single species of insect and usually a single species of plant in which the insect benefits and the plant is neither helped nor hurt. In addition to this fascinating example of a commensal relationship, Hackberry trees produce berries, also known as sugarberries, that provide fall hikers with a tasty treat. Just beyond the Hackberry trees lies one of Tinicum's White Mulberry trees. Introduced long ago from the Orient, they are exactly the same as the Red Mulberry trees you have passed, except their fruit is white when ripe and less tart in flavor.

After the dike curves to the left you finally arrive at a good viewing spot for the fresh-water tidal marsh. The vegetation here is quite diverse and contains Spatterdock, Pickerelweed, Arrow Arum, Broad-leaved Arrowhead (or Duck Potato), Great Bulrush, River Bulrush, Great Bur-reed, as well as smartweeds, knotweeds, cattails, and a scattering of Wild Rice. More distant parts of the marsh contain dense stands of Wild Rice, a fascinating plant that ranges from Georgia to Canada. In this area, however, it is restricted to fresh-water tidal marshes. Wild Rice was so highly valued by the North American Indians that they included harvesting rights in their treaties with the European settlers. It is the last plant to emerge in the spring (late May) and the first to die in the fall (early October).

The best time to observe Wild Rice is late July through early September when it is going to seed. At this time its distinctive flower/seed cluster makes it easy to recognize. During this time you will also see thousands of Red-winged Blackbirds and Bobolinks, among others, feeding on the abundant seeds.

At the end of this section of dike, where the trail again curves to the right and near the old dead tree (probably a White Oak judging by its shape), the vegetation in the impoundment becomes thicker. There are clumps of Purple Loosestrife and Common Buttonbush and large expanses of Spatterdock. This is the best place in the impoundment for waterfowl viewing, especially in April and October during the migrations. The Black-crowned Night-Herons have their rookery here (about 100 pairs strong) and wading birds such as Snowy Egrets, Great Egrets, and Great Blue Herons also tend to congregate.

As you move past the old dead tree the tidal marsh becomes a solid stand of cattails. This is a good spot to look for Marsh Wrens. The males not only call from just below the tops of the cattails, but usually build several nests while trying to attract a female. When the females arrive they usually build a nest of their own, ignoring the efforts of the males. Their nests are essentially nesting boxes or cavities, with a side entrance, all woven of cattail leaves and tied to the cattail stalks.

This area is a likely spot to see Muskrats, which also depend heavily on cattails. Muskrats are so named because of scent glands that they use for marking their territory and identifying each other. Man has no trouble recognizing Muskrats because they are the only mammal with a vertically flattened tail. Muskrats are supremely adapted for aquatic life; they use their tails for rudders, their hind feet have both webbing and stiff hairs that make efficient paddles, and their coats are thick and waterproof. Muskrats prefer swimming so much that they excavate canals in order to swim to drier parts of the marsh. They produce several litters of 2–8 young a year and their numbers can grow so large that they denude marsh vegetation. Their burrowing can cause leaks in dikes as well. Many animals will eat Muskrats if they catch them, but the main predators are Minks and Raccoons, neither of which is plentiful at Tinicum. The

Muskrat is the most commonly trapped animal in the United States (no trapping is allowed at Tinicum) and its fur is sold as "Marsh Rabbit." Muskrats were introduced to Europe for the value of their pelts, but today they are considered a serious pest, especially in the Netherlands, where they undermine the dikes.

As the dike curves to the left, the character of the tidal marsh again changes, this time to mudflats with clumps of Spatter-dock, Pickerelweed, Broad-leaved Arrowhead, and Arrow Arum. This section of the trail is infamous for the amount of

Pickerelweed

trash and debris along the dike. The debris collects because the current greatly slows here, allowing it to be deposited—a graphic example of how dumping upstream can affect the environment miles downstream. At the sign for the observation blind make a right and go into the wooden blind overlooking Darby Creek's mudflats. This is an excellent area for shorebirds if the season and tide are right. The best months are May, August, and September. The best time is 2–3 hours before high tide; the rising water gradually pushes the shorebirds toward you. A wide variety can be seen at Tinicum. Killdeer, Greater and Lesser Yellowlegs, Black-bellied (in the fall) and Semipalmated Plovers, Solitary, Pectoral, Semipalmated, and Least Sandpipers are the most common. Waterfowl, herons and egrets, Fish Crows, various gulls, Muskrats, an occasional Snapping Turtle, and rarely a Sora and Virginia Rail round things out nicely.

The observation blind marks the end of the dike trail. At this point several options are possible. Most obvious is to retrace your steps to the visitor center. This makes a round trip of 2.6 miles and allows you to see things you may have missed the first time. A second option is to continue around the impoundment, bearing left at the first trail sign, and follow the signs back to the visitor center for a round trip of 3.3 miles. This pleasant walk takes you through shrubby marshes, lowland woods, and old fields in various stages of succession. Along the way you can see American Bittersweet, Pale and Spotted Touch-me-nots, Bouncing Bet, Bigtooth Aspen, Eastern (Common) Cottonwood, Northern Water and Eastern Garter Snakes, Ring-necked Pheasant, American Woodcock, and a wide variety of songbirds and butterflies—in short, a worthwhile addition to your travels.

The third and longest option is for those who wish to see more of the tidal marsh, and Wild Rice in particular. To do this, continue past the blind and bear right, ignoring the first trail sign. After 0.75 miles you will arrive at a nice stand of Wild Rice. At this point you'll be on higher ground overlooking the marsh. If you continue along the narrow footpath you will come to a second observation blind that overlooks Darby Creek and its associated mudflats (another excellent area for shorebirds). Although this trail continues to Route 420, it is probably best to retrace your steps. The round trip totals about 4.5 miles.

No matter what route you choose you will see a diverse wetland area that survives in an urban situation because local citizens cared enough to protect it. Wetlands, marshes in particular, have been considered mosquito-infested wastelands for too long. Fortunately, people now realize their value for flood and pollution control, as well as their importance to the nation's fishing industry, and to sport fishermen, hunters, and trappers, and—not least—their aesthetic and scientific value to people who enjoy nature observation and seek to understand our world.

Dragonfly

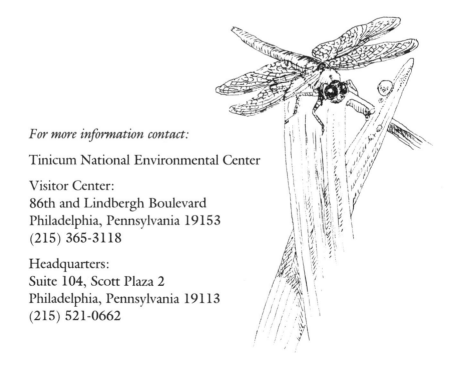

For more information contact:

Tinicum National Environmental Center

Visitor Center:
86th and Lindbergh Boulevard
Philadelphia, Pennsylvania 19153
(215) 365-3118

Headquarters:
Suite 104, Scott Plaza 2
Philadelphia, Pennsylvania 19113
(215) 521-0662

Directions to Tinicum National Environmental Center, Pennsylvania

From the City Line Avenue Exit of the Schuylkill Expressway (I-76), continue for 5.3 miles along U.S. 1 South (City Line Avenue) to the intersection with Route 3 (West Chester Pike). Pass through this intersection and go another 0.1 miles to the next light. Make a left on Lansdowne Avenue and drive another 3.7 miles to MacDade Boulevard. Make a right and stay in the left lane for 0.3 miles to the second light. Here proceed through the intersection onto Chester Pike (MacDade Boulevard veers to the right) and travel another 0.4 miles to the second light by a gas station. Make a left on Calcon Hook Road and drive 0.9 miles to the next light, which is Hook Road. Turn left, loop around the oil tank farm, and drive 0.6 miles to the next light by an apartment complex called "The Chalets" International City. Make a right at the light on Lindbergh Boulevard and drive 0.2 miles to the stop sign and the entrance to the Tinicum National Environmental Center on the right. Go through the gate and follow the gravel road for 0.3 miles to the parking lot by the visitor center. The dike road around the preserve begins just below here, but is closed to traffic and must be walked (or bicycled). A one-way trip from the Schuylkill Expressway takes approximately forty minutes.

There are several alternative routes to Tinicum from center city Philadelphia, but much of the area near the Philadelphia International Airport and Interstate 95 is under construction, so be ready for a myriad of detours.

A traditional route is via the George Platt Bridge (formerly the Penrose Avenue Bridge), which is presently under lengthy reconstruction. From the Schuylkill Expressway (I-76) take Exit 5 for the Airport and 26th Street. At the second light make a right and cross the bridge. Immediately after the bridge drive 0.4 miles and, following signs for I-95 South and Island Avenue, make a right. Travel another 0.4 miles to the second light and make a left on Bartram Avenue (a left at the first light

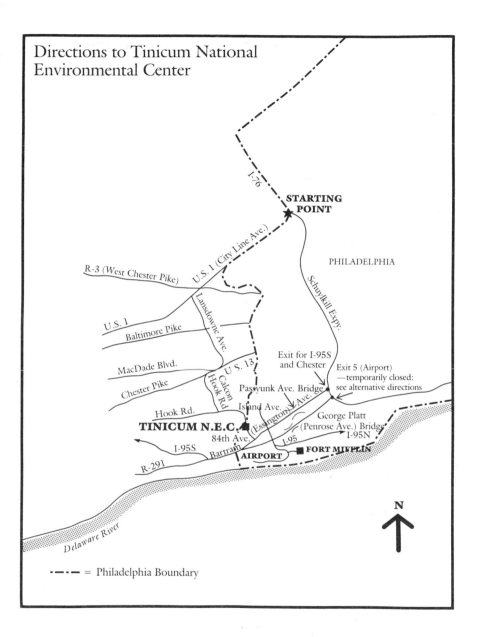

Directions to Tinicum National Environmental Center

STARTING POINT

PHILADELPHIA

I-76

U.S. 1 (City Line Ave.)

R-3 (West Chester Pike)

U.S. 1

Baltimore Pike

Lansdowne Ave.

Schuylkill Expy.

MacDade Blvd.

Chester Pike

U.S. 13

Calcon Hook Rd.

Exit for I-95S and Chester

Exit 5 (Airport) —temporarily closed: see alternative directions

Passyunk Ave. Bridge

Hook Rd.

Island Ave.

Essington Ave.

George Platt (Penrose Ave.) Bridge

TINICUM N.E.C.

84th Ave.

I-95N

I-95S

Bartram

I-95

FORT MIFFLIN

R-291

AIRPORT

N

Delaware River

-··-··- = Philadelphia Boundary

allows access to I-95 South via a recently constructed ramp). Drive 0.3 miles and make a right at the first light on 84th Avenue. Continue 0.7 miles to the second light and make a left at "The Chalets" International City on Lindbergh Boulevard. The entrance to Tinicum National Environmental Center is 0.2 miles further on your right.

At the time of this writing an easy method is to take the Schuylkill Expressway (I-76) east from center city. Stay in the right lane and take the exit for I-95 South and Chester. Drive 0.5 miles to the first light and make a right following the signs for I-95 South. Continue along Essington Avenue, cross the old Passyunk Avenue Bridge, and after 3.4 miles you will come to the intersection with Island Avenue (following signs for I-95 South all the time). Proceed straight on what is now Bartram Avenue, drive 0.3 miles, and make a right at the light on 84th Avenue. Stay in the left lane and drive 0.7 miles to the second light at "The Chalets" International City. Make a left on Lindbergh Boulevard and proceed 0.2 miles further to Tinicum's entrance on your right.

Fresh-Water Marshes and Related Fresh-Water Habitats of the Delaware Valley Region[1]

PENNSYLVANIA

Fresh-water marshes and related habitats often border the rivers and streams throughout southeastern Pennsylvania. Manmade impoundments also account for much of the fresh-water environs, especially in the Piedmont. Truly natural lakes occur most frequently in the more northern mountainous sections shaped long ago by glacier retreat and runoff. Many of the locales listed in the Deciduous Forests section contain some

---

[1]Let me thank Brian Moscatello and Franklin Haas for their help in compiling this listing.

fresh-water habitat, so check that listing. The areas mentioned here (even if a few are redundant) are locations where the fresh-water marsh, swamp, and so forth account for a significant percentage of the total habitat and are generally accessible to the public.

Brandywine River (Creek) Watershed, Chester County, Pennsylvania, with multiple accesses off Route 282, U.S. 322, and Route 100 (from north to south and into the state of Delaware). Extensive marshes and wooded swamps just north and south of U.S. 1 near Chadds Ford. Visit nearby Brandywine River Museum. Phone: (215) 459-1900.

Crum Creek Valley, Delaware County, near Media, Pennsylvania, between U.S. 1 and Baltimore Pike. Especially good for the secretive rails. Also contains deciduous woodlands.

Long Pond, Monroe County, near Long Pond, Pennsylvania, and the famous Pocono Raceway ("Motor Racing Capital of the World") off I-80 and Route 115. Excellent for marsh birds in general and the Alder (Traill's) Flycatcher. Located in the Poconos and surrounded by sections of boreal forests. See "The Mountains."

Marsh Creek State Park, Chester County, near Eagle, Pennsylvania, off Route 100. Also contains deciduous woodlands and successional fields. Phone: (215) 458-8515.

Middle Creek Wildlife Management Area, Lebanon and Lancaster Counties, near Kleinfeltersville, Pennsylvania, off U.S. 322 and Routes 501 and 897. Also contains extensive deciduous woodlands, successional fields, and croplands. Visitor center and museum. During the controlled goose-hunting season (September to the December closing date) access to much of the area is restricted. Phone (Pennsylvania Game Commission): (215) 926-3136.

Neshaminy State Park. See Deciduous Forests listing.

Octoraro Area. See Deciduous Forests listing.

Peace Valley Nature Center. See Deciduous Forests listing.

Pennsbury Manor State Park, Bucks County, near Tully-town, Pennsylvania, off U.S. 13. Includes nearby Upper and Lower Van Sciver Lakes, Manor Lake, Money Island (with deciduous woods), and some fresh-water tidal marsh along the Delaware River itself. Site of William Penn's seventeenth-century estate. Penn Warner Club manages the lakes and shoreline areas and access may be limited at times. Phone: (215) 295-7191.

Quakertown Marsh, Bucks County, near Quakertown, Pennsylvania, off Routes 309 and 313 (adjacent to Old Swamp Road).

NEW JERSEY

What was said for Pennsylvania also pertains to New Jersey and Delaware. In addition, along the Atlantic Coastal Plain—especially as one approaches Delaware Bay or the Atlantic Ocean—fresh-water habitats often become intimately associated with salt-water habitats. This mixing occurs gradually in the various estuaries of the tristate region where fresh water meets salt water (now called brackish). These estuaries are dynamic, ever-changing, unique ecosystems whose characteristics vary from season to season, depending on such conditions as weather, rainfall, tides, snowmelt from the previous winter, incursions of salt water from the ocean during droughts, and so forth. The close association between fresh-water and salt-water habitats can be even more dramatic, as seen at various National Wildlife Refuges and Wildlife Management Areas that dot the coastal areas of New Jersey and Delaware. Much of this proximity is artificial in that man diked the fresh-water and brackish impoundments during the 1930s and afterwards to provide feeding and resting grounds for waterfowl and shorebirds migrating along the Atlantic Flyway.

Brigantine Division of the Edwin B. Forsythe National Wildlife Refuge, Atlantic County, near Oceanville and Absecon, New Jersey, off U.S. 9 (10 miles from Atlantic City). Two large fresh-water impoundments (East and West Pools) plus extensive marshes along Doughty Creek host a great variety of wildlife, especially birds. Extensive salt-water marshes along outside perimeter of diked tour road. Some pine-oak woodlands and successional fields in more upland areas. Nature center. Phone: (609) 652-1665.

Cape May Point State Park, Cape May County, near Cape May Point, New Jersey, off Lighthouse Avenue (from the Garden State Parkway southern terminus, continue on Lafayette Street to Perry Street, bear right on Perry, which becomes Sunset Blvd., and eventually turn left on Lighthouse Avenue). Several nature trails wind past fresh-water marshes, wooded swamps, deciduous woodlands, and beach dunes. Premier hawk watching location in the region during the fall, along with spectacular concentrations of butterflies, especially Monarchs during their autumnal migration. Nature center. Phone: (609) 884-2159. See "The Barrier Beach and Island."

Charles Rogers Sanctuary (formerly **Princeton Wildlife Refuge**), Mercer County, near Princeton, New Jersey, off U.S. 1 and Routes 571 and 27. Visit the adjacent deciduous woodlands of the Princeton Institute Woods. See Deciduous Forests listing.

Great Swamp National Wildlife Refuge, Morris County, near Basking Ridge, New Jersey, off I-287. Remnant of Glacial Lake Passaic formed 10,000 years ago during the Wisconsin Glacier retreat. Fresh-water marshes and wooded swamps famous for Wood Ducks, Barred Owls, Bog Turtles, among others. Visitor center. Phone: (201) 647-1222. Visit adjacent Lord Stirling Park (Somerset County) with its similar habitats, nature center, and extensive boardwalk system. Although these areas are somewhat north of what is generally considered the Delaware Valley Region, they are well worth a visit. While in the area also visit Morristown National Historical Park (Morris County), the 1777 winter encampment of the Continental Army. Even further north, visit Troy Meadows, Morris

County, near Troy Hills off I-280—the largest cattail marsh in New Jersey.

Higbee Beach Wildlife Management Area. See Deciduous Forests listing.

Lester G. MacNamara Wildlife Management Area (formerly **Tuckahoe-Corbin City Tract**), Atlantic and Cape May Counties, near Tuckahoe, New Jersey, off Routes 50 and 631. Fresh-water marshes and impoundments along with salt-water and brackish marshes and pine-oak woodlands. Great birding. Phone: (609) 628-2103.

Manahawkin Wildlife Management Area, Ocean County, near Manahawkin, New Jersey, off Route 72 and U.S. 9. Very similar to Brigantine N.W.R. Former breeding locale for the rare Black Rail (present status?).

Mannington Meadows, Salem County, four miles north of Salem, New Jersey, off Route 45. Famous for the striking American Lotus (*Nelumbo*), a member of the water-lily family.

Peaslee Wildlife Management Area, Cumberland County, between Millville and Tuckahoe, New Jersey, between Routes 552 and 49. Also contains vast tracts of pine-oak and deciduous woodlands.

Pedricktown Marsh, Gloucester and Salem Counties, near Pedricktown, New Jersey, off I-295. Located along Oldman's Creek and famous for seeing the Ruff (a Eurasian shorebird) in April before the marsh vegetation emerges.

Rancocas State Park and Nature Center. Harbors fresh-water tidal marshes and large stands of Wild Rice. Phone: (609) 261-2495. See Deciduous Forests listing.

Timber-Beaver Swamp, Cape May County, between South Dennis and Swainton, New Jersey, off Routes 585 and 83, and U.S. 9. Above dam at Clint Millpond are fresh-water marshes and heavily wooded swamps; below are brackish and eventually salt-water marshes. Good location for Beaver, River Otter, and Muskrat.

Trenton Marsh (Roebling Memorial Park), Mercer County, Trenton, New Jersey, on Sewell Avenue off U.S. 206 from U.S. 1. Excellent fresh-water marsh with some wooded swamps, deciduous woods, and fields.

DELAWARE

Blackbird Creek (Taylor's Bridge), New Castle County, near Odessa and Taylor's Bridge, Delaware, off Route 9. Above the bridge are extensive fresh-water marshes; below are brackish and eventually salt-water marshes. Before canoeing the creek, check with Delaware Wildlands, Inc. Phone: (302) 834-1332. This organization owns and manages a great diversity of habitats in the state in addition to portions of this marsh. Canoes can be rented for this and other nearby trips from Wilderness Canoe Trips, Inc. in Wilmington. Phone: (302) 654- 2227. They can give information on the need for permission to canoe in areas here and elsewhere under private ownership.

Bombay Hook National Wildlife Refuge, Kent County, near Smyrna and Leipsic, Delaware, off Route 9. Several fresh-water impoundments (Raymond and Shearness Pools), fresh-water marshes (Bear Swamp and Finis Pools), and a wooded swamp (parts of Finis Pool) occur here as well as extensive salt-water marshes, deciduous woodlands, successional fields, and croplands. Generally similar to Brigantine, New Jersey, but more diversity. Nature center. Phone: (302) 653-9345.

Brandywine Creek State Park. See Deciduous Forests listing.

Churchman's Marsh, New Castle County, between Wilmington and Newport, Delaware, off Route 4. Only remnants now exist of the once famous fresh-water marshes surrounding much of nearby Wilmington.

Dragon Run Marsh, New Castle County, near Delaware City, Delaware, off Route 72. Former nesting site of a pair of Purple Gallinules during the late 1970s (a bird more typical of the Deep South). Canoe rental possible from Wilderness Canoe Trips, Inc. Phone: (302) 654-2227.

Little Creek Wildlife Area, Kent County, near Dover and Little Creek, Delaware, off Route 9 (about 15 miles south of Bombay Hook N.W.R.). Fantastic birding, especially waterfowl and shorebirds, and the northernmost breeding locale for the Black-necked Stilt (a typical southerner and westerner). Several accesses to this extensive area include Pickering Beach, the HQ. entrance road to the observation tower, and the Port Mahon Road. Phone (Division of Fish and Wildlife): (302) 736-4431.

Prime Hook National Wildlife Refuge, Sussex County, Milton, Delaware, between Milford and Lewes, off Routes 14 and 16. Combination of fresh-water, brackish, and salt-water marshes along Prime Hook Creek and Petersfield Ditch among others. Home of the Seaside Alder (found only along the coastal streams of the Delaware-Maryland border and in Oklahoma), Muskrat, River Otter, Black Rail, and Sedge (Short-billed Marsh) Wren—all local or rare species save the Muskrat. Nearby canoe rental available. Visitor center. Phone: (302) 684-8419.

Thousand Acre Marsh, New Castle County, near Delaware City, Delaware, off Routes 9 and 417 (Dutch Neck Road). Located just south of the eastern end of the Chesapeake-Delaware Canal, as is Dragon Run Marsh (just north of the canal). Largest fresh-water marsh in Delaware. Canoe rental possible from Wilderness Canoe Trips, Inc. Phone: (302) 654-2227.

Woodland Beach Wildlife Area, Kent County, near Smyrna, Delaware, off Routes 9, 6, and 82. The fresh-water Taylor's

Gut impoundment is separated from vast brackish and salt-water marshes to the east by a man-made sluice. Canoes can be rented from Wilderness Canoe Trips, Inc. Phone: (302) 654-2227.

Suggested Readings on the Fresh-Water Marsh and Other Fresh-Water Habitats

Angel, H., and Pat Wolseley. *The Water Naturalist*. New York: Facts on File, 1982.

Brown, A. L. *Ecology of Fresh Water*. Cambridge, Mass.: Harvard University Press, 1977.

Clark, John. *Coastal Ecosystems*. Washington, D.C.: The Conservation Foundation, 1974.

Coker, R. E. *Streams, Lakes, and Ponds*. Chapel Hill, N.C.: University of North Carolina Press, 1954.

Delaware Valley Regional Planning Commission. *Four Environmentally Significant Areas* (Delaware Estuary Coastal Zone Working Paper). Philadelphia: Pennsylvania Department of Environmental Resources, 1976.

Dills, Gary, et al. *Aquatic-Biotic Community Structure as an Indicator of Pollution* (PB-216-801). Washington, D.C.: U.S. Department of the Interior, Office of Water Resources Research, 1972.

Fisher, Alan. *Country Walks Near Philadelphia*. Boston: The Appalachian Mountain Club, 1983.

Freshwater Biology and Pollution Ecology Training Manual (PB-242-000). Washington, D.C.: U.S. Environmental Protection Agency, 1975.

Headstrom, Richard. *Adventures with Freshwater Animals*. New York: Dover Publications, 1983.

Hotchkiss, Neil. *Common Marsh, Underwater and Floating-leaved Plants of the United States and Canada*. New York: Dover Publications, 1972.

Hunt, Cynthia, and Robert M. Garrells. *Water: The Web of Life*. New York: W. W. Norton, 1972.

Klots, E. B. *New Field Book of Freshwater Life*. New York: G. P. Putnam & Sons, 1966.

Kroodsma, Donald E. "Marsh Wrenditions." *Natural History*, September 1983.

Larson, Joseph, and Richard Newton. *The Value of Wetlands to Man and Wildlife* (SP-125). Massachusetts: Cooperative Extension Service, University of Massachusetts, U.S. Dept. of Agriculture and County Extension Services, 1981.

McCormick, Jack, Robert R. Grant, and Ruth Patrick. *Two Studies of Tinicum Marsh*. Washington, D.C.: The Conservation Foundation, 1970.

McMillan, Vicky. "Dragonfly Monopoly." *Natural History*, July 1984.

Macan, T. T. *Ponds and Lakes*. New York: Crane, Russak, 1973.

Moyle, Peter B. "America's Carp." *Natural History*, September 1984.

Niering, William. *The Life of the Marsh*. New York: Our Living World of Nature Series, McGraw-Hill, 1966.

Odum, William E., Thomas J. Smith III, John K. Hoover, and Carole C. McIvor. *The Ecology of Tidal Freshwater Marshes of the United States East Coast: A Community Profile*. Washington, D.C.: U.S. Fish and Wildlife Service, FWS/OBS-83/17, 1984.

Popham, E. J. *Life in Fresh Water*. Cambridge, Mass.: Harvard University Press, 1961.

Reid, George. *Ecology of Inland Waters and Estuaries*. 2nd ed. New York: Van Nostrand Reinhold, 1976.

————. *Pond Life* (A Golden Guide). New York: Golden Press, 1967.

Thomas, Bill. *The Swamp*. New York: W. W. Norton, 1976.

"Tinicum—A Chronology." *The Beacon*. Philadelphia: Philadelphia Conservationists, March 1978.

Tinicum National Environmental Center: Master Plan. Washington, D.C.: U.S. Department of the Interior, Fish and Wildlife Service, 1980.

Usinger, Robert L. *The Life of Rivers and Streams*. New York: McGraw-Hill, 1967.

Wakefield, Penny. "Reducing the Federal Role in Wetlands Protection." *Environment*, December 1982.

Wetzel, R. *Limnology*. Philadelphia: Saunders, 1975.

Winterringer, Glen. *Some Plant Galls of Illinois* (no. 12). Illinois: Illinois State Museum, 1961.

the Mountains

LARRY M. RYMON
JACQUELYN L. KATZMIRE

The Delaware Water Gap National Recreation Area is a 72,000-acre national park encompassing a 35-mile stretch of the Delaware River between Pennsylvania and New Jersey. To the west in Pennsylvania, the river is bordered by the eastern-most edge of the great Appalachian Plateau, so heavily dissected by stream erosion and glaciation that it has lost the character of a plateau and appears now as the mountains and ridges known as the Poconos. To the east in New Jersey, the river is bordered by the Kittatinny Ridge, the most outstanding in a series of parallel ridges running northeast to southwest that make up the Ridge and Valley Province. Also called the Folded Appalachians, these ridges cross the northwest corner of New

Jersey and continue southwest into Pennsylvania through the area of the Delaware Water Gap. The Gap itself is one of the most spectacular features of the Pocono area; indeed, it is the best example of a water gap found anywhere in the United States.

The Recreation Area was originally authorized by Congress in 1965 in conjunction with the proposed Tocks Island Dam project. The lake created by the dam was to become a public recreational facility. Stiff resistance to the dam, spearheaded by local officials and residents, ultimately shelved the project. The Recreation Area was then placed under the authority of the National Park Service, to preserve the natural beauty and wilderness quality of the river and surrounding area. The park provides year-round recreational and educational opportunities. In summer, facilities are provided for swimming, picnicking, hiking, canoeing, and fishing. There are also guided walks and canoe trips with Park Service interpreters that emphasize the natural history and wildlife of the area. In winter, there is snowmobiling and crosscountry skiing. The Pocono Environmental Education Center (Pennsylvania) and the Wallpack Valley Environmental Education Center (New Jersey) provide students with the opportunity to study ecology and conservation in an "outdoor classroom."

Peters Valley (New Jersey) is a nearby community of artisans working in wood, metal, textiles, and photography. Resident artists' studios can be toured by appointment, and visitors are welcome at the information center, craft store, and annual craft fair. Millbrook (New Jersey) is an Early American country village that has been recreated to give visitors a taste of rural life in the early 1800s. It includes a blacksmith's shop, weaver's shop, shoemaker's shop, store, church, and several homes. More information about the park and a schedule of upcoming events can be obtained from Kittatinny Point Information Station in New Jersey, Dingmans Falls Visitor Center in Dingmans Ferry, Pennsylvania, or at Park Headquarters in Bushkill, Pennsylvania.

The mountains, ridges, and plateaus of the Poconos reveal a complex geologic past. Composed of sedimentary rocks—

sandstones, shales, limestones, and conglomerates—the Pocono region was once part of a much larger geographic formation called the Appalachian geosyncline, a shallow trough-like depression in the land surface. During Paleozoic time, between 600 and 270 million years ago, the geosyncline was sunk below a number of shallow inland seas that successively covered the area, interrupted at intervals by brief periods of uplift. Over these hundreds of millions of years, layer upon layer of sediment, amounting to some 12,000 feet, was deposited on the bottom of the ancient seas. Eventually the combination of weight and the earth's internal heat turned the layers of sediment into rock. Sand and small particles became sandstone, clay became shale, limey clay became limestone, and gravel and larger particles became conglomerates. In the early Silurian Period, about 425 million years ago, just before the land was uplifted for the final time, a layer of hard pebbles and quartz sand was spread over the sea floor as a coarse gravel that later hardened into the highly resistant rock known as the Shawangunk Conglomerate. The upthrust edge of this Shawangunk Conglomerate now forms Kittatinny Ridge.

At the end of the Carboniferous Period, 270 million years ago, tremendous pressure deep in the earth began to compress the rock layers. Many geologists believe this to have been caused by the shifting and slow, grinding collision of the crustal plates of the North American and African continents. Gradually the layers buckled, lifting the land surface out of the sea to form mountains towering 20,000 feet high, the ancient ancestors of our Appalachians. In some areas the compression was so great that the rock broke, exposing the ragged edges of the rock layers, now tilted at a sharp angle to the horizon. The buckling resulted in a series of northeast-southwest folds extending inland into northeast Pennsylvania including the present-day bed of the Delaware River. This section of Folded Appalachian rock formed the base of what would later become the Ridge and Valley Province, while the unfolded rock west of the river became the Appalachian Plateau Province.

Once the initial pressure had been relieved by the folding, the surface remained stationary for a very long time. Erosive forces went to work on the new land and during the long period of immobility, all of its features were worn away, reducing the entire area to a broad, rolling peneplain that extended all the way from the Appalachian Plateau to the sea in a single, gentle slope. The flat top of Kittatinny Ridge is a remnant of this ancient peneplain, across which the Delaware River wandered in a wide flat valley.

During the Cretaceous and Tertiary Periods, 135 to 2 million years ago, the land began to rise again, reaching its present elevation through a series of gradual uplifts. As the slope of the land increased, the streams and rivers began to flow faster, cutting into the rock underneath. The horizontal rocks of the Plateau section were deeply dissected by stream erosion while the Delaware carved the edge of the plateau into mountains and ridges. The folded rocks of the Ridge and Valley section were eroded differentially. The softer, more soluble rock layers were worn away to form valleys between the edges of the more resistant layers, which remained standing as ridges. At the same time, the Delaware River had begun the slow process of cutting its way through the hard Shawangunk Conglomerate. All the power of the river was concentrated on the small area where it crossed the Shawangunk, and in time, the Delaware's tributaries created Kittatinny Ridge as the Delaware itself created the Water Gap.

Some finishing touches were added when glaciers occupied the area as recently as 10,000 years ago. These were huge sheets of ice, high enough to cover the top of Kittatinny Ridge. Rock surfaces seen today were smoothed and rounded by the scraping action of the ice. Many surfaces show glacial striations or scratches left by huge rocks pushed along the base of the glacier. Whatever topsoil formerly existed was scraped away, exposing the rock beneath. When the climate finally warmed and the glacier melted back, most of the region was left covered with a layer of gravelly clay called glacial till. This combined effect produced the thin, stony soils that predominate in the Pocono area.

Historically, the region east of the Mississippi was covered by a continuous, well-nigh impenetrable forest. Overland routes were by and large impractical, due to the dense structure of the forest—stands of immense trees ranging 2 to 5 feet in diameter, standing 50 to 150 feet high. The forest floor was literally choked with the debris. Branches and fallen trunks were too thick to walk around or climb over, and this maze was further complicated by the ropy twining stems of grapevines. Travel through the Pocono region in the 1600s was restricted to Indian trails along either side of the Delaware; thus the Lenape Indians set the course for present-day roadways through the Gap.

White settlers eventually succeeded in destroying most of these forest giants and cleared the understory for farming and commerce. The urge to conquer the land was so great around the turn of the last century that small farms sprang up everywhere, even on the slopes and the very tops of the ridges. Because of the rapid erosion of the thin soil on the ridges, most such farms proved unproductive in the long run. They were abandoned to the long process of succession that continues to this day.

As you look more closely at the vegetative cover in the Poconos, it becomes increasingly apparent how confusing it is to explain, even for naturalists. Most of the region is covered by a Mixed Deciduous-Coniferous Forest whose characteristic trees are oak, Eastern White Pine, Eastern Hemlock, birch, aspen, and Red Cedar (Eastern). The problem of description arises because proportions of deciduous and coniferous trees and the particular species present vary greatly according to local conditions. Instead of a general pattern of vegetation, we have a composite of smaller individualized communities. This "localization effect" is the result of several influences.

To begin with, repeated glacial activity has left a mosaic of soil types plus discrete pockets of remnant northern plant communities (Sphagnum Moss—Black Spruce—Tamarack bogs). The ridge-and-valley configuration, particularly the steepness of a slope and the direction it faces, also contributes to the variation in cover. In addition, man has extensively altered cover through farming, logging, fire management, and the introduction of exotics such as Ailanthus (Tree-of-Heaven), European Larch, and Purple Loosestrife, as well as of diseases like the blight that destroyed the once prevalent American Chestnut.

As a result, practically every area in the Pocono region is covered by vegetation in some stage of regrowth or succession. In fact, the forest we see today has been cut at least three times. The present cover of mixed oak-conifer is a subclimax state, with oak filling the void left by the loss of the American Chestnut. This stage will eventually be succeeded by a Northern Hardwood climax forest, where maples and American Beech are codominant species in association with other hardwoods, Eastern Hemlock, and Eastern White Pine.

Finally, the Pocono area is the meeting place of the Canadian and Carolinian Life Zones. Plant and animal species of more typically southern distribution, such as Sassafras, Opossum, Common Persimmon, and Northern Mockingbird, overlap with species of more northerly distribution, such as the Snowshoe Hare (Rabbit), Eastern Coyote, Striped Maple, and Tamarack. The following general description outlines some of the identifiable plant communities that make up the Pocono region. As you explore, however, expect to find places where the vegetation does not correspond to these patterns at all.

Sunny, well-drained, south-to-west facing slopes along the lower half of the Delaware are mainly a mixed oak-hardwood forest. Dominant are Scarlet and Black Oak, in association with Chestnut, Northern Red, and White Oak. Since oaks hybridize, however, individual trees frequently show characteristics of several species. A few small Eastern Hemlocks, Eastern White Pines, and Red Cedars may be scattered among the oaks, as are small numbers of a wide variety of other hardwoods, including Tuliptree (Yellow-poplar), Red Maple, Sugar Maple, American Beech, Shagbark Hickory, Bitternut, White Ash, Box Elder (Ashleaf Maple), American Elm, and Black Cherry. Flowering Dogwood and Eastern Hophornbeam (Ironwood) grow in the understory along with Pink Azalea, Mapleleaf Viburnum, and Common Greenbrier. Gray Birch, Sweet (Black) Birch, Quaking Aspen, Bigtooth Aspen, American Basswood (American Linden), Sassafras, and Staghorn Sumac are found with Witch-hazel and Spicebush in disturbed areas such as the edges of openings in the forest cover. A thick accumulation of leaf litter covers the forest floor through which some bare rock shows. These southern slopes are very similar to the woodlands described in "The Eastern Deciduous Forest" chapter, except for the birches and aspens, which favor cooler, more northerly latitudes, or higher elevations of the mountains.

Shady and damp north-to-east facing slopes are covered by nearly equal numbers of deciduous and coniferous trees. Underneath, ferns grow profusely among the prominent outcroppings of rock that show everywhere between the trees. Among deciduous trees, the oaks and maples predominate, mainly Red and Sugar Maples and Northern Red Oak, with American Beech and some Yellow and Sweet Birches. Among the conifers, conditions favor the Eastern Hemlock, which is probably twice as numerous as the Eastern White Pine.

"Evergreen" is the term generally used to describe conifers because of their most salient characteristic: retaining green chlorophyll throughout the winter. To survive the extremes of weather, deciduous trees have evolved a "life-support cutback" system. The seasonal changes of falling temperatures and shrinking day length, and possibly other as yet unknown factors, trigger physiological changes that result in loss of foliage and a generalized slowing of their metabolic processes. Evergreens, on the other hand, have evolved a strategy to maintain their metabolic processes at a constant rate. Green chlorophyll is not lost, thus food manufacture via photosynthesis can continue. Conifers have also adapted to the lack of usable ground water during winter. Their shallow root system can absorb very small amounts of water penetrating from the surface, which occurs in gradual snow-melt. Also, the "needle" leaves expose a small surface area from which water can evaporate, and the thick waxy coating on the needles, called the cuticle, helps prevent moisture loss. The cuticle also helps regulate the internal temperature of the needle.

These same adaptations aid conifers under high temperatures and prolonged dry spells too. When faced with water-deprivation, deciduous trees show the same "cutback" response as in winter, whereas the conifers' shallow roots, needle-leaf structure, and thick cuticle enable them to carry on for a considerable period without noticeable effect. At present, the coniferous forests of the Poconos are showing signs of damage from the acid precipitation that threatens the entire Northeast. Eastern White Pines seem particularly vulnerable, and far too many of these stately conifers now display yellowed needles, bare branches, and dead terminal shoots.

In the flanks of the ridges are drainage ravines, carved by the action of small streams flowing to the Delaware. These ravines are filled almost exclusively with Eastern Hemlock–Native Rhododendron–Fern communities that thrive in the abundant moisture, low light, and shelter from wind. The ravines contain highly acidic soil, a major reason for the dominance of the rhododendrons and hemlocks. Decomposition of coniferous leaf litter, greatly slowed by cool temperatures and excess moisture, produces a very acidic *mor* or raw humus. Although weathering of the parent rock releases minerals into the soil that would help neutralize the acidity, the permeability of the underlying rock—mostly shales and sandstones—plus the high water content of the soil causes the minerals to be rapidly leached away. The organic acids build up in the soil, lowering the pH, which, in turn, affects the availability of various plant nutrients and determines which plants can survive in these areas. The pH is a chemical measure of acidity or alkalinity with a numerical range of 1 to 14. Pure water has a pH of 7 which is neutral. A pH below 6.5 is acidic, while that above 7.5 is alkaline. It has been theorized that the rhododendron thrives in acid soils because it is an inefficient absorber of iron, and at low pH (4.5–5.5) more iron becomes available, ensuring that the rhododendron will receive an adequate amount. The hemlock thrives here because its seedling can grow in the dense shade of the rhododendron thickets, which most trees cannot tolerate. As the hemlocks grow, they provide shade for the rhododendrons, and their litter maintains the acidity of the soil. In this way, the hemlock-rhododendron association becomes a self-perpetuating community.

Farther north along the river, the slopes of the plateau are much rockier and the soil layer thinner than those at the lower elevations. Deciduous cover of Chestnut, Black, Scarlet, and White Oak as well as Red Maple is interspersed with large stands of Eastern White Pine, mixed with Eastern Hemlock and some Red Pine. Small stands of Gray Birch, Quaking Aspen, and Bigtooth Aspen grow along the edges, and Striped Maple grows in the deciduous understory with Mountain Laurel, low-growing blueberries, Black Huckleberry, and Common Greenbrier. As the slopes become increasingly vertical near the top, large faces of bare rock are exposed, to which Scrub (Bear) Oak and Pitch Pine cling.

Some of the rock faces continuously crumble and slough off, forming a mound of loose rock at the base called a talus slope. These are rugged environments with extreme temperature changes and no protection from wind or rain. They are also dangerous places to attempt to explore. Red shale cliffs along Route 209 break up into long slivers of rock with very sharp edges. Lichens survive here, as do Spotted Knapweed (Starthistle), rock cresses, and stunted oaks, maples, and sumacs. When the slope of certain shales approaches a 70° angle, a special shale barrens community exists, dominated by Prickly-pear cactus. Although most water runs off these slopes, and their exposure to the sun creates very high surface temperatures, the Prickly-pear flourishes, seemingly oblivious to the harsh environment. In the Water Gap, sections of conglomeritic rock break up into football-sized pieces to form talus slopes. One of these is situated next to Interstate 80, and fear of rock slides led to the construction of a retaining wall and application of a fixative to the slope. Since then, Eastern Hemlocks and Gray Birches have successfully anchored themselves to the rock.

The top of the plateau still shows the effects of major disturbance by man. Forested areas that have recovered from timbering and clear-cutting are still primarily oak, but greater numbers of maples and American Beech indicate a gradual return to a Northern Hardwood climax forest—provided succession is allowed to continue uninterrupted. Until about 50 years ago, many areas were periodically burned, usually for commercial reasons such as blueberry production. These burn areas are now covered by thick scrub growth of Gray Birch, Quaking Aspen, Scrub Oak, Pitch Pine, and some Sweet Birch and Bigtooth Aspen. When the glaciers passed over the plateau and scraped away the topsoil, irregularities in the undersurface of the glacial ice were pressed into the rock by the weight, creating water-holding depressions in the surface of the plateau.

Larger holes were later filled in by the melting ice to form small glacial pothole lakes; good examples are Lake Lacawac in Pike County, Pennsylvania and Sunfish Pond on top of Kittatinny Ridge in New Jersey. Shallower depressions were partially filled in by the deposition of glacial till, creating boreal-type bogs and swamps. The top of the plateau is still pockmarked by glacial lakes and Sphagnum Moss swamps left behind by the retreating glaciers, such as the Cranberry–Black Spruce–Tamarack bog in Tannersville, Pennsylvania, about 10 miles west of the Gap.

MT. MINSI

The walk described in this chapter is located on Mt. Minsi, the name given the face of Kittatinny Ridge along the Pennsylvania side of the Water Gap (the face along the New Jersey side is called Mt. Tammany). The area was once part of a luxury resort on the east side of the town of Delaware Water Gap, Pennsylvania and is just slightly north of the Gap itself, which has since become part of the Delaware Water Gap National Recreation Area. The hotel building, called the Kittatinny House, stood on the spot that is now Resort Point Overlook (Gap Overlook 1) on Route 611. The starting point of the walk is at Lake Lenape on the next terrace of Mt. Minsi, directly above Resort Point. You will be following the old gravel road that leads from Lake Lenape along the second terrace of Mt. Minsi and up to the third terrace. This road also runs concurrently with the Appalachian Trail for a short way. Though less than a mile long, this walk takes you through several of the most distinctive communities that make up the Pocono region, and ends with a breath-taking view of the Delaware Water Gap from a glacier-marked, bare rock terrace known as Table Rock. The walk is basically easy, though two short sections could prove difficult for someone with a heart or breathing problem. Hiking boots are recommended if you want to explore the side trails, but for the main trail, sneakers or walking shoes are fine.

The walk begins in a section of Mixed Deciduous–Coniferous Forest. To the left, just beyond the gate, is a small sink

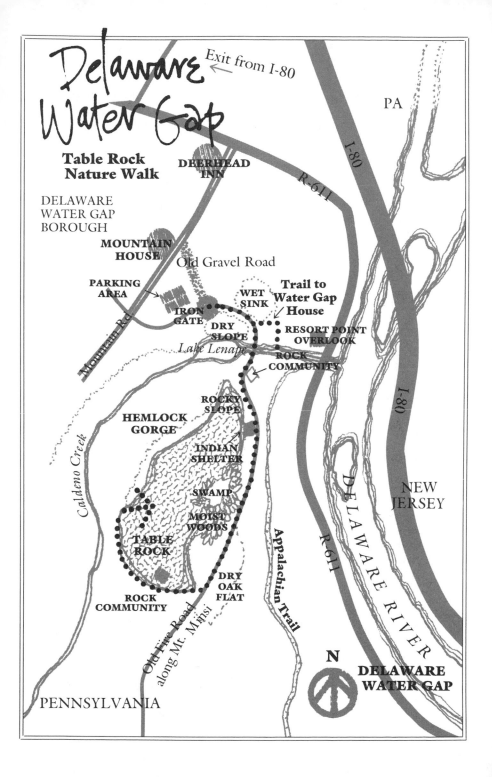

where water collects. The moist environment supports several large Eastern Hemlocks and White Oaks, but take note of three massive trees that dwarf everything around them. These are Swamp White Oaks, identified by the open, rounded structure, drooping branches, and beautiful foliage of dark green contrasting with silvery-white undersides. Swamp Whites are sure indicators of a water-retaining location. They are becoming a less common sight everywhere thanks to wholesale draining of wetland areas. This little sink had been partially drained by the borough of Delaware Water Gap, but remains wet enough to support these giants.

To the right is a drier slope with mixed oaks, Red and Sugar Maples, American Elm, and a couple of small Eastern Hemlocks. The great number of oaks means abundant acorns for squirrels, deer, and turkeys. You can see Gray and Red Squirrels dashing among the tree trunks almost any time, but it takes a wary observer to catch a Wild Turkey scratching its way upslope, or a White-tailed Deer nosing through the underbrush. The Wild Turkey had been brought close to extinction by the turn of the century, less from overshooting than from timbering, which eliminated stands of mature trees that produce the mast crops (acorns, nuts, and such) upon which the turkey depends. Careful management since then has restored this prized game bird all over the United States, particularly in the Northeast.

If you look closely at some of the acorns, you may see a tiny bore-hole, perfectly round. This is the work of the Acorn Weevil, cousin to the Boll Weevil. Weevils have an extremely long, tubelike snout, easily twice the length of their bodies, with tiny mandibles at the tip. They approach an acorn on the ground, extend their snout, and chew through the husk into the meat underneath, leaving the small hole as a calling card when finished.

In the branches overhead are familiar year-round residents, Black-capped Chickadees, Tufted Titmice, White-breasted Nuthatches, Downy Woodpeckers, Yellow-rumped (Myrtle) Warblers, and Blue Jays, but when spring bursts on the scene, these trees become a kaleidoscope of color as migrating warblers move through the area. Tennessee, Orange-crowned,

Nashville, Cape May, Bay-breasted, Worm-eating, and Connecticut Warblers are some of the rarer species that can be seen during spring migration. Those that remain to nest more or less regularly in the Poconos are the Black-and-white, Blue-winged, Yellow, Magnolia, Black-throated Blue, Black-throated Green, Blackburnian, Chestnut-sided, and Canada Warblers, Northern Waterthrush, Ovenbird, Common Yellowthroat, American Redstart, and sometimes the Golden-winged Warbler. Many of these nest on or near the ground in the low shrubs of the understory. Others choose small conifers such as spruce or young hemlock in which to build their nests

Wild Turkey

of small twigs, evergreen needles, grass, and spider webs. Yellow Warblers and American Redstarts fashion a tiny cup-shaped nest, 2 inches in diameter and 3 inches high, in the forks of shrubs or saplings, often in dense thickets that border roadsides, streamsides, or ponds. Although well concealed in almost every case, warblers' nests are commonly discovered by the Brown-headed Cowbird and parasitized with its egg. In many instances, when the intruder is found, the warbler will construct a new nest floor right over the cowbird's egg and its own, and lay a second clutch.

The slightly larger, less colorful vireos are also part of this montage: Solitary, Yellow-throated, White-eyed, and Warbling Vireos, and the common Red-eyed Vireo. All of these nest in the immediate vicinity as well as throughout the Delaware Valley, except the Solitary Vireo, which is common only in the Northern Mixed Hardwood–Coniferous Forests such as these.

The road represents a highly disturbed opening in the forest. The gravelly, debris-strewn waste areas along the sides are home to a number of trees, shrubs, and wildflowers associated with such areas. At the bottom of the slope, where water collects, you find Virginia Waterleaf, named perhaps for a species with succulent leaves, or perhaps from the gray-green "watermarks" on the leaves. With the Virginia Waterleaf is some Sweet Cicely, a member of the parsley family that blooms from June through August. The flower is nondescript, but the carrotlike roots exude a pleasant licorice or anise scent when crushed. On the left side is some Zigzag (Broad-leaved) Goldenrod, whose waxy bright yellow flower clusters are a cheerful note in late fall. Blue Wood Aster and White Wood Aster are also common here midsummer through fall, as are the thick patches of White Snakeroot and Spotted Touch-me-not (Jewelweed). White Snakeroot was once used to treat snakebite, but it is actually poisonous to man and animal. Cows that graze on this plant can transmit the poison through milk, making humans extremely ill. The crushed leaves of Spotted Touch-me-not make a good remedy for the itch of Poison-ivy, which is also found practically everywhere in the area. Spicebush grows along the road where there is sufficient moisture and the oak canopy lets some sunlight through.

Ahead on the left, a small sidetrail leads to the ruins of the old Water Gap House. This was a second hotel built on the resort grounds by William Brodhead, owner of the already established Kittatinny House. Work on the Water Gap House was begun just prior to the Civil War, suspended for the duration, and resumed afterward. The hotel was finally completed in 1873. Though less famous, Water Gap House surpassed Kittatinny in grandeur, and was the most expensive resort hotel in the area. In its heyday, the guest list included such notables as Fred Astaire and sister Adele, and President Teddy Roosevelt.

The road then curves right to Lake Lenape, a small shallow lake created by the damming of Caldeno Creek. The near side of the lake is bordered by the oak forest and a small patch of Common Buttonbush and Hazel (Smooth or Common) Alder next to the road. The far side of the lake is bordered by Eastern Hemlock–Native Rhododendron thickets that fill the entire ravine carved by Caldeno Creek. In late June and early July, these Rhododendrons, also called Great or Rosebay, are liter-

Rhododendron

ally covered with pale pink blooms, mirrored in the still surface of the lake. A small footpath takes you directly through the thicket along the cool, shady bank of the lake where you can find Early Meadow-rue growing by the water. Around you, nesting American Redstarts, and Black-throated Blue, Yellow, and Canada Warblers busy themselves among the rhododendrons, having found this an excellent spot to raise their young.

At present, much of the lake is choked by a profuse growth of Fanwort that has greatly reduced the variety and abundance of aquatic life. Fanwort is an aquatic plant of the genus *Cabomba*, commonly used in aquariums. It may have been introduced into the lake many years ago, along with Goldfish that are also found there now, having somehow managed to survive the Pocono winters. Fanwort produces large amounts of debris that undergo bacterial decomposition. As the bacteria break down the debris, they consume much of the oxygen dissolved in the water, which greatly diminishes the lake's capacity to support aquatic life.

Fragrant (White) Water-lilies grow in the one small spot of open water left. On the lily pads rest dainty, iridescent Bluet Damselflies, and a keen eye may spot Black-winged Damselflies clinging to the weedy growth at the edge of the lake. The White-tailed Skimmer, a pretty brown and white dragonfly, also breeds here. The male establishes a territory which he patrols constantly, guarding the female until she has deposited her eggs. The assorted dragonfly and damselfly nymphs (larvae) provide food for the few stunted sunfish and Brown Bullheads able to tolerate the oxygen-depleted water. Belted Kingfishers are seen here in summer, plunging into the water and sometimes rising with Goldfish clamped in their bills.

On summer evenings, as many as a dozen Little Brown Myotis (Bats) skim over the surface of the lake, scooping up night-flying midges and moths. The bat is one of man's closest relatives, outside of the primates, and the world's only flying mammal. It makes use of a highly developed echo-location system that allows it to navigate and locate prey in total darkness. Once pinpointed, the insect is caught in a pocket formed by the bat's tail and interfemoral membranes (those between the back legs) much like a baseball catcher uses a mitt. The bat retrieves the insect by mouth and consumes it while still on the wing. After eating its fill in early evening, the bat returns to roost and digest before going out to hunt again just before dawn. Little Browns are generally not migratory and, together with Big Brown Bats, hibernate during winter in nearby caves on the mountain slopes. Red, Silver-haired, and Hoary Bats also can be found in the area.

In the past, Muskrats have set up residence in the lake, but the population has remained sporadic, as has that of the Beaver. Caldeno Creek has a history of Beaver activity, but apparently there is not enough forage to support a colony. Beaver require trees that grow in open sunlight, such as birch and aspen, and the supply of these is small here. They are more abundant at higher elevations north and west of the Gap. There have been occasional sightings of River Otters fishing in the lake, and one winter they were observed sliding down a snow-covered bank near the outlet of the lake, a favorite play activity. These agile and loveable furbearers have been totally protected from trapping in Pennsylvania since 1952, but little was known about their habits and status here until 1976, when an otter research program was initiated at East Stroudsburg University, Pennsylvania. Since then, much has been learned. For example, the otter has long been accused of preying heavily on gamefish such as trout. However, food studies demonstrated that the otter's diet consists mainly of "rough" fish—those considered undesirable for sport fishing. The otter's future well-being in this state has grown enormously from this work. Over the past several years, nearly thirty live-trapped otters have been relocated in the northcentral part of the state, where overtrapping and the effects of acid mine runoff had reduced the population to a point where they were no longer producing young. It appears that the relocated otters are reproducing, and places like the Grand Canyon of Pennsylvania and surrounding tributaries of the Susquehanna and Allegheny Rivers should again see a thriving River Otter population.

Lenape Lake does support a number of amphibians and reptiles. The arrival of spring in the Water Gap is heralded by the noisy chorus of Northern Spring Peepers. Red-spotted Newts live and breed in the lake; their juvenile form, called Red Efts, can sometimes be seen marching about the forest floor. Those odd-looking bubbles on the surface of the water are the eyes of Pickerel Frogs, watching for their next meal. Eastern Painted Turtles haul themselves onto logs, rocks, and lakeshores to bask in the warmth of the sun, a pastime shared by Eastern Ribbon and Northern Water Snakes. American Toads begin trilling their nuptial song in May, and continue for two frantic weeks until the last of their sticky egg masses is secured to plants along the shore.

The upper reaches of Caldeno Creek are clean enough to support several species of salamanders, including the Northern Red, Northern Two-lined, Four-toed, and Spring. A little scouting in the surrounding woods, turning over rocks and logs, will produce Red-backed, or infrequently, Marbled and Spotted Salamanders. But development for resorts and second home construction have drastically diminished the habitat for salamanders, as well as for many other species. Once the most numerous of land vertebrates, amphibians like the salamander have been reduced to the fewest and least diverse of animals.

An excellent indicator of water quality is the presence of a Pocono native, the Brook Trout. Once common to all clear, cool, rushing tributaries of the Delaware and Lehigh watersheds, the "Brookie" has become relatively scarce as water quality has declined. Both the Brown Trout, introduced from Europe, and the Rainbow, a Pacific coast species, tolerate warmer, more polluted waters. The pink-fleshed natives are superior in fighting ability to their pale, hatchery-stocked cousins, and offer the purist fly-fisherman an experience never to be forgotten.

The outlet of the lake runs underneath the road. Then Caldeno Creek continues down the slope of Mt. Minsi to Route 611 on the terrace below, under Route 611, and down to the Delaware. A tiny trail follows Caldeno down the slope to Resort Point Overlook on Route 611, site of the old Kittatinny House, built by William A. Brodhead in the early 1800s. Its location on this terrace, 180 feet above the river valley, afforded guests an excellent view of the river and surrounding mountains, though the Water Gap itself was blocked by a lower ridge called Blockhead Mountain. Guests spent pleasant hours wandering marked trails along the face of the ridge and up through the ravine of Caldeno Creek. There they found delightful woodland retreats such as Eureka Falls, Rebecca's Bath, and Moss Grotto, emerged onto the next terrace at Lake Lenape, and could proceed up the slope to Table Rock. It was possible at that time to follow Caldeno Creek further up Mt. Minsi to its source at Hunter's Spring, but the ravine has been so washed out over the years that the trail has become too hazardous to travel. Eastern Hemlock and Native Rhododendron fill this ravine to the bottom at Route 611 and extend laterally along the lower slope for several hundred feet, crisscrossed by the old trails from Kittatinny House. This section provides good birding in winter. Evening Grosbeaks and Golden-crowned and Ruby-crowned Kinglets favor these evergreen glens, as do the less common Pine Grosbeaks and the elusive Pine Siskins. When arctic air blows out of the far north, local birders have found northern finches like White-winged and Red Crossbills and Common Redpolls.

At the side of the road across from the lake is a large, free-standing rock that is home to a community of plants characteristic of such rock ledges. These areas illustrate the process of primary succession—succession that begins with bare rock. The flat, round splotches of Pale Shield Lichen are usually the first living things to appear. The product of a symbiotic ("mutually beneficial") relationship between algae and fungi, lichens such as Pale Shield are the pioneers, the all-important first step in the progression. As moisture and bits of debris collect, beginning the build-up of a soil layer, the Pale Shield is followed by the upright branchlets of Reindeer Lichen, the tiny golf tees of Pixie-cup (Goblet) Lichen, and small patches of red-tipped "British Soldiers" (Red Crest or Match Stick Lichen). Mosses take hold next. Giant Club Moss pops up and will eventually cover much of the top of the ledge. The delicate frond-like branches of Fern Moss creep out onto the damp rock faces. Carpet Moss makes furry, bright green mounds. Mosses in turn catch larger debris, adding to the developing soil layer so that larger plants can grow. Ferns spread quickly through the new soil. Common Polypody covers flatter surfaces; Ebony Spleenwort wedges itself into the crevices. Fragile

Fern occasionally graces the rock with lacy, pale green fronds. In early spring, the green backdrop sets off the vivid scarlet blooms of Wild Columbine. On this particular rock, the soil has accumulated sufficiently to support a Mapleleaf Viburnum. This is of course a telescoped version of primary succession. In reality, the process takes a great many years.

Above the rock stands the dead stump of an Eastern White Pine. Too often, stumps such as this are cut for firewood in the mistaken belief that they are no longer a useful part of the forest community. Just the opposite is true. The crucial importance of standing deadwood cannot be overemphasized. These "den" trees provide food, shelter, and nest sites for a variety of inhabitants. In search of a meal, the Pileated Woodpecker chisels large oblong holes in the trunks of mature Eastern White Pines. The wounds are an invitation to wood-boring insects like Metallic Wood-borers and Long-horn Beetles. Eventually the tree dies. Decay enlarges the cavities which then become prime nest holes for Southern and Northern Flying Squirrels, Red and Gray Squirrels, Tufted Titmice, Black-capped Chickadees, Eastern Screech-Owls, Northern (Yellow-shafted) Flickers, Downy and Hairy Woodpeckers, and the Pileated itself. The decaying wood also provides refuge for numerous insects like Wood Roaches and earwigs. Termites feed exclusively on

MODEL OF PRIMARY AND SECONDARY SUCCESSION

Primary Succession

ROCK   **PALE SHIELD LICHEN** (algae-fungi)   **MOSSES**   **SOIL BUILD-UP VIA TRAPPING, ETC.**

dead wood and, more than any other organism, are responsible for recycling cellulose back into the ecosystem (if it weren't for termites, we'd be up to our eyebrows in dead wood). Black Bears and Raccoons search out the hidden insects, and their digging enlarges the cavities which can then be occupied by the Raccoons, Wood Ducks, Barred and Great Horned Owls.

Continuing up the hill from the lake, the road is lined with Sweet Birch and Witch-hazel, species typically found in disturbed environments. Sweet Birch is named for the wintergreen flavor of its twigs, a characteristic of several other birches. Underneath is a jumble of wildflowers, including Queen Anne's Lace, Wild Bergamot, Spotted Knapweed, Thimbleweed (Tall Anemone), and bedstraws. In midsummer you can treat yourself to tangy wild strawberries. These wildflower areas are rich with a diversity of insect life. Leaf Hoppers are everywhere, tiny wedge-shaped creatures in white, green, and even green-and-crimson striped. The Ambush Bug hides inside a flowerhead, waiting to grab the next insect that

Secondary Succession

FIRST FLOWERS

SHRUBS, WILDFLOWERS
Herbaceous Phase

CONIFER-HARDWOOD "pioneers"
Woody Phase

CLIMAX FOREST

lands there. Blister Beetles prefer yellow flowers and, if touched, secrete a caustic liquid (actually their own blood) that will cause blisters on human skin. The infamous Spanish Fly is a member of this family. Aphids congregate on succulent growing tips where they are preyed on by Green Lacewings (Aphid Lions) and Ladybird Beetles. Early spring brings the Mourning Cloak and Red-spotted Purple butterflies, followed in May or June by Black and Eastern Tiger Swallowtails. Later in summer, Orange Sulphur butterflies and an occasional Monarch can be seen.

To the right, the rocky face of the ridge has emerged and Table Rock is now directly above you. Note the layering of the sedimentary rock that forms the ridge. Mixed oaks cover this steep slope and Striped Maple can be found growing in the understory. Under the trees is a thick layer of leaves in which Marginal Shield Fern and Spinulose Shield Fern thrive. "Shield" refers to the sorii (pronounced "sore-eye," singular sorus), or areas on the leaflets where the spores are produced. Shield Ferns have round sorii which distinguish them from ferns with oblong sorii. The leaflets of Marginal Shield Ferns have rounded tips and sorii located at the extreme edges. Spinulose Shield Ferns have finely divided leaflets with pointed tips and sorii set slightly in from the edges.

Almost at the top of the hill, this slope becomes a nearly vertical cliff of exposed rock where only a few Northern Red and Chestnut Oaks have found pockets of soil to support them. Common Juniper can be seen at the edge of Table Rock above. In the face of the cliff is an Indian shelter, a rectangular opening chipped out of the rock. There are several such Indian shelters in cliffs along the river valley used by the Lenape and probably other tribes when traveling through the region. On one of the rock ledges just above the opening is a fairly large patch of Maidenhair Spleenwort, indicating that this particular ledge is composed of limestone.

Dry, rocky slopes like this make ideal sunning spots for our two remaining species of pit vipers, the Northern Copperhead and the Timber Rattlesnake. Both species have been severely reduced by land development and the indiscriminate use of biocides for pest control. Northern Copperheads were seen in the trail area in the past, but sightings have become very rare in recent years. Timber Rattlers are still seen occasionally, but most have apparently moved to the talus slopes and rocky outcroppings of the higher reaches. Man, in his ignorant and irrational fear of serpents, cheers at what he considers a triumph over an ancient enemy. In truth, these snakes and others eat considerable quantities of small rodents, providing an important control on populations that would otherwise rise to damaging proportions.

Just past the Indian shelter, the road levels off on the next terrace of the ridge. On the left, the Eastern Hemlock–Native Rhododendron gorge has given way to drier flats of mixed oaks and hardwoods, home to all manner of nesting birds indigenous to these woodlands, from Red-tailed Hawks to Yellow-billed Cuckoos to Chipping Sparrows. Black-and-white Warblers cling to the trunks, nuthatchlike, probing cracks for insects and larvae. A spot of orange in the treetops is a Northern (Baltimore) Oriole keeping an eye on his territory. A bright flash of crimson in the understory is a Scarlet Tanager displaying his finery to his green and yellow mate. On the forest floor, an Ovenbird, a ground-walking warbler, stalks about on oversized pink legs, pausing only to issue his loud, familiar *teach'-er, teach'-er, teach'-er* . . . call which often triggers the flute-like lilt of the nearby Wood Thrush.

Stands of oak such as this are prime targets for the Gypsy Moth caterpillar. Introduced into the United States around 1869 in an attempt to hybridize or substitute for the Silk Moth, the Gypsy Moth escaped captivity. It reached Pennsylvania early in this century but did not become a threat to forests until the 1960s. The immediate response of local governments was to begin a spraying program. DDT was used first, but as the moths built up immunity to it, a series of organophosphates were tried. All of these substances are deadly to hundreds of other insects, some of them extremely beneficial to man. For example, one of the organophosphates, Sevin, is particularly lethal to bees, who are the crucial pollinating agents for uncountable numbers of flowering plants. Also, spraying coincides with the nesting season of songbirds. Further, the elimination of so many nontarget insects means insufficient food for nestlings. A high rate of nestling death could go undetected for several years before it began to noticeably reduce the population, and by then, the effects could prove irreversible for some species. Alternatives to chemical spraying are needed that will not adversely affect the natural ecosystems. In fact, if simply left alone, Gypsy Moths will ultimately act as their own control. The population will increase until it has consumed all available food. With nothing left to eat, caterpillars die by the millions. The population undergoes a dramatic reduction from which it takes years to recover. Healthy, mature oaks can survive two or three consecutive defoliations without ill effect, and areas that were never sprayed, such as Hawk Mountain Sanctuary in Kempton, Pennsylvania, have survived extreme Gypsy Moth infestations, proving that passive handling of the problem is possible.

At the boundary of the Eastern Hemlock gorge and the oak flat, the Appalachian Trail splits to the left. Wild violets grow along the sides of both trails and the edge of the hemlocks is a good spot to find Round-lobed Hepatica. Ahead, the road loops around to the right a full 180°. In the bend of the loop is a small Sphagnum Moss swamp, one of the numerous glacial remnant swamps that dot the Poconos. This tiny swamp and the moist woodland around it support an amazing diversity of wildlife. In summer, the tangle of Mountain Laurel, Highbush Blueberry, and Common Greenbrier surrounding the swamp makes it inaccessible to any but the most determined hiker. Mountain Laurel is one of the most abundant understory plants of the mixed oak and hardwood forest (on acid soils). It is a very beautiful little shrub, with glossy, dark green foliage and dense clusters of pale pink blooms in late May and early June, often lasting as long as 2 to 3 weeks. Thickets of Mountain Laurel provide winter cover for White-tailed Deer, Eastern Cottontails (Rabbits), Snowshoe Hares, and Ruffed Grouse. Mountain Laurel is also one of the most important grouse foods in the Northeast. The grouse eat the leaves in fall, winter, and early spring when most other plants are bare. Deer also eat small quantities of leaves and twigs, which are poisonous to domestic livestock, though wild animals apparently are unaffected.

Similar swamps throughout the Poconos provide ideal day cover for River Otter, Mink, Beaver, Muskrat, and Black Bear, who also happens to love blueberries. The Black Bears of Pennsylvania are the largest in the world, with males weighing as much as 700 pounds. Over the last 10 years, the Black Bears in the Poconos have been intensively studied by Gary Alt, a biologist with the Pennsylvania Game Commission and long-time Pocono resident. His research has provided us with new

Black Bear

and sometimes startling information. For example, it was long thought that both males and females denned up underground during winter. Although this is true of Black Bears farther north in the Catskills, Alt discovered that among Pennsylvania bears, only the females den. The males build "beds" of twigs on sphagnum bogs or in swamps where they escape the worst of winter weather curled up in a state of dormancy. At present, there is an annual harvest of Black Bears ("harvest" is a game management term meaning the total number of animals that hunters are permitted to kill, calculated to keep the population balanced and, therefore, healthy), but the population continues to expand its range southward and eastward. Sightings of bears in the Water Gap area have increased noticeably in the last decade.

In winter, this swamp has served as a "yarding" area for White-tailed Deer. When snow accumulates to such a depth that deer cannot travel, they will "yard": they gather together in groups of 10 or 15 to over 100, then tramp down the snow in a relatively small circular area where they can share their body heat and move about freely until snow levels drop. But yarding can also backfire. Deer in a yard soon strip and eat all the browse from around the edges. If snow levels do not drop quickly enough, the entire group will starve to death.

The swamp is filled with tussocks of Sphagnum Moss, on top of which grow Native Rhododendron, Red Maple, and Mountain Winterberry (Largeleaf Holly), a member of the holly family. Royal Fern, Rice Cutgrass, and sedges grow along the edges. There is an interesting relationship between the Red Maple and the Native Rhododendron. The seeds of both sprout on the Sphagnum Moss tussocks, but the maple grows much more quickly. Its developing root system builds up a soil base on the tussock, but it cannot tolerate the excessive water for very long and eventually dies. The more water-tolerant rhododendron is then left with an ample soil base on which to grow.

Around the swamp, the moist woodland area of oaks and Eastern Hemlock provides food and nesting cover for Wild Turkey, Ruffed Grouse, and American Woodcock. Woodcocks nest on the ground, where their natural camouflage makes them almost impossible to see. If approached, they frequently will not flush from the nest until the intruder is only a few feet away. The Ruffed Grouse, although generally an abundant species here, undergoes radical changes in population. One environmental factor creating these population cycles is the fluctuation in mast crops (nuts, seeds, and berries) from year to year. Overall, Ruffed Grouse and Wild Turkey remain abundant because they can reproduce well on the calcium-poor acid soils of the Poconos. Calcium is necessary for the production of healthy eggs. Calcium-poor soils mean calcium-poor vegetation and mast, but because the grouse and turkey evolved on these soils, their metabolic systems are able to cope with the lack of calcium. By contrast, the introduced Ring-necked Pheasant reproduces poorly or not at all because its metabolic system has been unable to make this adjustment.

Both Red-shouldered and Broad-winged Hawks favor these moist woodlands for nesting. Turkey Vultures also nest here although they do not actually build a nest. They make a "scrape" nest on the ground beside a fallen tree, in a hollow log, or on a low rock ledge. The Northern Goshawk may occasionally be seen in these woods. A shy, secretive hawk of the forest, it has not adapted well to man's presence and sightings have become increasingly rare.

If you look closely at some of the taller trees, you may see that several inner branches have been girdled—a strip of bark has been completely removed from around the branch. This is the work of the Porcupine, who feeds on the inner bark of both conifers and hardwoods during the winter; in summer, it feeds on twigs, leaves, and buds. The adaptable Opossum has also found a niche in these woodland areas. A southern species by origin, the Opossum has gradually been extending its range northward into the Poconos. It has been successful in finding food and shelter but has not yet made some necessary physical adjustments. Having originated in a milder climate, the Opossum's naked ears, feet, and tail are vulnerable to the northern cold, and they are often seen missing bits of these appendages as a result of frostbite.

On the woodland floor, the wet soil supports a thick growth of huckleberries and Ground Pine, the largest of the club mosses, where Wood Turtles and Eastern Box Turtles rummage for slugs, snails, insects, mushrooms, berries, and anything else they can find. White-footed Mice and Short-tailed Shrews tunnel under the cover of leaves to look for food and to avoid the talons of Barred Owls and Eastern Screech-Owls living nearby. Closer to the water, the Star-nosed Mole, a good swimmer and diver, builds mounds of muck as large as a foot wide as it excavates its subterranean tunnels.

The back of the swamp is overlooked by a slope at the end of Table Rock terrace above. Growing on the tumbled rock ledges with Wild Columbine and Ebony Spleenwort is Herb-Robert, a member of the geranium family that blooms from May through October. Across the swamp, horsetails and Cutleaf (Leathery) Grape-fern grow where the drainage water from the upper slope collects before emptying into the swamp.

Once around the swamp, the road begins the final ascent. On the right is another free-standing rock where you can find a patch of Rose Moss, so named because the individual heads look like miniature roses. Along the sides of the road are Zig-zag Goldenrod, Early Goldenrod, and White Vervain. There is also some Hay-scented Fern, which grows in open areas, able to tolerate more sunlight than most other wood ferns. Halfway up the hill on the left is a large Bigtooth Aspen. In the fall, its leaves turn a vibrant golden yellow, attention-getting even among the other bright colors of the autumn forest.

Very soon you will have reached the top of the hill and reenter the hemlock ravine of the Caldeno Creek, heard flowing down the slope to the left. In the shade of the evergreens, Coltsfoot and White Avens grow by the side of the road with Blue-stemmed Goldenrod, and on the small bank to the right is Christmas Fern, Partridgeberry, and False Solomon's-seal. A few steps through the Eastern Hemlocks and you emerge onto the terrace of Table Rock.

The rugged vegetation on Table Rock represents various stages of long-term primary succession, based on the natural weathering of rock. Water penetrates the rock where it freezes and expands, opening up small cracks in the surface. Debris collects in the cracks and tiny plants like mosses and Sheep (Common) Sorrel begin to grow. Along the edge of the woods, carpets of Giant Club Moss have grown out onto the rock, giving Trailing Arbutus a base on which to grow. Continued freezing and plant growth erode more rock and enlarge the cracks until larger plants like grasses and goldenrods can become established. Across the surface of Table Rock is a gridwork of long cracks full of Little Bluestem prairie grass and Silver-rod, the only white goldenrod. With the soil held in place by the grasses and weeds, Scrub Oak, Pitch Pine, Common Juniper, and Staghorn Sumac get a toe hold, deepening the cracks with pressure exerted by their growing roots.

Table Rock was reputed to have been a favorite haunt of the Catamount ("cat-of-the-mountain"), or Mountain Lion, also called Cougar, Puma, and Panther. In 1870, L. W. Brodhead wrote an account of the killing of one of these great cats by his father on this very spot. Rare sightings of the much smaller Bobcat (15 to 35 pounds) have been made in terrace areas similar to Table Rock and on top of the plateau. Bobcats prey on small to mid-sized mammals, including the Snowshoe Hare, usually found in the more remote scrub thickets and bogs to the north.

Another inhabitant of the plateau is the Eastern Coyote, a relative newcomer to Pennsylvania. When the Gray Wolf was still widespread throughout the eastern United States, the Eastern Coyote was restricted to a few small populations in isolated mountain areas. Since the disappearance of the wolf, victim of relentless persecution, the coyote has slowly moved out of isolation to fill the open niche. The Eastern Coyote differs from the Western Coyote. It is larger, weighing up to 56 pounds, howls or barks very little, and is usually solitary. The Eastern Coyote population in the Poconos is apparently healthy and on the rise, as evidenced by the increased number of animals trapped, shot, and hit on the roads.

A little path along the outer edge of the Table Rock terrace opens up the panorama of the river valley 500 feet below. From this vantage point it is possible to watch the fall migration of raptors along the ridges—Broad-winged, Red-tailed, Sharp-shinned, and Cooper's Hawks, Ospreys, Bald Eagles, and a rare Golden Eagle. Such autumn spectacles occur along the entire Kittatinny Ridge in both New Jersey and Pennsylvania; Hawk Mountain, near Kempton, Pennsylvania, is the best known of many such lookouts. The "point" of the Gap on both sides of the river offers opportunities to see many of the species mentioned above while providing a haven from the throngs of hawk watchers often encountered at the more popular sites. A guide to some excellent viewing areas along the Appalachian Trail, published by Donald Heintzelman, is listed in the Suggested Readings at the end of this chapter.

In addition to providing a navigational landmark during migration, the ridges serve another, perhaps more important, purpose. The largest number of migrants move when northwest winds blow, and for good reason. Since the Appalachians and the Kittatinny Ridge generally run from northeast to southwest, the northwest winds strike the ridges at a nearly 90° angle, producing deflective, uplifting air currents. Migrating raptors can soar hundreds of miles on these currents, expending little energy. Further assistance is provided by rising thermals, columns of air that develop when the sun heats the morning ground moisture. This heated moisture rises to produce circulating air currents upon which soaring birds can ride almost effortlessly.

The Osprey, or Fish Hawk, a large raptor that feeds exclusively on fish, migrates regularly through the Water Gap; however, it has not nested here in several decades. In 1980, a cooperative program was undertaken by the Pennsylvania Game Commission, the National Audubon Society, and East Stroudsburg University to reestablish the Osprey as a nesting species. To date, 80 nestlings from healthy populations on the Chesapeake Bay have been brought to Pennsylvania and released into the wild. It is expected that when these birds reach maturity at 3 years of age they will return to their release sites to begin breeding. The status of the Osprey in Pennsylvania was recently changed from Extirpated (present but no longer breeding) to Endangered to assure maximum legal protection until the birds have firmly reestablished themselves as part of Pennsylvania's wildlife.

The Bald Eagle is becoming a more frequent sight along this part of the river, particularly in the winter. Its numbers have increased greatly over the last ten years and it is now a regular part of the winter community. Bald Eagles frequent the sheltered coves and sections of rapids where the water stays open all winter long, enabling them to catch fish, their main food. The population usually peaks in January and February, when as many as 18 to 20 birds may be in the immediate vicinity. A reintroduction program similar to that for the Osprey is underway. Although Bald Eagles nest in Pennsylvania, they do so in only one location on the northwest border of the state. The Pennsylvania Game Commission hopes to expand Bald Eagle nesting to all parts of the state; so far, 24 eaglets have been brought from wild nests in Saskatchewan, Canada, and released.

Our destination lies at the very end of the path by the chain link fence, offering a magnificent view of the Delaware Water Gap, still partially obscured by Blockhead Mountain. It is staggering to contemplate how many millions of tons of rock have been removed from that great cleft by the Delaware River, a process that is continuing as we watch. The sight seems a fitting conclusion to this first small journey through the Poconos, a region we hope will not be further damaged by our increasingly technological civilization. If we are wise with our resources, we can pass on the heritage of a sound environment to the generations that follow.

For more information contact:

Delaware Water Gap National Recreation Area
Bushkill, Pennsylvania 18324
Phone: (717) 588-6637

Kittatinny Point Information Station and Visitor Center
Interstate 80
Delaware Water Gap, New Jersey
Phone: (201) 496-4458

Red Eft

114   *The Mountains*

Those interested in canoe tours/rentals for the Delaware River, contact among others:

Adventure Tours, Inc. Phone: (717) 223-0505

Kittatinny Canoes, Inc. Phone: (717) 828-2700 or 2338

Directions to the Pocono Mountains, Pennsylvania, and the Delaware Water Gap National Recreation Area, Pennsylvania and New Jersey

The Pocono Mountains, with Stroudsburg as its conventional hub, is within a 100-mile, two-and-a-half hour drive of Philadelphia. From the Valley Forge–King of Prussia entrance to the Pennsylvania Turnpike (which can be reached via Interstate 76 West [Schuylkill Expressway] from Philadelphia), bear right after the toll gate, following the signs for the Northeast Extension (New Jersey East and Allentown North). Drive east 7.6 miles along the turnpike and bear right at the exit for the Northeast Extension (Route 9). Travel 55.3 miles, and turn off at Exit 34 (Mahoning Valley) for Stroudsburg via U.S. 209. Drive 0.5 miles on the off-ramp to the toll booth ($1.55 in 1985). Bearing right, travel another 0.2 miles to the stop sign and turn right on U.S. 209 North. Drive 31.2 miles on U.S. 209 North to Marshall's Creek (Exit 52); U.S. 209 North runs concurrently with Route 33 West for approximately 2 miles between Sciota and Snydersville, then bears right to join Interstate 80 East at Stroudsburg. U.S. 209 North leaves Interstate 80 at Exit 52 (Marshall's Creek). To reach the location of the walk, continue on Interstate 80 East 1 mile further to the Delaware Water Gap (Exit 53). Take the Delaware Water Gap Exit and proceed to the stoplight. Turn left on Route 611 South and drive 0.2 miles looking for the Deerhead Inn on the right side of Route 611

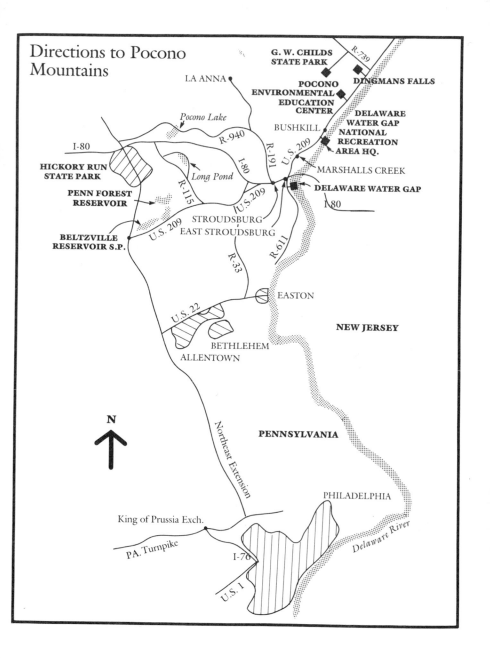

Directions to Pocono Mountains

G. W. CHILDS STATE PARK

LA ANNA

R-739

DINGMANS FALLS

POCONO ENVIRONMENTAL EDUCATION CENTER

DELAWARE WATER GAP NATIONAL RECREATION AREA HQ.

BUSHKILL

Pocono Lake

R-940

I-80

I-80

MARSHALLS CREEK

HICKORY RUN STATE PARK

Long Pond

R-191

U.S. 209

R-115

U.S. 209

DELAWARE WATER GAP

PENN FOREST RESERVOIR

U.S. 209

I-80

STROUDSBURG

EAST STROUDSBURG

BELTZVILLE RESERVOIR S.P.

R-33

R-611

EASTON

NEW JERSEY

U.S. 22

BETHLEHEM

ALLENTOWN

N

PENNSYLVANIA

Northeast Extension

PHILADELPHIA

King of Prussia Exch.

P.A. Turnpike

I-76

Delaware River

U.S. 1

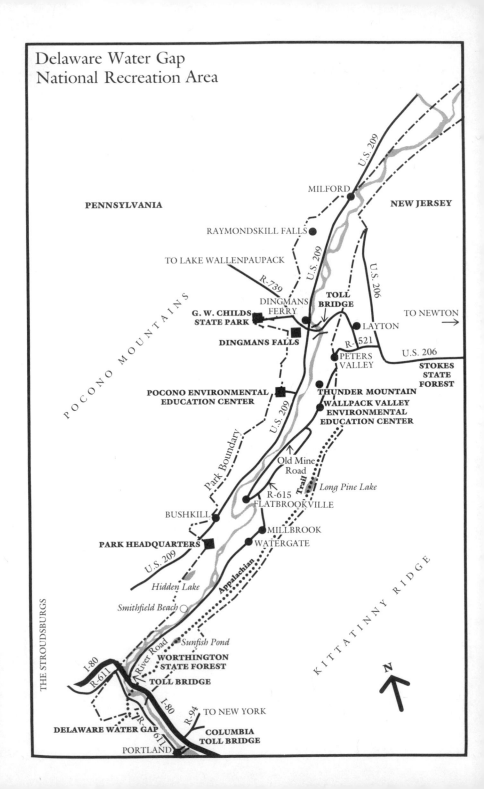

Delaware Water Gap
National Recreation Area

PENNSYLVANIA

NEW JERSEY

MILFORD

RAYMONDSKILL FALLS

TO LAKE WALLENPAUPACK

R-739

U.S. 209

U.S. 206

DINGMANS
FERRY

**TOLL
BRIDGE**

**G. W. CHILDS
STATE PARK**

LAYTON

TO NEWTON

DINGMANS FALLS

R-521

PETERS
VALLEY

U.S. 206

P O C O N O   M O U N T A I N S

**STOKES
STATE
FOREST**

**POCONO ENVIRONMENTAL
EDUCATION CENTER**

THUNDER MOUNTAIN

**WALLPACK VALLEY
ENVIRONMENTAL
EDUCATION CENTER**

U.S. 209

Park Boundary

Old Mine
Road

R-615

Long Pine Lake

Appalachian Trail

FLATBROOKVILLE

BUSHKILL

MILLBROOK

PARK HEADQUARTERS

WATERGATE

U.S. 209

Hidden Lake

Smithfield Beach

Appalachian

K I T T A T I N N Y   R I D G E

River Road

Sunfish Pond

THE STROUDSBURGS

**WORTHINGTON
STATE FOREST**

I-80

R-611

TOLL BRIDGE

N

I-80

R-94

TO NEW YORK

R-611

R-611

DELAWARE WATER GAP

**COLUMBIA
TOLL BRIDGE**

PORTLAND

South. Immediately past the Deerhead, turn right on Mountain Road and head up the hill approximately 0.25 miles until you see the Mountain House Restaurant on the right. On the left, directly across from the Mountain House, is a gravel road. Follow this road for several hundred feet until you see the iron gate across the road and a parking area on the right. The gate marks the beginning of the walk.

To reach the upper parts of the Delaware Water Gap National Recreation Area, take U.S. 209 North from Marshall's Creek exit (Exit 52) for 9.9 miles. Make a right at the sign for the Delaware Water Gap National Recreation Area; the headquarters is 0.8 miles further up the road (River Road).

After leaving the Gap Recreation Area headquarters, turn right on U.S. 209 North. Drive 1.8 miles to the blinking light in Bushkill (Bushkill Falls is 2 miles to the left). Proceed past the blinking light on U.S. 209 North for another 6.8 miles to the entrance for the Pocono Environmental Education Center (PEEC). Make a left at the sign (keep a sharp eye) and wind up the steep grade for 0.9 miles to the headquarters (open weekends) and pick up the regional bird list and map of the area trails.

After leaving the PEEC, turn left on U.S. 209 North. Travel 4.6 miles and immediately before a blinking signal and at the sign for Dingmans Falls make a left on a paved road. Drive 0.5 miles and bear right at the fork. The parking lot and visitor center are 0.7 miles further. Stop by the Dingmans Falls Visitor Center (run by the National Park Service) for lists of the area's flora and fauna, trail maps, and exhibits on the natural history of the region. Check for information on guided tours of the falls area led by naturalists.

After leaving Dingmans Falls, turn left on U.S. 209 North, immediately cross the small bridge and slow down at the blinking traffic light only 0.2 miles further. Turn left here on Route 739 North, and following the signs for G. W. Childs State Park, drive 1.2 miles. Bear left at the fork in the road (Route 739 North continues straight here). Travel 1.7 miles to another sign for G. W. Childs State Park. Immediately before this sign there is a small parking lot on your left next to an historic old mill. Alternatively, you can park in a much larger lot by turning left on another paved road at the Childs State Park sign. The lot is 0.1 miles down the road.

Mountains of the Delaware Valley Region

This section includes other mountainous habitats in various locales throughout the Appalachian Mountains of our region. Examples are found along the Kittatinny Ridge of the Ridge and Valley Province of northwestern New Jersey and eastern Pennsylvania and also in the Pocono Mountains of the Appalachian Plateau Province of northeastern Pennsylvania. The term Poconos is used by many to refer to the latter and also to much of the adjacent Kittatinny Ridge running through the Delaware Water Gap.

PENNSYLVANIA

Bake Oven Knob, Lehigh County, near New Tripoli, Pennsylvania, off Route 309. Similar to Hawk Mountain Sanctuary but less crowded on fall weekends, Bake Oven Knob is located about fifteen miles to the northeast along the Kittatinny Ridge.

Beltzville State Park, Carbon County, near Weissport, Pennsylvania, off Route 9 (N.E. Ext. Pa. Tpk.) and U.S. 209. Contains large fresh-water lake. Also visit nearby Wild Creek Reservoir and Penn Forest Reservoir with their surrounding coniferous and deciduous woodlands. Visitor center (closed weekends), bulletin board. Phone: (215) 377-0045.

Big Pocono State Park, Monroe County, near Scotrun, Pennsylvania, off I-80 and Route 715. Good location for the Black Bear. Visitor center. Phone: (717) 894-8336 or 894-8337.

Bruce Lake State Forest Natural Area, Pike County, near

Blooming Grove, Pennsylvania, off I-84 and Route 390. Extensive wetlands including some northern bog habitat. Excellent birding, especially nesting warblers of the boreal forest ecosystem. Phone (c/o Tobyhanna State Park): (717) 894-8336.

Devil's Hole (State Game Land no. 221), Monroe County, near Mount Pocono, Pennsylvania, off Routes 611 and 940. Excellent for typical Poconos flora and fauna.

Dingmans Falls, Pike County, near Dingmans Ferry, Pennsylvania, off U.S. 209 (part of the Delaware Water Gap National Recreation Area). Famous for its shady boreal forest trail past two grand waterfalls, Dingmans and Silver Thread. Nature center and naturalist guided tours May through October. Phone: (717) 828-7802.

George W. Childs State Park, Pike County, near Dingmans Ferry, Pennsylvania, off U.S. 209 and Route 739 (located in the Delaware Water Gap National Recreation Area). Three smaller waterfalls and historic ruins. Summer weekend interpretive tours. Phone (Delaware Water Gap N.R.A.): (717) 588-6637.

Hawk Mountain Sanctuary, Berks County, between Drehersville and Kempton, Pennsylvania, off Routes 895 and 61. Excellent year-round birding, especially famous for its autumn raptor flights. Interesting geological formations, such as the River of Rocks. Nature center and bookstore. Phone: (215) 756-6961.

Hickory Run State Park, Carbon County, near White Haven, Pennsylvania, off I-80 and Route 534. Varied habitats excellent for typical Poconos flora and fauna. Also famous for Boulder Field, a geological wonder and a National Natural Landmark. Visitor center and naturalist guided tours in season. Phone: (717) 443-9991.

Lacawac Sanctuary, Pike County, near Greentown and Lake

Wallenpaupack, Pennsylvania, off I-84 and Route 507. South-ernmost unpolluted glacial lake (Lacawac Lake) in our region with remnant acidic bog habitat. Owned by The Nature Conservancy and open by appointment only. Nature center. Phone: (717) 689-9494.

Lackawanna State Park, Lackawanna County, between Fleet-ville and Waverly, Pennsylvania, off Routes 407 and 438. Visitor center. Phone: (717) 945-3239.

Pennsylvania State Game Land no. 180, Pike County, near Lords Valley, Pennsylvania, between I-84 and U.S. 6. Location of Shohola Waterfowl Management Area. Famous for Wood Duck, Ruffed Grouse, Beaver, and Snowshoe Hare (Rabbit).

Pocono Environmental Education Center, Pike County, near Dingmans Ferry, Pennsylvania, off U.S. 209 (part of the Delaware Water Gap National Recreation Area). Varied habitats including coniferous and deciduous woodlands, fresh-water streams and ponds, successional fields, and so forth. Famous for its fossil slopes. Nature center and full schedule of ecology-related events. Phone: (717) 828-2319.

Pocono Lake, Monroe County, Pocono Lake, Pennsylvania, off Route 940. Stands of boreal forests and acidic bogs still sur-round portions of the lake.

Promised Land State Park, Pike County, near Greentown and Skytop, Pennsylvania, off Route 390 (near Bruce Lake State Forest Natural Area). Good location for the Black Bear. Nature center and extensive hiking trails. Phone: (717) 676-3428.

Ricketts Glen State Park Natural Area, Luzerne County, near Red Rock, Pennsylvania, off Routes 487 and 118. Primitive wilderness with many waterfalls and virgin, never-logged coniferous forests. Visitor center. Phone: (717) 477-5675.

Tannersville Cranberry Bog Preserve, Monroe County, near

Tannersville, Pennsylvania, off Route 611. Boreal forest, including Black Spruce and Tamarack, and an acidic Sphagnum Moss bog (Pitcher-plant and sundews). Owned by The Nature Conservancy and open by appointment through the Meesing Nature Center. Nature center and boardwalk trail. Phone: (717) 992-7334.

Tobyhanna State Park, Monroe County, near Tobyhanna, Pennsylvania, off Routes 611 and 423. Nature center. Phone: (717) 894-8336. Visit adjacent Gouldsboro State Park.

NEW JERSEY

Mt. Tammany, Warren County, near Kittatinny Point Information Center, New Jersey, off I-80 (part of the Delaware Water Gap National Recreation Area). The New Jersey counterpart to Mt. Minsi. Visitor center. Phone: (201) 496-4458.

Raccoon Ridge, Warren County, near Blairstown and Walnut Valley, New Jersey, off Route 94. Famous for its autumn raptor migration along the Kittatinny Ridge. Similar to Hawk Mountain Sanctuary, Pennsylvania. Rugged trail begins at Yards Creek Pump Storage Station on Walnut Valley Road.

Stokes State Forest, Sussex County, near Tuttles Corner, New Jersey, off U.S. 206. Visit famous primeval Tillman Ravine for Canadian-zone flora and fauna. Across the Delaware River from Dingmans Falls, Pennsylvania. Visitor center. Phone: (201) 948-3770.

Worthington State Park, Warren County, near Kittatinny Point Information Center, New Jersey, off River Road and I-80 (located in the Delaware Water Gap National Recreation Area). The blue-blazed trail to Sunfish Pond is a major attraction. Visitor center. Phone: (201) 841-9575.

Suggested Readings on the Mountains: The Appalachians, Including the Poconos and Kittatinny Ridge

Argow, Keith. *Appalachian Natural Areas Directory*. Rev. ed. Washington, D.C.: Society of American Foresters, 1976.

Bertland, D. N., P. M. Valence, and R. J. Woodling. *The Minisink: A Chronicle of One of America's First and Last Frontiers*. Four-County Task Force on the Tocks Island Dam Project, 1975.

Brett, James J., and Alexander C. Nagy. *Feathers in the Wind*. Kempton, Pa.: Hawk Mountain Sanctuary Association, 1973.

Brodhead, Luke W. *Delaware Water Gap: Its Scenery, Legends, and Early History*. Philadelphia: Sherman, 1870.

Brooks, Maurice. *The Appalachians*. Boston: Houghton Mifflin, 1965.

———. *The Life of the Mountains*. New York: Our Living World of Nature Series, McGraw-Hill, 1967.

Broun, Maurice. *Hawks Aloft: The Story of Hawk Mountain*. New York: Dodd, Mead, 1949.

Calder, Nigel. *The Restless Earth: A Report on the New Geology*. New York: Viking Press, 1972.

Fulcomer, Kathleen, and Roger Corbett. *The Delaware River: A Resource and Guide Book to the River and Valley*. Springfield, Va.: Seneca Press, 1981.

Gill, John D., and William Healy. *Shrubs and Vines for Northeastern Wildlife*. Upper Darby, Pa.: U.S.D.A. Forest Service General Technical Report NE-9, Northeast Forest Experimental Station, 1974.

Grimm, William C. *The Trees of Pennsylvania*. Harrisburg, Pa.: Stackpole and Heck, 1950.

Harwood, Michael. *The View From Hawk Mountain*. New York: Charles Scribner & Sons, 1973.

Heintzelman, Donald S. *A Guide to Eastern Hawk Watching*. University Park, Pa.: Pennsylvania State University Press, 1976.

———. *Autumn Hawk Flights: The Migrations in Eastern*

North America. New Brunswick, N.J.: Rutgers University Press, 1975.

Hurlbut, Cornelius S., Jr., and Cornelius Klein. *Manual of Minerology*. 19th ed. New York: John Wiley & Sons, 1977.

Knepp, Thomas A. *The Poconos: A Handbook and Guide to Pennsylvania's Vacation Land*. Stroudsburg, Pa.: T. Knepp, 1966.

Lane, F. C. *The Story of Mountains*. Garden City, N.Y.: Doubleday, 1951.

Menzies, Elizabeth. *Before the Water*. New Brunswick, N.J.: Rutgers University Press, 1966.

Miller, Russell, and The Editors of Time-Life Books. *Continents in Collision*. Alexandria, Va.: Planet Earth, Time-Life Books, 1983.

Milne, Lorus J., Margery Milne, and The Editors of Time-Life Books. *The Mountains*. Rev. ed. New York: Life Nature Library, Time-Life Books, 1967.

Pirkle, E. C., and W. H. Yoho. *Natural Regions of the United States*. 2nd ed. Dubuque, Iowa: Kendall, Hunt, 1977.

Shepps, Vincent C. *Pennsylvania and the Ice Age*. Harrisburg, Pa.: Pennsylvania Topographic and Geologic Service, Education Series no. 6, Pennsylvania Department of Environmental Resources, 1962.

Street, Phillips B. "Birds of the Pocono Mountains, 1890–1954." *Cassinia* 41 (1954): 3–76.

———. "Birds of the Pocono Mountains, 1955–1975." *Cassinia* 55 (1974–75): 3–16.

Subitzki, Seymour, ed. *Selected Areas in New Jersey and Eastern Pennsylvania and Guide Excursions*. New Brunswick, N.J.: Rutgers University Press, 1969.

Vankat, John L. *The Natural Vegetation of North America*. New York: John Wiley & Sons, 1979.

Wilhusen, J. P. *Geology of the Appalachian Trail in Pennsylvania*. Harrisburg, Pa.: Pennsylvania Geological Survey, Series no. 4, Commonwealth of Pennsylvania, 1983.

Wyckoff, Jerome. *Rock, Time, and Landforms*. New York: Harper & Row, 1966.

Young, Patrick. *Drifting Continents, Shifting Seas*. New York: Franklin Watts, 1976.

The Pine Barrens

LOUIS HARRIS

The Pine Barrens is an area of approximately 2,000 square miles lying in the outer Atlantic Coastal Plain of southern New Jersey. It is the largest wilderness area east of the Mississippi, a fact that surprises even many New Jersey residents. Once extensively logged and mined for bog iron, it was largely bypassed and forgotten during the industrialization of the nineteenth and early twentieth centuries.

The Pine Barrens are aptly named, for they are indeed barren when compared with the profusion of plant and animal life found in the rolling deciduous forests to the west and north. But a number of attractive streams wind their way through the cedar and cranberry bogs and the scrubby pine and oak woodlands of this immense area. Although not spectacular, the alert visitor comes to love the subtle beauties of this flat, sandy land.

The Barrens of today reflect a long geologic process. Approximately 200 million years ago, as the continental plates of North America and Africa began to separate, sediments from the Piedmont were washed and swept onto the broadening Atlantic Coastal Plain, covering the ancient bedrock. Subsequently, about 100 million years ago, the coastal plain submerged beneath the sea. Over the ensuing millions of years the sea advanced and withdrew numerous times, layering the thick deposits of sand that make up the Cohansey Formation on which most of the Pine Barrens sits. (This formation holds a large subterranean "lake" of pure water, an aquifer that underlies much of the Pine Barrens.) When the Atlantic Ocean retreated for the last time some 5 million years ago, vegetation finally became firmly established.

Present Pine Barrens flora, however, has probably been in place only since the most recent glaciation some 10,000 years ago. The southern tip of the Wisconsin Glacier stood about 40 miles above the northern border of the Pine Barrens; consequently the land was subject to an arctic climate and the flora would have been tundral. As the ice retreated, the present flora advanced from the south and west to occupy the now more hospitable land.

The two walks outlined in this chapter lie within the confines of the Wharton Tract, a forest of approximately 100,000 acres purchased by New Jersey in 1954 from the estate of Joseph Wharton, a Philadelphia financier. Mr. Wharton had obtained the lands some 80 years previously in the hope of supplying Philadelphia with the pure water of the Pines. The New Jersey legislature got wind of his intent, however, and prohibited such export. Though the lands were offered for sale to the state as early as 1912, it took 43 years for the deed to be accomplished.

In the era preceding and immediately following the War of Independence, there were numerous small towns scattered throughout the Pines. Many have completely disappeared and others can be recognized only by scant remains.

Perhaps of most interest is the village of Batsto, an iron-making village in the revolutionary era that supplied Washington's army with cannon and shot. The village prospered through the War of 1812, but went into decline after the discovery of iron and coal in the mountains of Pennsylvania. There were attempts to establish other economic bases for survival, including the manufacture of glass, paper, and charcoal, but by the late nineteenth century the site had been essentially abandoned. In recent years the state of New Jersey has seen to its reconstruction as an historical model. It is now much as it was some 200 years before, and well worth a visit.

PLEASANT MILLS–BATSTO

Just west of Batsto is the community of Pleasant Mills. Our first walk will commence behind the Pleasant Mills United Methodist Church, which has stood at this site since 1808 and was preceded by other churches in the general area back to the early 1700s. A number of revolutionary era local notables are buried in the small graveyard adjoining the church. The sparse settlement today makes it difficult to believe that Pleasant Mills was a prospering area of numerous enterprises in the mid-1700s. Follow the dirt road that passes behind the church and over Nescochague Creek. If there is water in the depressions on this road, do not be alarmed; the water is shallow and should give a conventional vehicle no trouble. You will soon cross an old barge canal whose original purpose was to move materials from Batsto Forge to the Mullica River. Then you will arrive at a parking area on your left, where you should leave your car.

You will observe a number of different environments on this walk. As you leave your car and pass between the concrete posts put there in the wan hope of stopping four-wheel traffic, you walk along a sandy road into a stand of Pitch Pines, the tree that "dominates" the Barrens. The Pitch Pine is especially adapted to withstanding fire, which is a common occurrence in these environs both historically and today. After a fire, new pine trees develop from basal sprouts out of the old root systems which have survived. Also, fire pops open the pine cones and releases seeds to start a new generation. As well, many fire-damaged pines sprout new growth through the charred bark of

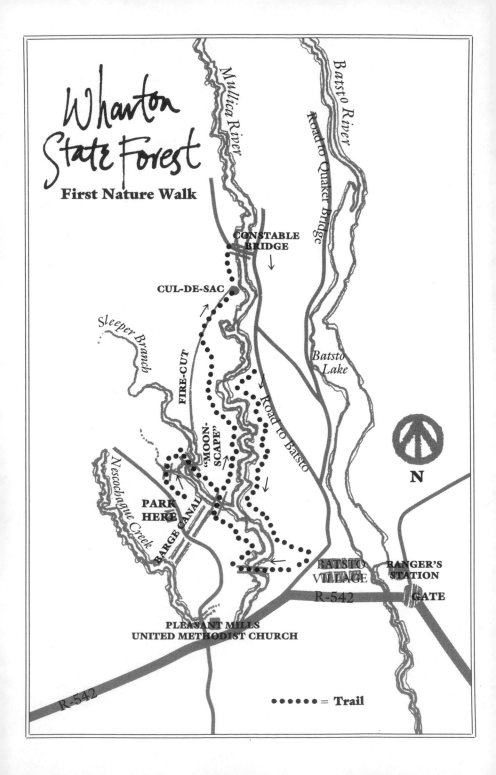

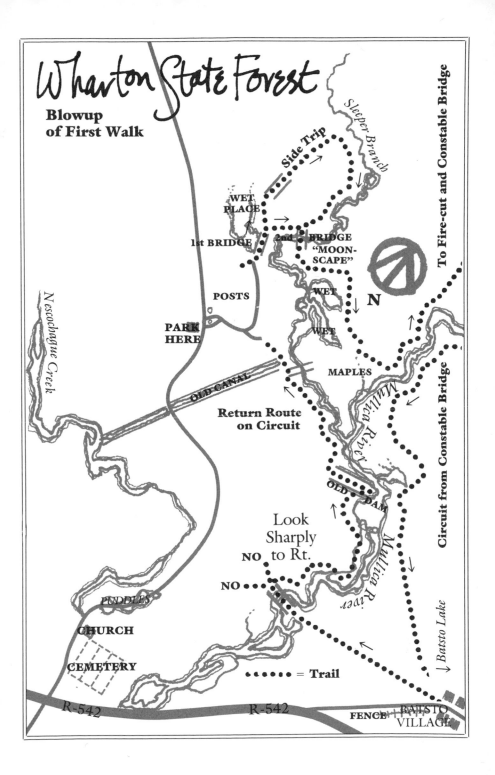

their trunks. Thus, the Pitch Pine has the competitive edge over the oaks, which are dependent mainly on regeneration from basal sprouts. There is limited undergrowth around here—huckleberries, blueberries, and so forth.

Take your first left, a somewhat obscure road, and as you bend right toward a small wooden footbridge, the understory thickens. At the bridge you enter a separate "microenvironment," a perennially wet area. Young Atlantic (Southern) White Cedars crowd the watery way. One can find Leatherleaf, Thread-leaved and Spatulate-leaved Sundews, Sphagnum Moss, Fragrant (White) Water-lily, bladderworts, Rose Pogonia (a common orchid of the pinelands), Large Cranberry, pipeworts, clubmosses, and so forth. The surface of the water sometimes has a thin "oily" layer; this is a film of iron leached from the soils by the acid water.

Proceed past Red Maples, and then more Atlantic White Cedars and Pitch Pines. The next footbridge (in some disrepair) crosses the Sleeper Branch of the Mullica River, a stream of varied dimensions, whose "flood plain" is easily discerned. During a wet spring the entire span of the bridge crosses water; by midsummer, only the first two sections do so. By late July, Virginia Meadow-beauty is in bloom. Before that Bullhead-lily, Fragrant Water-lily, and Yellow Loosestrife (Swamp Candles) with their spikes of yellow, starlike flowers, have lit the dark stream. Here too are Coast (Sweet) Pepperbush (also known as Summersweet), Staggerbush, and Sheep Laurel.

On crossing the bridge one enters a circular area surrounded by pines, a kind of "back-of-the-moon" scape. In May the ground is strewn with Golden-heather's (*Hudsonia*) yellow flowers and later with the white stars of Pine-barren Sandwort. Such areas are thought to be sites where colliers once made charcoal, and which the pines are just now reclaiming. Around the perimeter by mid-July you may see the thin, grasslike blade of Redroot (also known as "bog thief" because it tends to crowd cranberry bogs), which soon displays its wooly, dull yellow flowers. Specimens of Inkberry (Low Gallberry Holly), the most numerous of the hollies in the Pines, also dot the perimeter.

Bear to the right, continuing around the perimeter of the circle. Look into the stream and contiguous wet area for a variety of grasses and flowers that change with the season. Note the various shades of drab, brown Earth Stars (a fungus) which are found on the ground at any season. A number of mushrooms and lichens are also present. Throughout the year one can see hardy specimens of Match Stick Lichen (known to some as "British Soldiers" because of their conspicuous red bonnets) on the bridge posts and amidst the Pine-barren Sandwort scattered over the "moon-scape." As one proceeds, Sandmyrtle, which blooms in a glorious profusion of small white five-pointed flowers by mid-May, becomes more numerous.

Keeping the stream and the contiguous swampy area to your right, proceed through a more open area of dazzling white sand. Turn left at the T intersect. Proceed until the trail, which can be obscure but is usually heavily marked with footprints, bears left and heads north. To your right, however, just beyond a line of pine trees and demarcated by a shallow depression, is a spit of land that runs out to the Mullica. Should you walk along this "beach," note the Red Maples at the Mullica's edge. I've watched them grow for 17 years, and yet in all that time they've scarcely doubled in size.

Your journey, however, is to the north. As you proceed you will note the introduction of Blackjack and Scrub (Bear) Oaks, as the upper story transforms into a spindly, scrubby mixture of pine and oaks. The understory contains grasses, lichens, Sheep Laurel and an occasional Mountain Laurel, huckleberries, greenbriers, Swamp Sweetbells, Sandmyrtle, Golden-heather, Staggerbush, and so on. The meanders of the Mullica afford attractive sights. Be alert as the path moves away from the river, but do not be daunted; you can proceed north as directed if you keep a sharp eye for the trail. Again, keep the river and contiguous thick growth to your right.

Once you find a fire-cut (freshly cut at the time of this writing), the rest is easy. Proceed north along the fire-cut, noting depressed areas as you pass through. There is a boggy spot that can be crossed on grassy hummocks (Tussock Sedge) or on small timbers laid down by those who have preceded you. You will find yourself at a cul-de-sac; go left until you intersect with a road running east-west. Turn right at this intersection and proceed to Constable Bridge as it crosses the Mullica River. (Consult the maps at the end of this chapter.)

Bear in mind that the rest of the circuit is somewhat longer than what is already behind you. You may choose to reverse your steps. Should you do so, the point where you entered the fire-cut will be obscured by now. Follow the fire-cut approximately 350 feet from the wet place at the cul-de-sac. Where the fire-cut veers off to the west (right), look sharply for the now concealed path that retraces your steps south.

There is no great harm if you follow the fire-cut back; it will take you near the first "moon-scape." In fact, if you have an excellent sense of direction or the good sense to have a compass and topographical map, it is a delight to walk across the land between the Mullica and Sleeper Branch. Despite the seeming wildness, it is in fact rather tame, and you are bounded by the two streams, both of which flow south. Their juncture marks a natural end to this southern excursion.

If you choose to make the whole circuit, cross Constable Bridge and take the first road to your right, which goes south. Note the Bracken Fern which dominates the lower story in many places throughout the Pines, though scarce here. Sourgum (Black Gum or Black Tupelo), Sweetgum, and Northern Red Oak are present. Tall Huckleberry (Dangleberry) and the earlier huckleberries, here and elsewhere, make for a pleasant midsummer snack. As you proceed, look for a fairly well-defined road to your right. Once on the road, keep the river and adjacent growth close to your right as you look for the break that leads to the Mullica.

There are attractive vistas as you walk south along the meandering Mullica's beaches, several of which are delightful places for picnics and a swim. (A walk in the bed of this and other Pines rivers can be fun; they tend to be shallow. Old sneakers protect feet, but watch out for underwater stakes.) In midsummer a striking white flower, Slender Marsh-pink (white variant), blooms along the banks. Earlier, Lance-leaved Violet can be seen in most of the same places; here and there Coppery St. Johnswort as well as Common St. Johnswort may appear. Sundews, which supplement a nitrogen-poor diet by trapping small insects in beads of sticky "dew," add to the floral beauty in July as they bloom white and pink, depending on the variety. Along the river banks, west and east, are a number of grasses and closer to the water a variety of rushes and sedges.

Once you have passed the last "beach" and are on the trail you will pass through a stand of pines and then a mixed forest of pines and deciduous trees as you proceed toward Batsto. Be careful—there are several openings to your left. Continue until the trail definitely veers to the left, and follow it until you arrive at a road. Note the fence that marks the boundary of Batsto. Follow the fence, bearing right, until you arrive at a narrow break and a path to the village. Once at the gate take a look along this path. In May there are Pink Lady's-slippers (Moccasin-flower), among the more common of the Pine Barren's orchids, plus an occasional white variety.

If you have time, a walk through the village can be quite enjoyable. In any case, the path to the right of the road and away from Batsto leads back to your car. Along this path in May and June look for Frostweed and American Ipecac, later Cowwheat and Path Rush. There is a small group of Pipsissewa, and a short way down the path a solitary patch of Crowberry (blooms February to March), probably a transplant from elsewhere in the Pines. Wintergreen (Checkerberry) is conspicuous here and there (and also on the path from Constable Bridge). Northern Bayberry, Maleberry, Sassafras, and Post Oak also can be noted.

Now cross a wide wooden footbridge. The trail from the footbridge takes an immediate right (do look sharply and carefully for the most immediate). Proceed along the west bank of the Mullica among Atlantic White Cedar and Red Maple as well as the Inkberry, Staggerbush, blueberries, and huckleberries found in the area's wet places. You will note increasing evidence of human use as you approach a rampart, the remains of a long ago washed-away dam that impounded so-called "New Pond." By midsummer this clutter becomes almost as distressing as the heat and humidity. Mid-July to early September is not the happiest of times to be here. Spring, early summer, and fall are better, and winter can be a delight too.

As you approach the rampart, you may find that the river covers the contiguous flood plain. If so, look for the trail that traverses higher, wooded ground. Once upon the rampart proceed to your left; then drop off to your right onto a sandy way as soon as you can comfortably do so. Continue along the edge of the Sleeper Branch of the Mullica and look carefully for a narrow wooden footbridge (often disassembled). Once level with this bridge you may take the trail to your left that leads to the road and the concrete posts that mark the parking area. Or you may use the bridge, if passable, and continue a short way until you cross an orange swath of sand. Immediately take a left and proceed along the trail which you will recognize as the one you followed from the "back-of-the-moon" scape at the beginning of your trip. Arrive at the bridge which recrosses Sleeper Branch and proceed left to the very first footbridge. Continue to your car.

If you have the time and inclination you might consider an interesting side-trip. As you approached the second small footbridge at the commencement of the trip there is a path to the left; it leads to a circuit of open sandy places spotted with pines. Here are some of the area's original nature trails. When first I walked them I fancied myself in a bonzai garden (but each to his own imagining). No great care is needed here. Simply keep the water and thickly grown places to your right as you move around the perimeters. Occasional posts can be seen, remnants of markers for the nature trails. Pitch Pine, some huckleberries, Red Maple, and Atlantic White Cedar are the dominant growth here. Golden-heather and Pine-barren Sandwort dot the ground, though they are patchy.

As you near the end of these circles you will come to a broad wooden walk across a wet area. If you missed it, go back and look into the swampy region just north. By midsummer this is heavy in Thread-leaved Sundew and clubmosses. Rose Pogonia and Goldencrest are numerous also in midsummer.

At the wooden walk, Pitcher-plants (another of the insectivorous plants of these piney woods) bloom from about mid-May through early June. Note the pitcher-shaped leaves, lined on the inside by incurving, spiney hairs that prevent insects which have entered the bowl from reversing their steps. Eventually they fall into the pool of enzyme-laden water in the "pitcher" and die. Now continue on the trail to the first bridge near the beginning of your trip.

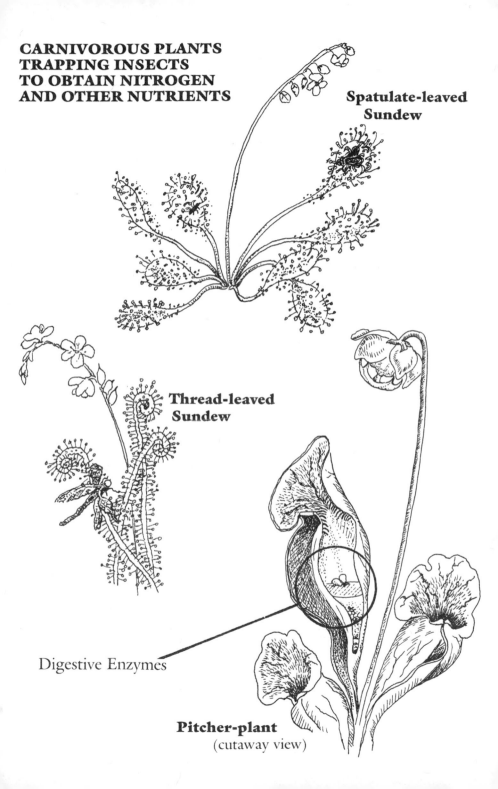

CARNIVOROUS PLANTS TRAPPING INSECTS TO OBTAIN NITROGEN AND OTHER NUTRIENTS

Spatulate-leaved Sundew

Thread-leaved Sundew

Digestive Enzymes

Pitcher-plant
(cutaway view)

WILDLIFE OF THE PINE BARRENS

Just as the appellation "Barrens" well describes the terrain and flora of this sparse, sometimes monotonous land, so too it describes the animal life. The wildlife tends to be dispersed and infrequently seen or heard, in contrast to the experience of a walk through upland deciduous woods. I will list only those species I have seen myself, with occasional reference to others presumed to be about or that are "famous" inhabitants of the pinelands. More complete lists of local fauna and flora are obtainable at the ranger's station at Batsto.

With some luck you might spot a White-tailed Deer, but usually you must settle for tracks. Gray and especially Red Squirrels can be seen, though evidence of their presence, such as disintegrated pine cones, is much more frequent than a sighting. You will cross the tunnelling of the Eastern (Common) Mole from time to time. The tracks of Opossum and Raccoon are seen here and there. Beaver, which were reintroduced to the Pines some years ago, are quite active in parts of the Wharton Tract—for instance, at Batona Camp Site, across the road from the Caranza Memorial—but signs are infrequent along the walks described here. The Little Brown Myotis (Bat) flutters in the twilight. The Red, but more commonly, the Gray, Fox makes an occasional appearance. Evidence of Muskrat (including an occasional swimmer) can be found at stream and bog sides.

The more common birds (if we leave out the spring and fall migrants), divided roughly into two groups, are each found in separate but adjoining habitats. First are the drier areas, including thickets and pine-oak woods. Here you might see the Ruffed Grouse, which occasionally delights the ear with its drumming and startles the unwary as it explodes from under foot. Among the more likely sightings: Northern (Yellow-shafted) Flicker, Downy Woodpecker, the Eastern Wood-Pewee with its plaintive whistle, the ubiquitous and friendly Carolina Chickadee, Blue Jay, Tufted Titmouse, White-breasted Nuthatch, Brown Thrasher (which can fill the air with more song than any other bird in the Wharton Tract), the common

Pine Warbler (which arrives in eager flights by late March to early April, punctuating the silent woods with its monotonous trill), the very common Prairie Warbler, Common Yellow-throat, Chipping Sparrow (whose song is often hard to distinguish from the Pine Warbler's, though it's a late comer), and the Rufous-sided Towhee, the bird most characteristic of the Pines. Some years, the Common Nighthawk is seen in the Atsion vicinity. The Whip-poor-will can be heard at night and is sometimes spotted resting on the sandy roads.

The following birds are found at river's edge and in cedar bogs: Yellow-billed Cuckoo, Eastern Kingbird, Great Crested Flycatcher (with its harsh call so appropriate to this land), Eastern Phoebe, Gray Catbird, Black-and-white Warbler, Prothonotary Warbler, Ovenbird, Hooded Warbler, and the frisky American Redstart.

I have seen the Northern Pine Snake, Northern Black Racer, Eastern Kingsnake, and Northern Water Snake. Scarlet and Corn Snakes might be seen as well. The Timber Rattlesnake is occasionally found in the Pines; I have not seen one in the area of these two walks. The Northern Pine Snake is much preyed upon by poachers and is now uncommon, even endangered.

Beaver

Pine Warbler

The Eastern Box Turtle can be quite numerous in the spring. Eastern Painted Turtles are generally spotted at or near streams, while the larger Red-bellied Turtle favors lakes and open bogs. So do Spotted Turtles, which you are most likely to see in the spring. The Northern Fence Lizard is common elsewhere in the Pines, i.e., between Batona Camp Site and Apple Pie Hill, but seldom seen on these walks. The furtive Ground Skink is probably here as well as the Five-lined Skink.

A number of frogs reside in the Pines. The most famous is the endangered Pine Barrens Treefrog. Though primarily a nocturnal amphibian, its "quacking" can also be heard on overcast days, generally in the vicinity of bogs and ponds. Northern Spring Peepers (and the New Jersey Chorus Frog) fill the spring air with glorious piping. Carpenter and Southern Leopard Frogs are here, the former banging out its workbench song from virtually every pond and sluggish river bed.

Damselflies and dragonflies are at the streams, ponds, and adjacent woods. Along the roads Tiger Beetles flit before one's footfall. In spring a small black wasp works the roadbeds with feverish assiduousness. Butterflies are represented by a number of Swallowtails, especially Black and Eastern Tiger. As well, that harbinger of spring, the Mourning Cloak, can be seen as early as March. Spring Azures dot spring, early summer, and fall days. An occasional member of the skipper and elfin families is evident. In late summer and early fall Field Crickets can be abundant.

The Deer Fly, a pest of summer, can make your walk miserable if you fail to bring insect repellent. Ticks are numerous in the spring and present through summer and fall. Be sure to check yourself thoroughly for them once home. From late summer to fall's first chill the Chigger can be pesky; use repellent liberally on ankles, calves, and waist, and stay out of grassy places.

I have touched upon many of the common plants and animals to be seen and heard in these regions, but there are many more. Enjoy discovering them!

Pine Barrens Treefrog

LOWER FORGE WILDERNESS AREA

Our second walk requires less caution and attention to detail than the first: it is a straightforward course that mainly follows pineland roads, though there are other options, including a portion of the Batona Trail. (The Batona Trail, chartered and built by the Batona Hiking Club of Philadelphia in 1961, is now a 41-mile hiking trail extending from Ongs Hat in Lebanon State Forest to and through the Wharton State Forest, terminating at Evans Bridge on Route 563. Maps are available at the ranger's stations of Lebanon and Wharton State Forests.)

Follow general directions at the end of this chapter to the Atsion Ranger's Station on Route 206. Immediately south of the ranger's station take the dirt road on your left to Quaker Bridge, approximately 4 miles to the southeast. If you lack four-wheel drive, do not cross the bridge. Park on the west side. If you have four-wheel drive, you can cross the bridge depending on conditions; then take an immediate left and proceed approximately 1 mile north, parking to the side just before the entry to Lower Forge Wilderness Area. On the one hand, your walk would commence at the bridge; on the other, at the entry to Lower Forge.

Quaker Bridge is said to have been first constructed in 1772 by Quakers to ensure a safe trip to Meeting in Tuckerton. There had been several drownings at this site before the bridge was built. It was at Quaker Bridge in 1805 (or 1808) that the famous Curly Grass Fern was discovered. There have been subsequent notations of its presence to the present time. If interested, look into the cedar bog and swampy areas on either side of the road some 40–50 yards from the bridge as you approach from Atsion. Remember, you will have to look closely, literally with your nose to the ground, because it is a tiny plant. The original find was viewed as monumental, with botanists coming far and wide to participate in the discovery.

There is a variety of plants in the vicinity of the bridge: Sweetbay (Swamp) Magnolia, Swamp Honeysuckle, Atlantic

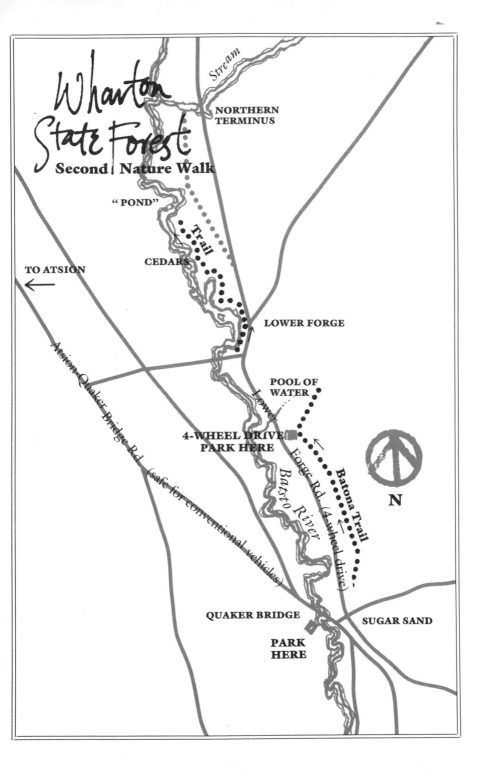

(Southern) White Cedar, Red Maple, Common Buttonbush, Fragrant (White) Water-lily, Broad-leaved Arrowhead, Large Cranberry, Sphagnum Moss, Moth and Common Mulleins, Coast (Sweet) Pepperbush, Tall Huckleberry (Dangleberry), Swamp Sweetbells, Highbush Blueberry, Sour-gum (Black Gum or Black Tupelo), Inkberry (Low Gallberry Holly), and of course the ubiquitous Pitch Pine. The wet woods about the bridge have a variety of greenbriers.

From Quaker Bridge take the immediate left north. A number of oaks can be seen as one proceeds along the road toward Lower Forge including Chestnut, Chinkapin, Black, Scrub (Bear), Blackjack, and White. Pine-barren Sandwort, Golden-heather (*Hudsonia*), low huckleberries, and Cow-wheat mark the margin of the road. An occasional bedstraw may be seen in summer.

Some 150 feet north of the bridge look carefully for a double pink blaze on your right. Once found, choose whether to follow the pink blazes up the Batona Trail or continue on the road. Either way, in approximately 1 mile you will come to the orange blaze designating entry to Lower Forge. If on the trail, get back on the road (the trail veers right—you go straight).

If you choose the Batona Trail, you will enter a mixed pine and deciduous forest, a world of shadow and sunlight. Although not the most striking section of the trail, it is attractive enough. If you choose to drive or walk up the road to Lower Forge, you will pass through a relatively sparse piney woods with the Batsto River to the left bordered by stands of Atlantic White Cedar bordering the river. The ground cover is mixed huckleberries, Pine-barren Sandwort, Golden-heather, and so forth. The sand on the road can be quite loose and deep, what local people call "sugar sand." It creates some difficulty as one walks and much more grievous difficulty for any vehicle without four-wheel drive.

At the entry to Lower Forge Wilderness Area the road dips into a wet place. In the spring, and whenever it rains, there is water here; generally there is only a pool, but occasionally a stream flows through. Be certain to ford to the left in spring; usually there is a makeshift bridge of fallen timber, but you could still get your feet wet. Leatherleaf is thick along the eastern border of the pool. Also note Sphagnum Moss, an American Holly, Sweetbay Magnolia, brambles, and, in midsummer, the Virginia Meadow-beauty. In the surrounding area find Red Maple, Pitch Pine, Sour-gum, Gray Birch, Northern Bayberry, Inkberry, Swamp Sweetbells, and Atlantic White Cedar. On slightly higher ground there are Sheep Laurel, Scrub, Blackjack, and White Oaks, as well as Sassafras and huckleberries.

Proceeding north along the road one comes to a peculiar site. A city tree, Ailanthus, or Tree-of-Heaven, has invaded the pines. A community of small specimens struggles to survive. (Perhaps you noted a group in the vicinity of Quaker Bridge as well.) Also notice a subtle change in the pine trees as Shortleaf Pine, another fire-resistant species that sprouts after burning, displaces the usual Pitch Pine, though not for long. Note the much smaller cones of the Shortleaf variety. Otherwise, there is little to distinguish them, unless one looks at the needles. The Shortleaf has bundles of two as opposed to bundles of three for the Pitch Pine.

Along the road are the usual Golden-heather, Pine-barren Sandwort, Tall Huckleberry, and Highbush Blueberry. Bush-clovers were conspicuous here and there during the summer of 1985. Proceed past the Lower Forge Campsite (a "wilderness" campsite accessible by foot off the Batona Trail, and by canoe from the Batsto River, which remains just to your left). Shortly you will come to a fork in the road; at this and each subsequent fork, take the way to the left.

Note the handsome stand of Atlantic White Cedar to your left and note the parklike area opening up on your right, with scattered Pitch Pines and undergrowth of oaks, Pine-barren Sandwort, Golden-heather, huckleberries, and so on. There are occasional larger deciduous trees, particularly Sour-gum. Continue along the winding road past an ever-thicker lower story of Sheep Laurel, Inkberry, greenbriers, and Staggerbush, as well as a solitary, well-developed broad-leafed Mountain Laurel. The area to your right continues open, offering views deep into the woods and inviting a crosscountry walk.

Shortly you will come to a moderate rise. Stay with the "main" road and arrive at a crest. To your left will be the tops of Atlantic White Cedars that seem closer than they really are. Walk forward and look down into a pondlike watery area. It is an oxbow in the river, but in spring or after heavy rain gives the appearance of a pond or small woodland lake. In spring, when the Leatherleaf is in full bloom (April to May), the "pond" is surrounded with tiny, white bell-shaped flowers—a sight to behold. Besides Leatherleaf, there are Swamp Sweet-bells, Large Cranberry, Sphagnum Moss, Red Maple, a sapling Bigtooth Aspen, and so forth. In summer, Spatulate-leaved Sundew sparkles in the shallows next to the small beach, and pipeworts give the appearance of ivory hatpins. In fall, Sickle-leaved Golden-aster, Common St. Johnswort, and Canadian St. Johnswort (a rather small plant) are found here. Bur-reeds, Bullhead-lily (yellow), and Fragrant Water-lily as well as grasses and reeds crowd the water by late summer.

After you have sated yourself here, continue on the road that winds high above the Batsto, affording lovely glimpses into the dark waters. If you should be here late June to early July, you may see Pickering's Morning-glory abloom. This is a most un-common plant, found only in the Pine Barrens of New Jersey, and strange in appearance for a morning-glory. A small stand is scattered about in this vicinity. The plants are entirely incon-spicuous except when blooming. Proceed, staying with the ma-jor (and upland) road as the river bends farther away.

Take a road that shunts to your right to a T intersection. Turn left, and you soon end at a stream that perennially crosses the road. This stream carries the run-off from Mannis Duck Pond, an artificial pond whose name describes its probable original use. You are at the northern terminus of this circuit; it is an attractive spot. Cinnamon Fern unfolds here in the spring. Common Polypody Fern is nearby. Bur-reeds and Broad-leaved Arrowhead as well as pipeworts have their sea-son. In spring, Golden Club, a familiar marker for that season in pineland ponds, bogs, and stream beds is here in small num-bers. At some bogs, however, Golden Club can be seen in the hundreds during spring. I find the reflection of the cedars in the water here almost captivating. A walk up the road as it con-tinues north is quite pleasant, but not part of this day's itiner-ary. It is time to return south.

Look carefully for your road, which is somewhat obscured,

and retrace your steps to the "pond"; then follow the road until it turns sharply away from the stand of Atlantic White Cedars that are now to your right. Note the path that proceeds parallel to the cedars. Go this way. There are two or three narrow trails you might take which lead into the cedar stand and bog. Go carefully if you do; though this is a seemingly safe bog, it is not always so. In general, it is best to be accompanied and to tread lightly when exploring unfamiliar cedar bogs.

After the cedar stand you will pass a series of approaches to the Batsto River, some of which have small beaches. The beach below Lower Forge Campsite is an attractive place to swim; there is also a straight view down the river that can be beautiful on a summer or fall day. Stay with the path until you T-intersect with a short road that terminates at the Batsto (note the posts driven into the river bottom). Just before arriving at this intersection you will pass a small patch of Pink Lady's-slippers (Moccasin-flower) that blooms in mid-May. Look again if you missed them, since they are somewhat hidden by the undergrowth.

Pink Lady's-slipper

Continue until you reach the road you first entered on; turn right and proceed back to the "wet place," and thence to your car. Before you leave the short road to the Batsto, note Sweet-fern. Crush a few leaves (not too many) and enjoy the fragrance. In the fall look for Sweet Goldenrod, whose leaves have an anise-like smell when crushed. A small number of young Winged (Shining) Sumac are at the intersection with the road that leads to your car.

You have completed the second circuit. There is less variety here, and more starkness, but I feel that this area captures the true essence of the Pine Barrens. Flowers are found in small numbers. Many stand alone. There is a solitariness here that contrasts with the profusion of the rich woods to the west. But that is the magic of this place. It is an experience in singularities rather than numbers.

For more information contact:

Wharton State Forest
Batsto, R.D. 1
Hammonton, New Jersey 08037
Phone: (609) 561-0024

Directions to Wharton State Forest, New Jersey

To reach Wharton State Forest from Philadelphia, Pennsylvania, proceed from the intersection of U.S. 1 (City Line Avenue) and the Schuylkill Expressway (I-76 East). Enter the Schuylkill Expressway (I-76 East) and drive 0.7 miles along the ramp, then bear left on U.S. 1 North (Roosevelt Boulevard). Drive 7.2 miles to Robbins Avenue following the signs for the Tacony-Palmyra Bridge. Make a right on Robbins Avenue (U.S. 13 North) and travel 1.6 miles; then bear left for the bridge at the light. Cross the bridge and pay the 25-cent (1985) toll. This is now Route 73 South. Drive 9.9 miles on

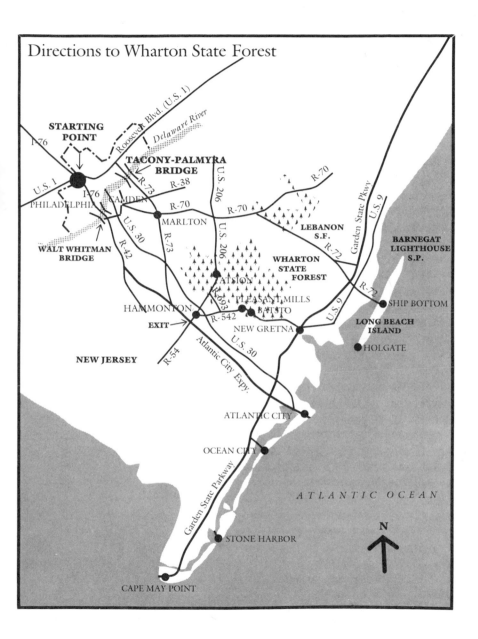

Directions to Wharton State Forest

STARTING POINT

I-76

Roosevelt Blvd. (U.S. 1)

Delaware River

TACONY-PALMYRA BRIDGE

U.S. 1

I-76

PHILADELPHIA

CAMDEN

R-73

R-38

U.S. 206

R-70

R-70

R-70

MARLTON

WALT WHITMAN BRIDGE

U.S. 30

R-73

R-42

U.S. 206

R-70

LEBANON S.F.

Garden State Pkwy.

U.S. 9

BARNEGAT LIGHTHOUSE S.P.

WHARTON STATE FOREST

ATSION

R-72

R-72

HAMMONTON

R-693

PLEASANT MILLS

BATSTO

U.S. 9

SHIP BOTTOM

EXIT

R-542

NEW GRETNA

LONG BEACH ISLAND

NEW JERSEY

R-54

Atlantic City Expy.

U.S. 30

HOLGATE

ATLANTIC CITY

OCEAN CITY

Garden State Parkway

ATLANTIC OCEAN

N

STONE HARBOR

CAPE MAY POINT

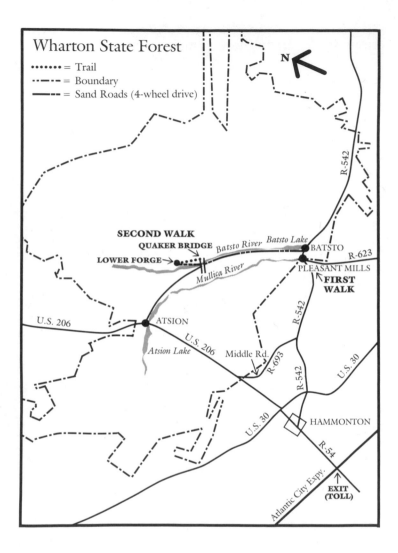

Wharton State Forest

• • • • • • = Trail
— • — • — = Boundary
——— • — = Sand Roads (4-wheel drive)

N

SECOND WALK
QUAKER BRIDGE   Batsto River   Batsto Lake
LOWER FORGE→   BATSTO
                          Mullica River   R-623
                                        PLEASANT MILLS
                                              ↖FIRST
                                                WALK

U.S. 206   ATSION
                                 U.S. 206
              Atsion Lake   Middle Rd.   R-542
                                         R-693   U.S. 30

                                                   U.S. 30

                                    U.S. 30   HAMMONTON

                                               R-54

                         Atlantic City Expy.   **EXIT**
                                                (TOLL)

Route 73 South until you reach a circle. Go three-quarters of the way around the circle and follow the signs for Lakehurst and Route 70 East. Travel 10.2 miles along Route 70 East to the second circle. One-quarter of the way around the circle bear right on U.S. 206 South. Drive 10.2 miles to the Atsion Ranger's Station on your left (Atsion Lake is just ahead on your right). After stopping at the ranger's station to check maps and road conditions follow the dirt road to the left southeast for approximately 4 miles to Quaker Bridge and the second walk. This road may be difficult for conventional vehicles after rainy weather (inquire at the ranger's station).

To reach the first walk, which commences at the Pleasant Mills–Batsto area, leave the Atsion Ranger's Station heading south on U.S. 206 South. Drive 4.3 miles and bear left on Middle Road following the signs for Batsto Village. After 1.3 miles bear left again on Myrtle Avenue, still following the signs for Batsto Village. Another 0.1 miles further this short road empties left on Route 693 East. Drive 2.7 miles along this paved road, pass the local airport, and turn left at the stop sign on Route 542 East. Travel 3.6 miles to the Pleasant Mills United Methodist Church, and turn left on the dirt road (Route 623 heads to the right opposite the church and cemetery). Follow the dirt road past the church, cross the bridge, and in 0.5 miles you will arrive at an earthen parking lot where you will begin the first walk.

To reach nearby Batsto Village, leave the church and turn left on Route 542 East. Drive past the fenced-in village on your left and after 0.9 miles turn left into the entrance. Bear left in 0.3 miles and shortly (0.1 miles) you will arrive at the parking lot for both Batsto and the Wharton State Forest Visitor Center. Stop here for maps and more information. You can also view the exhibits and book store. A tour of historic Batsto Village, which has been carefully restored by the State of New Jersey, is well worthwhile.

Alternative ways of reaching Wharton State Forest from Philadelphia include taking the Vine Street Exit off I-76 East (Schuylkill Expressway) and crossing the Ben Franklin Bridge (toll of 75 cents in 1985). Take U.S. 30 East (Admiral Wilson Boulevard) to the Airport Circle. There, bear left up the ramp following the signs for Routes 38 and 70. As you come down the ramp bear right on Route 70 East. Proceed on Route 70 East to Marlton, New Jersey, where it intersects with Route 73 South. Stay on Route 70 East and proceed as explained before.

Another way is to follow the general directions to Stone Harbor, New Jersey (see "The Salt-Water Marsh"). From Philadelphia cross the Walt Whitman Bridge (toll of 75 cents in 1985) and eventually pick up the Atlantic City Expressway. Then drive 15.7 miles east to the Hammonton Exit (Exit 28). Bear right to the exact change toll booth (25 cents in 1985). At the stop sign 0.1 miles past the toll booth turn left on Route 54 North (becomes U.S. 206 above U.S. 30). Drive 2.1 miles and in the center of Hammonton's business district turn right on Route 542 East following the sign for Batsto Village. Travel 1.6 miles on Route 542 East and make a right at the light on U.S. 30 East (White Horse Pike). Almost immediately (0.1 miles further) turn left on the continuation of Route 542 East (Pleasant Mills Road). Now drive 6.1 miles along Route 542 East to the Pleasant Mills United Methodist Church and the first walk. To reach the Atsion Ranger's Station and the second walk, backtrack 3.6 miles from the church to Route 693 West and proceed as outlined before.

A one-way trip from Philadelphia takes approximately 1 hour and 10 minutes.

Other Areas in the Pine Barrens of New Jersey

The Pine Barrens is an approximately 2,000-square-mile tract. Numerous small towns and crossroads neighborhoods punctuate this area, but large tracts remain a wilderness—not pristine, but nonetheless wild. Scattered throughout are a number of public lands that expose one to the diversity of the pinelands.

Wharton State Forest, Atlantic, Camden, and Burlington Counties, Hammonton, New Jersey. Phone: (609) 561-0024.

The two walks outlined in this chapter lie within the confines of Wharton State Forest, which is approximately 110,000 acres in size. There are other areas of interest within this tract:

Atsion Recreation Area, at the junction of Route 206 and Atsion Road. Here a lake, impounded in revolutionary times to power an iron mill, has been converted into a bathing area with access to boating. Just across U.S. 206 from the recreation area is a ranger's station where information and topographic maps can be obtained. Phone: (609) 268-0444. Nearby is the boarded-up Atsion Mansion. Cabins and campsites are available along the lake.

Batsto Village, off Route 542, just east of the entry to the first walk. The principal ranger's station for the Wharton State Forest is situated at Batsto Village. Information and topographic maps are available. There is also a bookstore where nature material and books concerning the area may be purchased. Replicas of Batsto products and memorabilia are sold here as well. Batsto is a repaired and reconstructed revolutionary era iron-making village. It includes the Iron Master's Mansion, purchased and added to by Joseph Wharton. Tours are available from Memorial Day to Labor Day for a fee. The village is accessible throughout the year, but there is an entry fee for automobiles through the summer season. Phone: (609) 561-0024.

Lebanon State Forest, occupying approximately 30,000 acres in Burlington and Ocean Counties, New Lisbon, New Jersey 08064, north of the Wharton Tract. Access to the local ranger's station lies off Route 72 just south of Four Mile Circle at the junction of Routes 70 and 72. Phone: (609) 726-1191. Just follow the local signs. Information and topographic maps are available. There is a nature center open from Memorial Day to Labor Day with a naturalist on duty. Walks with the naturalist can be arranged. Interesting areas within the Forest include:

Pakim Pond Recreation Area, easily found by following signs. It includes a small public beach with picnic tables and bath house. Three rustic cabins next to the pond are available for rental; check for information at the ranger's station. During the summer season there is a fee for access to Pakim Pond.

Reeves Bogs (ask for directions at the ranger's station) is of interest in that working bogs, where cranberry culture can be observed, are contiguous with other bogs that have gone through succession for some years. The cranberry harvest can be witnessed around Columbus Day.

Whitesbog, continuous with and part of Lebanon State Forest, holds a significant place in the development of the blueberry as a commercial crop. It can be reached by continuing east on Route 70 some 6.7 miles from Four Mile Circle to Route 530. Take a left there and continue 1.2 miles to the entrance to Whitesbog on the right. There is an information center, a number of historic buildings, and of course the bogs— an extensive area devoted to blueberry culture.

Penn State Forest, Burlington County, c/o Bass River State Forest, New Jersey, east of Route 563. Phone: (609) 296-1114. Access road is to the left; go south on Route 563 approximately 7 miles south of Chatsworth (Chatsworth is often viewed as lying in the center of the Pines and has been referred to as the "capital" of the Pines). Lake Oswego, an attractive man-made impoundment, is delightful for picnicking almost any time of the year.

Bass River State Forest, Burlington County, New Gretna, New Jersey 08224, east of the junction of Spur 563 and Route 542. Phone: (609) 296-1114. Lake Absegami is an attractive recreational area with a beach and bath house. Cabins fringing the lake can be rented. There is a ranger's station and a nature center which is open 5 days a week from Memorial Day to Labor Day. A naturalist is available and tours can be arranged. Access is clearly marked by signs and local routes.

The Pygmy or Dwarf Forest (also called **The Plains**), Burlington and Ocean Counties, New Jersey, bracketing Route 72, approximately 12 miles from Four Mile Circle east of Lebanon State Forest. There has been much debate as to why the trees are so stunted here. In large areas mature pines and oaks stand no higher than 4 to 5 feet. This area is only a short distance away from Lebanon State Forest and well worth a look.

The Batona Trail, begun in 1961 by the Batona Hiking Club of Philadelphia, is now 41 miles long and extends from Ongs Hat at the northwestern corner of Lebanon State Forest to Evans Bridge at the west branch of the Wading River on Route 563. Camping is allowed at designated sites. Maps, information, and permits can be obtained at ranger's stations in Lebanon and Wharton State Forests. The trail is a meandering combination of old roads and hiking trails that traverses a variety of pineland terrain and ecosystems.

Apple Pie Hill, one of the high points of the Pines, topped with a fire tower that commands a panoramic view of a large area of the Pines, is accessible on the Batona Trail from Route 532. It can also be reached by four-wheel drive vehicle.

Pine Barren Rivers. There are many small rivers and streams traversing the Pines. Of note are those that border and transect the Wharton State Forest. On the west is the Mullica River; centrally located is the Batsto River; and on the east side are the two branches of the Wading River. All are delightful for canoeing. Canoes can be rented from a number of suppliers. Telephone numbers are obtainable through the yellow pages of the Camden and Burlington County Directories.

Suggested Readings on the Pine Barrens of New Jersey

Beck, Henry Charlton. *Forgotten Towns of Southern New Jersey.* New Brunswick, N.J.: Rutgers University Press, 1961.
———. *More Forgotten Towns of Southern New Jersey.* New Brunswick, N.J.: Rutgers University Press, 1963.
Buell, M. F., and J. E. Cantlon. "Effects of Prescribed Burning on Ground Cover in the New Jersey Pine Region." *Ecology* 34 (1953): 520–28.
Cawley, J., and M. Cawley. *Exploring the Little Rivers of New Jersey.* New Brunswick, N.J.: Rutgers University Press, 1971.

Conant, Roger. "Notes on the Distribution of Reptiles and Amphibians in the Pine Barrens of New Jersey." *New Jersey Nature News* 17 (1962): 16–21.

Connor, Paul. "Notes on the Mammals of a New Jersey Pine Barrens Area." *Journal of Mammalogy* 34 (1953): 227–35.

Cook, George H. *Geology of New Jersey*. Newark, N.J.: New Jersey Geological Survey, 1968.

Fables, David G. "Breeding Birds of the New Jersey Pine Barrens." *New Jersey Nature News* 17 (1962): 60–64.

Forman, Richard T., ed. *Pine Barrens: Ecosystem and Landscape*. New York: Academic Press, 1979.

Harshberger, John W. *The Vegetation of the New Jersey Pine Barrens*. New York: Dover Publications, 1970.

Little, S., Jr., and E. B. Moore. "The Ecological Role of Prescribed Burns in the Pine-Oak Forests of Southern New Jersey." *Ecology* 30 (1949): 223–33.

McCormick, Jack. *The Pine Barrens: A Preliminary Ecological Inventory*. Trenton, N.J.: New Jersey State Museum, 1970. (Exhaustive bibliography.)

——— and M. F. Buell. "The Plains: Pigmy Forests of the New Jersey Pine Barrens, a Review and Annotated Bibliography." *New Jersey Academy of Science Bulletin* 13 (1968): 20–34.

McPhee, John. *The Pine Barrens*. New York: Farrar, Straus & Giroux, 1968. (A pleasant overview of the land and its inhabitants.)

———. "The People of New Jersey's Pine Barrens." *National Geographic*, January 1974.

Nixdorf, Bert. *Hikes and Bike Rides for the Delaware Valley and Southern New Jersey*. A pamphlet published by Bert Nixdorf, 1976. (Emphasis on the Pine Barrens. Available in some local book stores.)

Pierce, Arthur D. *Iron in the Pines*. New Brunswick, N.J.: Rutgers University Press, 1957.

Richards, H. G. "The Geological History of the New Jersey Pine Barrens." *New Jersey Nature News* 15 (1960): 146–51.

"The Pine Barrens of New Jersey." (A symposium sponsored

by the Ecological Society of America.) *Bartonia*, December 1952.

Thomas, Lester S. *The Pine Barrens of New Jersey*. Rev. ed. Trenton, N.J.: New Jersey Department of Environmental Protection, 1983. (A pamphlet available at ranger's stations and a very handy list of animal and plant life.)

Weygandt, Cornelius. *Wharton Tract Plant Life*. Trenton, N.J.: New Jersey Department of Conservation and Economic Development, 1965.

The Salt-Water Marsh

ANNE GALLI

The salt marshes that lie along the Delaware Bay and behind the barrier islands of southern New Jersey's Atlantic Coast are a vast habitat of 245,000 acres. Easily identified by their uninterrupted vista of waving grasses, the marshes are often overlooked and unvisited even when easily accessible.

The marshes have been disdained as swampy havens for biting insects and unfit places for humans since colonial times. This reputation is unfortunate. The marshes as well as other shallow-water estuarine habitats—mud flats, tidal creeks, sounds, inlets, and bays—are not only rich in food resources but one of our most productive ecosystems. A place where land meets the sea, these salt marshes are home for varied flora and fauna that offer opportunities for aesthetic enjoyment as well as instruction.

The best time to venture into a salt marsh is in the fall, from late August through October. Migrating and late-nesting birds abound, marsh and upland border plants are in bloom, and the air and water temperatures are comfortable. With luck, the biting insect population will have dwindled.

WETLANDS INSTITUTE

The ideal beginning of an acquaintance with salt marshes is at the Wetlands Institute in Cape May County, New Jersey. The Institute, which sits amidst an expanse of relatively undisturbed coastal salt marsh, can be reached from the Garden State Parkway. Turn left at the traffic light at mile post 10 and follow Stone Harbor Boulevard east across the marshes. The Boulevard was built atop the bed of a former railroad line that brought the first summer tourists to New Jersey beaches. The marshes you view as you approach appear the same as they did to those earlier visitors.

The Wetlands Institute is situated on the south side of the Boulevard a half-mile west of the Borough of Stone Harbor and within the boundaries of the Township of Middle. Its striking cedar shake building, designed by noted architect Malcolm Wells, has been open to the public since 1972. Funds for the facility and 6,000 acres of surrounding wetlands came from private, corporate, and foundation gifts through the efforts of Herbert Mills, the Institute's founder, in association with the World Wildlife Fund. Subsequent transfer of the land to the New Jersey Green Acres program assures its open space status. The public is welcome to explore the salt marsh and visit the museum, bookstore, and observation tower. The Institute sponsors many nature activities for members and non-members, including an annual weekend coastal festival, salt marsh safaris, school field trips, birdwatching expeditions, workshops, and courses on a wide range of subjects from wild foods to children's ecology and nature art. A seasonal schedule of events and a newsletter are available upon request. Dormitory accommodations serve students and visiting groups. Research laboratories are administered in cooperation with Lehigh University.

Begin your journey into the world of the salt marsh by climbing the spiral staircase of the Wetlands Institute's observation tower. This bird's-eye view of the salt marsh will help you understand the relationship of the marsh and neighboring habitats, the barrier island to the east and the upland forest to the west. Look first to the east to the barrier island known as Seven Mile Beach, and beyond to the Atlantic Ocean. Your view is framed by the roofline of homes in the Borough of Stone Harbor. Like most of New Jersey's barrier islands, it is now almost completely developed with homes and summer recreational facilities. To imagine how the island appeared to the colonists, you have to see the remnant patches of natural vegetation which still remain in the 21-acre Stone Harbor Bird Sanctuary (located between Second and Third Avenues at 111th to 117th Streets) and on the southernmost tip of the island beyond 123rd Street.

Barrier islands are vital to the formation of salt marshes. The islands absorb the energy of waves and storms along the ocean front, thereby sheltering the back bays and providing quiet, relatively shallow-water areas which can be colonized by the grasses which form the salt marsh. The barrier islands are separated by inlets which connect the ocean to the bays. The low bridge you see along the horizon spans a portion of Hereford Inlet. The bridge connects Stone Harbor to Nummy Island, a large salt marsh island you may want to visit.

Turn now and look over the salt marsh that surrounds the Wetlands Institute. A myriad of tidal ponds, channels, and creeks interrupts the surface of the grass. Throughout the year, differing patterns of color and texture are evident across the marsh. These patterns are indicative of the various species of plants that grow depending on subtle changes of marsh elevation and tidal inundation. Along the banks of creeks and channels is a narrow band of intense green. Here Saltmarsh Cordgrass grows taller and more vigorously than elsewhere. In spring, the sun shining on the dark mud of creek banks warms the soil and new shoots of grass "green up" quickly. In fall, when the expanse of marsh has turned brown, the ribbon of green remains late into the season. The profuse blossoms of the Saltmarsh Cordgrass top the band of green with a cap of gold. This band of green and gold defines the tiniest creeks even where open water is not evident.

At higher elevations, Salt Hay (Saltmeadow Cordgrass) is the predominant grass. In late September and through October, patches of brilliant scarlet punctuate the grassy meadows. Of the three species of glasswort that grow in the marsh, it is the two annuals, Dwarf Glasswort and Slender Glasswort, that add these hues of red and orange.

Step onto the tower balcony and walk around to the northeast side. The horizon serves as a backdrop for the trees of the forested upland. The marsh, which stretches for three miles between the barrier island and the upland, is a vital link between land and sea. It absorbs storm and wave energy, thereby protecting the mainland from flooding. The marshes also stabilize the shoreline by trapping sand and silt, filter pollutants and excess nutrients from upland runoff, and act as a barrier to the landward seep of salt water into underground fresh-water reservoirs. Salt marshes also serve as a nursery ground for an amazing number of commercially and recreationally important fish and shellfish.

Turn one more corner on the tower and look across the Boulevard to the small housing development. This community exemplifies the land-use philosophy of the 1950s and 1960s when marshes were considered wasteland useful only when bulkheaded and filled for development. The era of environmental awareness in the late 1960s, fortunately, drew into focus the heretofore unrecognized benefits of wetlands to both the natural world and society. In 1973 the New Jersey Wetlands Act was finally implemented after earlier passage by the state legislature. It passed none too soon. From 1953 to 1973 approximately 1,900 acres per year of tidal wetlands were filled or dredged for development. Since the installation of regulations associated with the Wetlands Act in 1973 the development of tidal wetlands has only been permitted to special public interest projects. The New Jersey Wetlands Act has allies. The Federal Clean Water Act requires a permit for dredging or filling wetlands. In addition, the U.S. Army Corps of Engineers, in cooperation with the U.S. Fish and Wildlife Service, the National Marine Fisheries Service, and the U.S. Environmental Protection Service, has administered a program that restricts the transformation of wetlands to those projects which are water dependent. Thus the state and federal agencies have acted generally in concert to protect an irreplaceable resource—the tidal wetlands.

You have perhaps noticed that trees and shrubs are absent from the marsh except within the bulkheads or along the elevated trail that runs south from the parking lot to Scotch Bonnet Creek. Tides control their distribution. Trees and shrubs are tolerant neither of salt-water flooding nor the shearing action of rising and falling ice in winter. They grow only on higher elevations. Often such elevated sites are the result of human activity. Traditionally, sand and silt dredged from channels were dumped onto the marsh, creating dredge spoil islands and destroying marsh vegetation. Through the process called succession, these elevated sites eventually become vegetated with shrubs, trees, and other nonmarsh species. Three dredge spoil islands, in different stages of vegetation, can be seen from the tower. Look north beyond the housing development.

Before you descend from the tower, look for wildlife in the area. In September and October, hundreds of migrating Tree Swallows gather on the telephone lines which run from the street to the building. Quiet for only moments, the swallows swoop, all on cue, to the Northern Bayberry bushes to feed on the waxy gray fruit. Quick as a wink, the Tree Swallows eat the berries, swirl up and away—perhaps to alight again on the wire or perhaps to move to other shrubs not yet stripped of berries. Young and adults flock together, the mature birds with iridescent blue backs often outnumbering the plain brown adolescents.

Now scan the marsh for birds. The larger species can often be seen from the tower. At this distance, the Snowy Egret and the Great (Common) Egret are easily confused. Both appear as long-necked, long-legged white birds standing in ponds or along creek banks. But a few minutes' observation will reveal the difference. The Great Egret is a slow, methodical feeder, spending much time waiting for prey to come within striking distance. In contrast is the Snowy Egret's frenzied dancing as it chases fish in the shallow waters. Should a Snowy Egret fly by, its striking yellow feet provide still another clue to its identity.

American Oystercatchers feed on the delectable bivalve for which they are named. These birds often rest on the open mud flat to the southwest of the Institute. Focus your binoculars over the wind anemometer for their distinct black and white form with the prominent red bill. You may also see a Clapper Rail scurry across the exposed mud bottom of the creek at low tide. Herring Gulls are easily spotted from the tower. They are fond of dropping clams or mussels onto the sandy path of the nature trail.

You should visit the small museum at the end of the hall after you descend from the tower. The exhibits focus on plants and animals of the marsh and other coastal habitats of the Delaware Valley. Particularly interesting are the live animals displayed in the salt-water aquaria. Most of the animals have been caught within a half-mile of the Institute during trawling expeditions for research or visiting groups. Because many species of salt marsh fish are not caught with the traditional hook and line, more unusual methods must be used to collect them. An otter trawl is a special net for towing behind a slowly moving boat. Weighted to ride along a creek bottom, the net funnels slow-moving, sessile, and bottom-dwelling fish and invertebrates into a bag. Hoisted onto the deck and opened, the trawl reveals the inhabitants of the creek—and catches are never twice the same. More spectacular catches include small sharks, most often Dogfish (Sand) Sharks, and an occasional ray. Most frustrating is a net full of mussels, or worse, "goobers"—basketball-sized chunks of salt marsh sod which have tumbled into the water from the creek banks. Always to expect the unexpected is the rule when trawling. A word of caution: Never try this technique yourself. It is illegal without a special collector's permit. All animals unneeded for further study are returned to the water. Occasionally, an unusual specimen caught by a local resident is donated to the aquaria.

The Lined Seahorse in the aquarium is a favorite of staff and visitors alike. It normally inhabits the irregular bottoms of the marsh channels from March to November and moves to deeper coastal waters for the winter. Male seahorses with unborn young in their pouches are occasionally caught during the warm summer months. Fortunate is the visitor who witnesses the birth of these tiny fish. The Northern Pipefish, a close relative of the seahorse, shares the unusual behavior of males' carrying the eggs in a brood pouch. Both fishes have slender snouts, stiff bodies, and protruding eyes. The Northern Pipefish has an eel-like body and is often thought to be an eel. In fact, the American Eel is a common salt marsh resident and small specimens may be seen in the aquaria, usually hidden beneath the rocks or in the gravel.

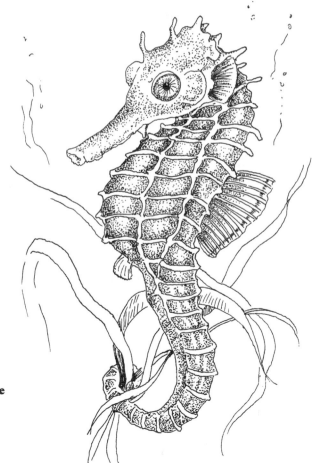

Lined Seahorse

Research conducted by Institute personnel has documented 112 species of fish in the southern New Jersey coastal embayments and nearshore waters. Small specimens of Oyster Toadfish, Spotted Hake and Red Hake (Ling), Mummichog (known to kids and fishermen as "minnies" or minnows), Atlantic (Common) Silverside, Threespine and Fourspine Sticklebacks, Black Sea Bass, Cobia, Common (Crevalle) Jack, Northern Kingfish, Spotfin Butterflyfish, White Mullet, Crested Blenny, Northern (Common) Sea Robin, Summer and Winter Flounders, Orange Filefish, Northern Puffer, and others randomly populate the aquaria. Even if you make a special effort to catch fish during a walk through the marsh, most of those mentioned will not be found. Seasonal migration behavior and habitat preferences make them hard to catch without special equipment. So enjoy those on view in the aquaria and recognize that salt marshes are the nursery ground and cafeteria for many fish.

Mollusks—snails and bivalves such as oysters and clams whose bodies are enclosed in hard calcareous shells—comprise another important group of salt marsh animals. A small exhibit identifying local shelled creatures is available for your reference.

Now let's visit the salt marsh. Ask at the bookstore for a guide sheet to the salt marsh nature trail. The trail begins on the far side of the staff parking lot to the right of the building. Actually a gravel road built years ago by a would-be developer, the trail is a dry route to Scotch Bonnet Creek. At the start of the trail, on your left along the marsh edge, Common Reed Grass (*Phragmites*) waves large fluffy plumes atop tall stalks. Often growing in dense stands, this exotic plant has limited value for wildlife. It is considered a pest because it competes with more valuable native plants. Along the trail, it serves as a screen through which you can peer at the shallow ponds in this corner of the marsh.

During spring and fall migration many species of shorebirds feed in the ponds, within easy range of your camera. Greater and Lesser Yellowlegs are slim, gray sandpipers with long, thin bills. Their bright yellow legs and larger size make them easily distinguishable from other sandpipers in the pond. They are not, however, easily differentiated from each other unless side

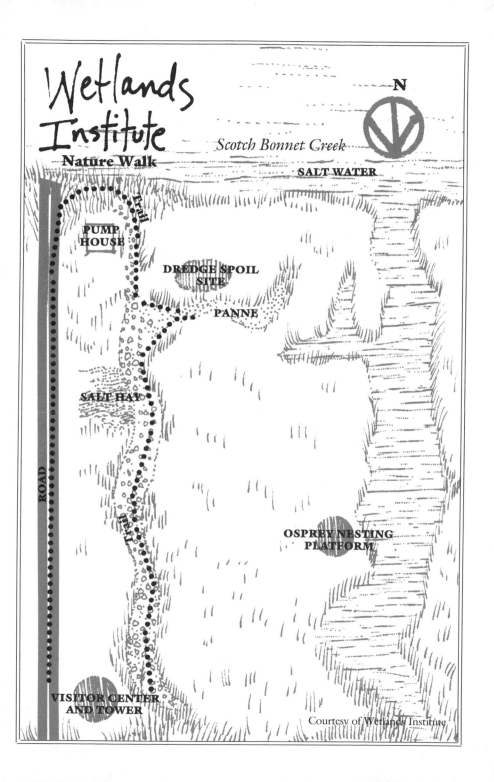

by side, and many a discussion has occurred among birders trying to distinguish them. The Lesser Yellowlegs is the more common species and has a softer call with fewer notes. Dunlin and Least and Semipalmated Sandpipers also feed here in spring and fall.

Shorebirds in fall plumage are difficult to identify, especially the small sparrow-sized sandpipers known collectively as "peep." This is a good spot to begin unravelling the complexities of shorebird identification. First, compare sizes. Least Sandpipers are smallest, with yellow or green legs and slight bills. Semipalmated Sandpipers are noticeably larger, with heavier bills and blackish legs. Dunlin are larger still and in early fall may still show remnants of rusty red on the back and a black belly patch. They are always distinguishable by their long, stout bill with a slight downward droop at the tip. Be on the lookout for the uncommon Western Sandpipers and White-rumped Sandpipers. Black-bellied Plovers, resplendent in their black "bib and tucker" of spring, are no less conspicuous in fall when their large size, stocky shape, hunched plover stance, and short bulbous-tipped bill give them away. In flight, this plover's underwing feathers form a dark, distinctive axillary patch. The smaller Semipalmated Plover is "marsh mud brown" above and white below, with a single dark breast band. It blends beautifully with the dark earth of the pond edges.

A surprise one spring were three Stilt Sandpipers, which stayed for several days in the ponds. This species is more frequently seen during their autumnal migration, along with the more numerous Spotted and Pectoral Sandpipers and Short-billed Dowitchers. In late spring, female Mallards and American Black Ducks bring their fluffy young to the pond. Herons and egrets, including Great Egrets, Snowy Egrets, Tricolored (Louisiana) Herons, Little Blue Herons, Cattle Egrets, Black-crowned and occasional Yellow-crowned Night-Herons, and Glossy Ibis are seen spring through fall. If the winter is mild, a few Great and Snowy Egrets may remain. The Great Blue Herons arrive in numbers in fall and stay until spring. In winter and early spring Brant are present, and wintering Snow Geese can be found in huge flocks, especially in marshes along the Delaware Bay.

Before you continue along the trail, check the trees for the many species of songbirds and warblers that use the bordering garden shrubs and trees as an oasis for cover and food. During spring migration (May), a wave of migrants may include American Redstart, Black-and-white, Yellow-rumped (Myrtle), Yellow, and Chestnut-sided Warblers, Blue-gray Gnatcatcher, Northern (Baltimore) Oriole, Rose-breasted Grosbeak, and Scarlet Tanager. Northern Cardinals, Northern Mockingbirds, and House Finches are permanent garden residents. Beware! Poison-ivy grows in abundance along the path. Despite its irritant properties for humans, its berries are a wonderful food for many birds.

The shrubs and trees of the roadbed provide both nesting and roosting sites for many species of birds. Red-winged Blackbirds abound. They are highly territorial, chasing Fish Crows and even Ospreys that fly over during the nesting sea-

Osprey

son. Short-eared Owls may be flushed from sparse shrubs along the marsh edge during winter. Northern Harriers (Marsh Hawks) cruise low over the vegetation each day, fall through spring, in search of rodents. In late fall, sparrows search for seeds from weeds and grasses. A careful observer may identify Song, Swamp, and Savannah Sparrows and Dark-eyed (Slate-colored) Juncos. Seaside and Sharp-tailed Sparrows nest in the marsh grass on the far side of the pond. Their raspy, buzzy calls give them away, for their habit of popping up out of the grass, flying low, and then dropping quickly out of sight makes them difficult to see.

A particularly conspicuous salt marsh resident in early spring is the Willet. Arriving in late March, these large shorebirds spend the next several weeks courting, displaying, and establishing territories along the roadbed. When standing still, which they rarely do during courtship, Willets blend surprisingly well into their surroundings. Overall grayish in color, with long legs and long bill, they flash a striking black and white wing pattern when displaying or flying. Their insistent call— *will-et, will-et*, which they often sound from atop the Institute's roof from which it reverberates through the laboratories—has been known to elicit unrepeatable comments from scientists trying to concentrate on a research project. Willets become quiet once incubation has begun. I have often been startled by a brooding Willet flushed from a nest within two or three feet of me.

As you move down the road, Northern Bayberry becomes the dominant shrub. The dark green, thick leaves are toothed toward the tip. Pinch a leaf and you will smell the pungent aroma of "bayberry candles." Female shrubs form clusters of waxy gray berries in late summer. The berries are still gathered for candle making. An important wildlife food, the berries are consumed by Tree Swallows, Northern (Yellow-shafted) Flickers, and wintering Yellow-rumped Warblers. This shrub inhabits the upland rather than the marsh. It occurs on the highest crest of the road in combination with other plants more characteristic of dry upland habitats. Species that may be familiar to you include Winged (Shining) Sumac, Red Cedar (Eastern),

Black Cherry, Yarrow, Pokeweed, Common and Great Rag-weeds, Wild Bean, Queen Anne's Lace, Common Evening-primrose, plantains, and others. These plants can withstand an occasional salt-water flooding during severe northeast storms. Although not occurring on this site, other salt marsh border plants include Virginia Creeper, Common Mullein, Camphor-weed, wild grapes, and the showy pink-blossomed Marsh Mallow.

Between late March and early August, stop at trail marker 4 for a look at the Ospreys on the nesting platform built on the marsh specifically for them. Traditional tree nesters on the bar-rier islands, Ospreys were displaced by human development. Fortunately, they were able to adapt their nesting habits and now use man-made structures such as duck blinds and channel markers. The pair at this site usually return from their South American wintering grounds in late March.

Preliminary nesting activity of Ospreys includes gathering sticks, marsh grass, and algae to build up and line the old nest. During incubation, one of the adults (usually the female) often sits low in the nest, barely visible above the rim. The male is frequently absent during the day, returning in early evening to roost on the pole at the edge of the platform. Both adults seem to prefer perching on stakes at the far end of the marsh or on the ground across the creek away from the nest. Here they feed on the fish that the male catches in the bay, ocean, or perhaps gravel pit ponds inland. The young hatch from May to early July and are able to fly within six to eight weeks.

When the Ospreys are in residence, please do not venture be-yond the trail edge. Such activity is frowned on by Institute personnel, since it may have dire consequences for the Osprey's eggs or young. Long-time residents of the coast can remember when Ospreys were so numerous that "every telephone pole" had a nest. The population declined drastically in New Jersey in the mid-1900s. Human disturbance of nests, physiological impact of pesticides, and the loss of nesting habitats on the bar-rier islands all combined to make the Osprey an endangered species in New Jersey.

The late Joseph Jacobs, one of the first people to build nest-

ing platforms in the salt marsh, helped significantly to preserve
the Osprey as a breeding species in Cape May County between
1950 and 1970. The exemplary management techniques pio-
neered by Joe Jacobs were supplemented by egg transplants
from southern populations (with lower pesticide levels) into
the nests of local Ospreys. Today the Osprey population has
increased to the point that, in early 1984, it was the first species
ever removed from the endangered list in the state! Continued
vigilance is necessary to assure that the Osprey will forever delight the nature enthusiast.

Following the Ospreys' departure in early fall, the platform
may be used by a Belted Kingfisher scanning the creek for
food, by migrating Tree Swallows in search of a dry landing
spot, or by an occasional Herring Gull or Fish Crow. To those
unfamiliar with coastal areas, the Fish Crow may seem indis-
tinguishable from the familiar American (Common) Crow of
your neighborhood. Both species occur in Cape May County
and offer an identification challenge to the birdwatcher. The
Fish Crow favors coastal marshes and beaches, and may sometimes be found along rivers as far inland as Pennsylvania.
Smaller and more slender than the American Crow, it is best
distinguished by its nasal, falsetto call. Fish Crows feed on
marsh invertebrates, carrion, bird and turtle eggs, insects, and
berries.

As you follow the trail from the road onto the bare patch of
ground called a salt panne, you will notice the change in vegetation resulting from a decrease in elevation. Northern Bayberry is replaced by Groundsel-tree. Although these two
shrubs grow adjacent to one another, Groundsel-tree is always
found toward the marsh side at an almost imperceptibly lower
elevation. Groundsel-tree is most conspicuous in late September and October when the creamy white, silky seed tufts appear
on the female shrubs. Marsh-elder is a shrub which invades the
higher marsh border at an elevation slightly above the high tide
line. Easily confused with Groundsel-tree, it may be distinguished by the opposite arrangement of the leaves and the hard
brown seeds dangling from its uppermost stems.

Below the shrubby transition zone, the high marsh is usually dominated by Salt Hay or Saltmeadow Cordgrass and by Spike (Salt) Grass. These species sometimes grow side by side or intermingle. Salt Hay is a fine, wiry grass. Its narrow leaves are rolled inward and appear round. The leaves of Spike Grass are flatter and are arranged in one plane only on opposite sides of the stem. The stems of Salt Hay are so fine that they tend to bend, forming swirled grassy mats. Historically, Salt Hay was used as fodder for cattle and sheep. Today it is used for mulch and is still harvested from marshes along Delaware Bay. Only small patches of Salt Hay are growing along the trail, but you may see some near the end of the road. Pause at trail marker 5 and part the thick mat of Spike Grass growing there. On even the hottest, driest days of summer the ground below the grass is damp and covered with a carpet of green algae. Look carefully and you will find an abundance of tiny brown Salt Marsh Snails. Adult snails are not aquatic. They possess a lung and breathe air. They feed on algae growing on the peat surface and are in turn eaten by fish which gain access to the higher marsh on flood tides. They are also eaten by marsh birds, especially during storm tides, when the snails must climb the grass stalks in order to remain above water. The bright red dots which you may see in the grass mat are Marsh Mites. A hand lens will magnify their lovely body structure.

Other higher-level marsh plants are distributed between the road and the panne. A distinct band of Sea-lavender extends along the border of the marsh. It coincides with the line of dead *Phragmites* stems and other flotsam and jetsam collectively called "wrack." This hodgepodge is washed up by high tides. In late summer this zone is a mist of tiny purple flowers of Sea-lavender. The wiry stalks remain into winter, as do the green basal rosettes of next year's flowering plants. Sea-blite grows singly or in small clumps. A bushy annual with fleshy, somewhat succulent linear leaves, its pale gray-green color is your first clue that this plant is worth investigating. In late summer and early fall, tiny green blossoms appear on the top sections of the plant. The seeds provide food for marsh birds. Three types of glassworts (also known as saltworts), first noted from the tower, also grow here. These plants have distinctive

PROFILE OF A SALT-WATER MARSH

Phragmites

Seaside Goldenrod
　　Northern Bayberry

　　　　Marsh-elder

　　　　　　Groundsel-tree
　　　　　　　　Pond and Spike Grass
　　　　　　　　　　Glassworts

spine-tipped stems. The common names are confused and confusing. We will refer to the three as: Dwarf Glasswort or Samphire, Slender Glasswort, and Woody Glasswort. The first two are annuals; the latter is a perennial with a woody stem. All have succulent, jointed branches, are conspicuously leafless, and in summer assume a wonderful jade color. I delight in introducing children to these plants. They are astounded when I eat a piece. The fleshy, branching annuals are crunchy with a salty tang; in fact, the colonists used them for pickles. All three species occur along the edge of the panne.

You have been walking on a salt marsh panne, a sandy strip devoid of plants. This site and other barren spots throughout the marsh are shallow depressions that flood during above-normal tides. They do not drain following tidal retreat. As a result, water remains on the surface until removed through evaporation. The high concentration of salts that remain inhibits colonization of the depression by even salt-tolerant marsh

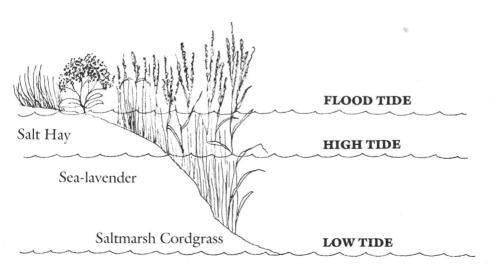

plants. When the panne is dry, you should observe tiny balls of sand resembling anthills dotting the surface. Although you may not see the owners of these little pyramids, they are an indication of the presence of earwigs—golden insects bearing pincers on their rear segments. After the panne has been washed by tides, the earwigs can often be found clinging to the undersides of scattered shell fragments. The shells are dropped by Herring Gulls in an effort to open them. A lucky visitor may be able to watch a gull repeatedly drop and retrieve a clam or mussel until it breaks, exposing the soft-bodied mollusk inside.

Evidence of yet another resident of the marsh are the small holes hidden between blades of grass near the water. Patience! Watch for a moment and you may be rewarded by a Fiddler Crab popping out of its burrow. One of the male claws is greatly enlarged for mating display before the female. Fiddler Crabs feed on plant and animal remains which they find in sand and mud. In turn, the crabs are fed upon by Clapper Rails, Night-Herons, and Whimbrels, the latter a spring and fall visitor whose long downcurved bill is designed to probe into crab burrows.

At low tide, your feet will stay dry even at the edge of the pond. As you approach, ripples may break the water surface as small fish dart from their hiding places. Most common are the Mummichogs or Killifish. Females are larger than males and drab grayish in color. The males have iridescent silver-blue bands during the breeding season. Sheepshead Minnows, deep-bodied and camouflaged with olive drab blotches, scurry about the pond in schools. A show-off during the breeding season, the male's back becomes steel blue and his belly and fins a rakish splash of yellow-orange.

On a calm day the water of the pond is still and clear. Look below the surface at the bumps on the muddy bottom. Don't be surprised if the bumps move, revealing a Mud Snail in its blue-black shell, or a Hermit Crab. Pick up a crab if you can reach it without stepping into the water. Caution: the ground beneath the grass is firm but the pond bottom is not! Hermit Crabs lack exoskeletons so they must find a protective covering elsewhere and routinely appropriate the shells of dead Mud Snails. A fuzzy growth covers the shell only when it is inhabited by a Hermit Crab. Referred to as "Snail Fur," the growth is a colony of hydroid animals encased in calcareous tubes. The hydroids sweep the water for food particles and ride free as the crabs move from place to place. Search for a Blue Crab, the most famous of the marsh residents. A gourmet's delight, they usually inhabit deeper channels and creeks, but occasionally one may be seen scurrying across the pond bottom.

A salt marsh is dotted with many pools and ponds. The pool where you are standing is connected to a large channel via a system of small creeks. Its water changes daily with the tides. The surface is usually clear and the salinity stable. Some pools are more isolated. They receive water only during rains or spring tides. Sheets of algae grow in these ponds, obscuring the water and giving the surface a scummy appearance. Fish washed in on high tides are trapped for weeks or months in the ponds. The fish survive, however, despite an environment where the salinity varies due to evaporation during dry times and dilution after heavy rains. The ponds are often ringed with egrets, herons, gulls, and terns feeding on the abundant fish in late summer and early fall. One wonders, given the large number of predators, how any fish can survive and, conversely, how each individual predator can find enough food. Daily, the location of the crowd changes as the birds exploit pond after pond.

Continue your journey on the panne toward the creek and small building which is the Institute's pumphouse. The pumps pull salt water from the creek to the greenhouse research laboratories. When you reach Scotch Bonnet Creek, look between the clumps of marsh grass for the Ribbed Mussel half-buried in the peat. Push aside the blades of Rockweed (Brown Algae) to find them. Notice as you do the air bladders on the blades of Rockweed. These floaters lift the plant to the water surface at high tide. In this way it is exposed to the sun's rays, which are crucial for photosynthesis. Firmly embedded in the peat, Ribbed Mussels provide substrate (a hard surface) which not only Rockweed but barnacles latch onto.

A barnacle is a crustacean, a relative of the crab. Adults are sessile, fixed to a hard substrate. They spend their lives standing on their heads, kicking food into their mouths with their feathery legs. Unlike other crustaceans, barnacles do not molt. The plates in which they are encased enlarge as the soft parts grow.

Live Horseshoe Crabs can be plucked from the water of Scotch Bonnet Creek on the high tides of spring. Horseshoe Crabs come in peak numbers to sandy beaches to lay their eggs between the full-moon high tides of May and June. Concentrated primarily along Delaware Bay, they also make their way into creeks and channels of the Atlantic Coast marshes. Later in the season, portions of their carapaces wash ashore; with enough pieces you may be able to reconstruct this prehistoric "monster."

Horseshoe Crabs are not crabs at all but are closely related to spiders. The two-part body is jointed, as are the six pairs of appendages. The tail or telson is used as a rudder or to help a crab right itself when it has been beached on its back by waves. To clear up popular misconceptions, the telson is not a stinging organ nor are Horseshoe Crabs harmful. The crab's shell provides a firm surface for attachment of other organisms such as slipper shells, flat worms, barnacles, bryozoans (moss-animals), and tube-dwelling worms.

Low tide exposes a wide mud flat extending from the bank to the waterline. Egrets, herons, sandpipers, and plovers feed here. Mud Snails, with muscular feet, glide over the ooze, scraping up algae as they go. Clumps of bright green Sea Lettuce spot the flats. Often this folded sheet of algae conceals the tubes of the Plumed Worm. A segmented marine worm with bristle or paddlelike "feet," the Plumed Worm constructs a skinlike tube for protection. The above-ground portion is encrusted with plant or shell fragments. The lower part of the tube gradually tapers to three feet below the ground. A number of polychaete worms inhabit the marsh. Most can be discovered only by digging through the sand or mud in which they burrow. They are an important food for birds and fish.

Across the creek from the Wetlands Institute is Ring Island. The island is home for the largest colony of Laughing Gulls in the world. A cacophony of sound rises forth from late spring through summer, as thousands of nesting Laughing Gulls squabble with neighbors and the young beg incessantly for food. Laughing Gulls build nests atop the wrack—mounds of dead plant stalks deposited on the marsh by high tides. When spring tides inundate the marsh, the activity and the calls rise to a frenzy as many nests and eggs are swept away. The birds must start all over again.

The strategy of nesting on the wrack is shared by three other closely related species: Forster's Tern, Common Tern, and Black Skimmer. The terns lay eggs in shallow depressions molded into flat rafts of dead plant material. Forster's Terns have always nested on marshes, salt or fresh. The Common Tern was traditionally a beach-nesting species, but it has adapted to the loss of beach habitat in recent years by switching to the salt marsh. Black Skimmers utilize both nesting strategies. In Cape May County they continue to nest on sandy beaches or sandy pannes on marsh islands. In Ocean County, the Barnegat Bay population nests on salt marsh wrack, while other colonies return annually to the barrier island beaches. The Black Skimmer and the smallest of the terns, the Least (Little) Tern, are both endangered in New Jersey. The continual disturbance as a result of human activity on the beaches devastates nesting and raising of the young. The Least Tern has not yet adapted to marsh nesting. The terns and Black Skimmer are dependent on the marsh for small fish as food.

On your return via the road, you might observe other wildlife. Reptiles are occasionally represented by such snakes as the Northern Black Racer and Northern Water Snake and several species of turtles. The Snapping Turtle occurs in fresh to brackish waters and the Eastern Mud and Eastern Painted Turtles and the Northern Diamondback Terrapin in the more saline estuarine waters of the coast. The best time to look for the Diamondback is during the nesting season in June and July, when females appear on land in search of dry sandy sites for egg-laying. The sand and gravel road is a perfect nesting area and you might be lucky enough to sight a female digging a nest. When egg-laying is complete, the terrapin will fill the hole, and sweep the area with her hind legs to conceal the nest. Animals with keener senses than ours, such as rats, Long-tailed Weasels, Striped Skunks, or Raccoons, have located nests and enjoyed a meal of turtle eggs. Holes with fragments of eggshell scattered about are evidence of such predators. Hatchling terrapins may

Northern Diamondback Terrapin

appear in late summer, or they may overwinter in the ground. Emerging in May, the inch-and-a-half baby terrapins are a wonderful discovery for school children visiting the Institute.

The only amphibian found in the vicinity of the tidal marsh is the Fowler's Toad. They frequent fresh-water pools on the high marsh. These pools receive occasional tidal inundation and toads have been found in pools with salinity up to 10 parts per thousand, a lot for an amphibian.

Goldenrods bloom along the road in late summer and fall. The showiest is Seaside Goldenrod. Its compact plume of blossoms attract migrating Monarch butterflies, royally hued in orange and black, that flit from flower to flower. The abundance of Monarchs varies from year to year, but only adults are seen on the marsh since the Common Milkweed on which the larvae feed does not grow here. A large, attractive species occasionally found in either the caterpillar (larval) or pupal stage is the Cecropia Moth, which overwinters in a brown papery cocoon attached lengthwise to a twig, usually Northern Bayberry. The caterpillar, which grows to four inches, is bright green with parallel rows of colorful tubercles on its back. The striking adult moth is rarely seen, as it is active at night.

Pearly Everlasting, a field flower, also grows in open patches along the margins of the path. It is a larval food of the American Painted Lady, a member of the widespread group of thistle butterflies. This butterfly's wings are brownish with yellow, orange, and white blotches. Two large eyespots on the underside of the wing are a distinctive feature of this species. Two other butterflies, more localized indicators of salt marshes, can be observed in season. Drab little creatures with robust mothlike bodies, the Broad-winged Skipper and the Salt Marsh Skipper favor Queen Anne's Lace and Yarrow, respectively.

The salt marsh's notoriety as a home for biting insects may be deserved. Three groups of insects, Salt Marsh Mosquitos, Greenhead Flies, and Biting Midges account for this reputation. The larvae of all three insects are true marsh residents. Greenhead Fly and Biting Midge larvae occur in the ground; Salt Marsh Mosquito wigglers live in isolated marsh pools. On strong winds, adult mosquitos can be blown from marsh to beach, creating havoc for bikini-clad tourists. To maintain proper perspective, remember that the abundance of insects is an important food source for marsh birds and fish. Human visitors to the salt marsh can increase their comfort by dressing appropriately and avoiding conditions favoring the insects.

The majority of salt marsh insects are not well known, but they are important to the food chain. Most noticeable are grasshoppers, crickets, plant hoppers, dragonflies, and various beetles and bugs. Experts enumerate four-hundred kinds of insect residents in salt marshes, with perhaps fifty species truly representative of the marsh habitat.

Few mammal species actually live their entire lives in the salt marsh. Most that do are small and occupy the upper marsh. Nocturnal by habit and infrequently seen, their presence is known from tracks in rainwater puddles or by their droppings. At intervals, the remains of small rodents, particularly shrews and Eastern Meadow Voles, may be found on the path. The Norway Rat is often present. The Marsh Rice Rat is more selective, occurring only under specific habitat conditions. Raccoons, Striped Skunks, and Long-tailed Weasels forage through the marsh edge. The weasels are particularly aggressive, feeding on other small mammals and on terrapin or bird eggs. During hunting season, White-tailed Deer appear in the marsh, seeking refuge. River Otters, too, are residents of the marsh; shy and nocturnal, they are rarely seen.

The Muskrat is a marsh native, particularly numerous in the brackish areas along Delaware Bay where their cone-shaped houses dot acre after acre of marsh. Muskrats tend to be territorial, ranging within 200 yards of home. Although they are active year-round, they are nocturnal and spend a great deal of time in their houses and tunnels, or in the water.

The salt marsh is a fantastic world, vital to the existence of many plants and animals and to man. Too long misunderstood, it has often been feared and abused. I must confess some apprehension when I first ventured onto its grassy expanse. But like any new acquaintance, it can become a friend after a time.

Before you leave the Wetlands Institute you might stop at the Tidepool Shop in the lobby. They have many books on salt marshes and other coastal topics. Institute personnel are happy to assist you and answer any questions.

If the herons and egrets feeding on the tidal marsh catch your fancy you may like to visit the Stone Harbor Bird Sanctuary at 3rd Avenue and 114th Street, just 5 minutes away. During the summer nearly a dozen species of herons and egrets nest in the 21-acre refuge. At dusk the birds return to the sanctuary to roost for the night. The display of hundreds of incoming birds is spectacular. The sanctuary is one of only two municipally owned rookeries in the world and is visited annually by thousands of tourists.

Perhaps you missed the American Oystercatcher or a sandpiper high on your most-wanted bird list. Nummy Island should be your next stop, particularly if the tide is high. When the mud flats bordering the tidal creeks become flooded, sandpipers, plovers, egrets, and herons use the pools higher on the marsh for feeding. Nummy Island can provide good birding at this time. The plants and animals in this section of marsh are basically the same as previously described for the Wetlands Institute.

For more information contact:

Wetlands Institute
P.O. Box 398
Stone Harbor Boulevard
Stone Harbor, New Jersey 08247
Phone: (609) 368-1211

Fiddler Crab

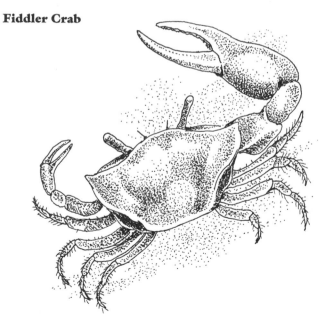

Directions to Stone Harbor, New Jersey (Wetlands Institute and Stone Harbor Point)

From the City Line Avenue entrance onto the Schuylkill Expressway (I-76 East) travel 10.4 miles following the signs for New Jersey to the toll booth at the Walt Whitman Bridge. After paying the toll (75 cents in 1985), cross the bridge and follow the signs for the North-South Freeway and Atlantic City. Drive 4.4 miles from the toll booth to Route 42 South. Drive 7.8 miles along Route 42 South and bear left on the Atlantic City Expressway. Travel 26.4 miles on the expressway to the Great Egg Harbor toll booth ($1.00 in 1985). From here travel another 9.9 miles along the expressway to the Garden State Parkway South (Exit 7 South for Ocean City and Cape May). Bear right on the Garden State Parkway South and drive 27.1 miles to the Stone Harbor Exit (Exit 10B). Along the way you will pass two toll booths each requiring 25 cents in 1985. At the light for the Stone Harbor Exit turn left on Stone Harbor Boulevard (Route 29) and drive 2.8 miles east to the Wetlands Institute on your right. The parking lot, museum, observation tower, and start of the nature trail welcome you almost immediately. A one-way trip from Philadelphia takes approximately one hour and forty-five minutes.

To reach Stone Harbor Point, the southernmost mile of the barrier island of Seven Mile Beach, leave the Wetlands Institute parking lot and turn right on Stone Harbor Boulevard (Route 29). Drive 0.7 miles east, crossing the bridge over the Intracoastal Waterway, to the first light in the town of Stone Harbor. Here make a right on Ocean Drive (3rd Avenue) and drive 1 mile to the parking lot of the Stone Harbor Bird Sanctuary (on your left) at 114th Street. The Sanctuary stretches from 111th to 117th Street and is between 2nd and 3rd Avenues.

After stopping at this famous heronry, turn left (south) on Ocean Drive (3rd Avenue) and at the first left 0.2 miles further turn on 117th Street (here one can also continue along Ocean

Directions to Stone Harbor

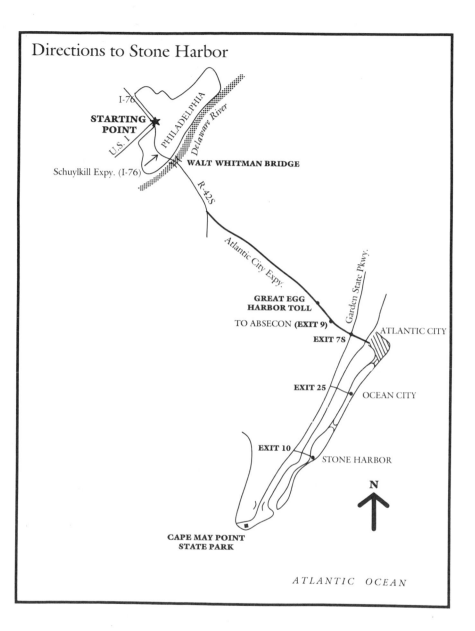

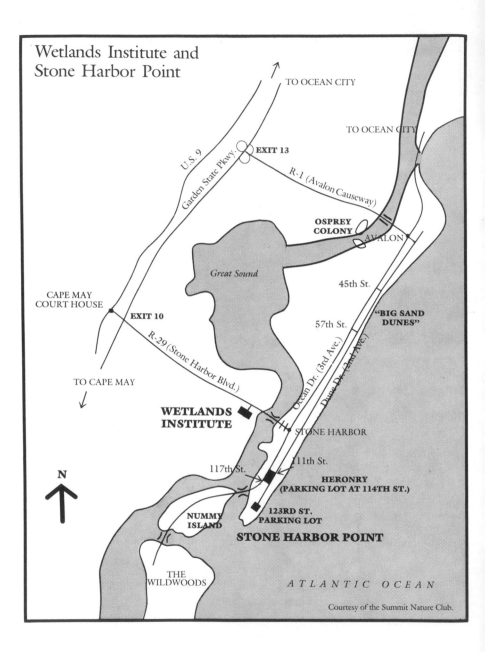

Wetlands Institute and Stone Harbor Point

TO OCEAN CITY

TO OCEAN CITY

U.S. 9

Garden State Pkwy.

EXIT 13

R-1 (Avalon Causeway)

OSPREY COLONY

AVALON

Great Sound

45th St.

CAPE MAY COURT HOUSE

EXIT 10

"BIG SAND DUNES"

57th St.

R-29 (Stone Harbor Blvd.)

Ocean Dr. (3rd Ave.)

Dune Dr. (2nd Ave.)

TO CAPE MAY

WETLANDS INSTITUTE

STONE HARBOR

N

117th St.

111th St.

HERONRY (PARKING LOT AT 114TH ST.)

123RD ST. PARKING LOT

NUMMY ISLAND

STONE HARBOR POINT

THE WILDWOODS

ATLANTIC OCEAN

Courtesy of the Summit Nature Club.

Drive for another 0.5 miles to the bridge for Nummy Island and its vast salt marshes). Drive 0.1 miles on 117th Street to the stop sign and make a right on 2nd Avenue. Travel south 0.3 miles along 2nd Avenue to the large parking lot at 123rd Street on the oceanfront. South of here is Stone Harbor Point and the beginning of the nature walk (about a 10-minute drive from the Wetlands Institute).

To reach the "Big Sand Dunes" in Avalon return to the Stone Harbor Bird Sanctuary. From here backtrack north on Ocean Drive (3rd Avenue) for 1.0 mile to Stone Harbor Boulevard. Continue north on Ocean Drive past this intersection and drive 2.0 miles to 57th Street in Avalon. Turn right on 57th Street, drive 0.1 miles and at the stop sign turn left on 2nd Avenue (Dune Drive). The dunes are on the right stretching from 57th to 45th Street in Avalon (about 0.7 miles). From 45th Street continue 0.8 miles north on 2nd Avenue to the second light in town. Turn left here and drive 3.3 miles west on the Avalon Causeway. Cross over the Intracoastal Waterway to the entrance for the Garden State Parkway North and Philadelphia.

Salt-Water Marshes of the Delaware Valley Region

Salt-water marshes are often associated with other habitats, including fresh-water marshes, estuaries, barrier beaches and islands, woodlands, and so on. The areas mentioned here (even if some are redundant) are locations where the salt-water marsh accounts for a significant percentage of the total habitat and which are generally accessible to the public. Many of these locales are Wildlife Management Areas open to hunting and fishing. Caution is advised during the hunting season. Call (609) 785-0455 for more general information on many of these areas and (609) 628-3219 for additional educational information.

NEW JERSEY

Absecon Wildlife Management Area, Atlantic County, near Absecon, New Jersey, surrounded by U.S. 9, U.S. 30, and Route 87. Many parcels of salt-water marsh behind Brigantine Island and Atlantic City. Fishing, crabbing, birding, sailing available. Public boat ramp off Route 9 near Absecon.

Atlantic County Park. See Deciduous Forests listing.

Barnegat Division of the Edwin B. Forsythe National Wildlife Refuge, Ocean County, between Manahawkin and Barnegat, New Jersey, off U.S. 9. Adjacent to the Manahawkin Wildlife Management Area and across from Long Beach Island. For more information see the Brigantine heading below or the Fresh-Water Marshes listing.

Brigantine Division of the Edwin B. Forsythe National Wildlife Refuge. The salt-water marsh is the dominant habitat of this vast refuge and surrounds the outside perimeter of the auto tour on the diked road. The Leeds Eco-Trail (leaflet available) samples the salt-water marsh plus other habitats. For more information see Fresh-Water Marshes listing.

Corson's Inlet State Park. Extensive salt-water marshes and tidal channels are found on the western side of Ocean Drive. See Barrier Beaches and Islands listing.

Dennis Creek Wildlife Management Area, Cape May County, near Dennisville, New Jersey, off Route 47 (Delaware Bay). Public boat ramp. Visit adjacent Belleplain State Forest with its mixed pine-oak woodlands. Phone: (609) 861-2404.

Dix Wildlife Management Area, Cumberland County, near Fairton and Sea Breeze, New Jersey, off Route 553 and Back Neck Road (Delaware Bay). Also contains some wooded swamps and deciduous woodlands.

Egg Island – Berrytown Wildlife Management Area (Dividing Creek), Cumberland County, near Dividing Creek and Port Norris, New Jersey, off Route 553 (Delaware Bay). Excellent birding.

Fortescue Wildlife Management Area, Cumberland County, near Newport and Fortescue, New Jersey, off Route 553 (Delaware Bay). Famous for large numbers of migrating and wintering Snow Geese.

Hackensack Meadowlands Environment Center, Bergen County, near Lyndhurst, New Jersey, off Routes 17 and 3. The HMEC is an educational and research facility located in the heart of one of the nation's most urbanized wetlands. The Environment Center is perched over the Kingsland Creek Marsh in the Hackensack River estuary on the eastern face of the Bergen County Landfill. The facility includes an auditorium, classrooms, lecture and conference rooms, diked impoundment, live animal exhibits, planetarium, and a museum scheduled to open in early 1986.

Although north of the Delaware Valley Region, the Meadowlands is well worth a visit and serves as a model for man's impact—past, present, and future—on our estuaries and wetlands. Near the Meadowlands Sports Complex and with the Manhattan skyline dominating the view to the east. Nature center. Phone: (201) 460-8300 or 460-1700.

Heislerville Wildlife Management Area, Cumberland County, near Heislerville and Delmont, New Jersey, off Route 47 with access from Matts Landing, East Point, and Thompsons Beach Roads (Delaware Bay). Diverse habitats including diked haying marshes (Salt Hay), impoundments, extensive salt-water marshes, and uplands. East Point Light (partially restored lighthouse) open for special events.

Killcohook National Wildlife Refuge, Salem County, near Harrisonville and Salem, New Jersey, off Route 49 (Delaware Bay). Under administration of Brigantine Division of the Edwin B. Forsythe National Wildlife Refuge. See Fresh-Water Marshes listing.

Lester G. MacNamara Wildlife Management Area (formerly **Tuckahoe—Corbin City Tract**). See Fresh-Water Marshes listing.

Mad Horse Creek Wildlife Management Area, Salem County, near Canton, New Jersey (south of Salem), off Route 49 and Canton Road (Delaware Bay).

Manahawkin Wildlife Management Area. See Fresh-Water Marshes listing.

Nummy Island, Cape May County, between Stone Harbor and the Wildwoods, New Jersey, off Ocean Drive. Accessible from the road; park on the shoulder. Several shallow pools, mudflats, and tidal marshes near the road provide feeding habitat for herons, egrets, and migrating shorebirds. Visit nearby Stone Harbor Bird Sanctuary on Ocean Drive at 114th Street (nesting site for herons and egrets). For more information see this chapter and "The Barrier Beach and Island."

Port Republic Wildlife Management Area, Atlantic County, between Port Republic and New Gretna, New Jersey, off U.S. 9, Garden State Parkway, Route 575, and Mill Street. Some upland field habitat adjoins the extensive salt-water marshes bordering the Mullica River, which also flows through the Pine Barrens. Auto trail.

Tuckerton Meadows (Great Bay Boulevard Wildlife Management Area), Ocean County, south of Tuckerton, New Jersey, off U.S. 9 and Great Bay Boulevard. Across Beach Haven Inlet from Holgate (Long Beach Island). Extensive salt-water marshes with their typical flora on either side of Great Bay Boulevard with great shorebirding at the end of the road on the mudflats exposed during low tide. Rutgers University Marine Field Station housed in former Coast Guard Station nearby.

DELAWARE

Augustine Wildlife Area, New Castle County, near Bay View Beach and Port Penn, Delaware, off Route 9. Extensive salt-water marshes with brackish and fresh-water marshes as one moves inland (westward). Nearby woodland area is an important Great Blue Heron nesting colony.

Blackbird Creek (Taylor's Bridge). Extensive brackish and salt-water marshes below Taylor's Bridge and at nearby Appoquinimink Wildlife Area just to the north. See Fresh-Water Marshes listing.

Bombay Hook National Wildlife Refuge. Great variety of habitats with vast salt-water marshes along outside perimeter of much of the diked tour road, especially opposite the fresh-water impoundments. Visit historic Allee House on the refuge grounds. See Fresh-Water Marshes listing.

Canary Creek and Old Mill Creek Marshes, Sussex County, near Lewes, Delaware, off Route 1 (14). Adjacent to the University of Delaware Marine Studies Complex.

Port Mahon, Kent County, near Little Creek, Delaware, off Route 9 and Port Mahon Road (south of Bombay Hook N.W.R. and north of Little Creek Wildlife Area). Drive east on Port Mahon Road past the first fresh-water impoundment on your right, which is part of Little Creek Wildlife Area. Continue along Port Mahon Road for several miles past salt-water and brackish marshes and the Delaware Bay.

Prime Hook National Wildlife Refuge. Large expanses of brackish and salt-water marshes along the roads through the refuge to Broadkill, Fowler, and Prime Hook beaches. See Fresh-Water Marshes listing.

Route 9, New Castle and Kent Counties, running from the Chesapeake-Delaware Canal near Delaware City, Delaware, south along the coast almost to the Dover Air Force Base. Many streams run under Route 9 and vast stretches of brackish and salt-water marshes border these numerous creeks as they enter Delaware Bay (including several mentioned by name in this section).

Woodland Beach Wildlife Area. Extensive salt-water marshes to the bayside (east) of the Taylor's Gut sluice. See Fresh-Water Marshes listing.

Suggested Readings on the Salt-Water Marsh

Many of the following books will contain pertinent sections on the fresh-water marsh and the barrier beach and island as they are often intimately associated with the salt-water marsh. Also included are texts on estuaries with brackish waters that result from the dynamic mixing of both fresh and salt water.

Amos, William H. *The Life of the Seashore*. New York: Our Living World of Nature Series, McGraw-Hill, 1966.

Beard, Lisa. *A Kettle of Fish: Salt Water Fishes of the Mid-Atlantic Coast*. Stone Harbor, N.J.: The Wetlands Institute, 1981.

Beard, Wendy. *A Salt Marsh Through the Seasons*. Stone Harbor, N.J.: The Wetlands Institute, 1979.

Carlson, Cathy, and John Fowler. *The Salt Marsh of Southern New Jersey*. Pomona, N.J.: Center for Environmental Research, Stockton State College, 1980.

Clark, John R. *Coastal Ecosystem Management*. New York: The Conservation Foundation, John Wiley & Sons, 1977.

Daiber, Franklin C. *Animals of the Tidal Marsh*. New York: Van Nostrand Reinhold, 1982.

Gosner, K. L. *A Field Guide to the Atlantic Seashore*. Boston: Houghton Mifflin, 1979.

Governor's Task Force. *The Coastal Zone of Delaware*. Newark,

Del.: College of Marine Studies, University of Delaware, 1972.

Green, J. *Biology of Estuarine Animals*. Seattle, Wash.: University of Washington Press, 1968.

Lauff, G., ed. *Estuaries*. Washington, D.C.: American Association for the Advancement of Science, 1967.

Lippson, A. J., and R. L. Lippson. *Life in the Chesapeake Bay*. Baltimore, Md.: Johns Hopkins University Press, 1984.

Lomax, Joseph L., Joan M. Galli, and Anne E. Galli. *The Wildlife of Cape May County, New Jersey*. Pomona, N.J.: Center for Environmental Research, Stockton State College, 1980.

Meanley, Brooke. *Birds and Marshes of the Chesapeake Bay Country*. Cambridge, Md.: Tidewater, 1975.

Newcomb, Carol E. *Salt Marsh Flowers of Southern New Jersey*. Franklin Lakes, N.J.: New Jersey Audubon Society, 1978.

Niering, William. *The Life of the Marsh*. New York: Our Living World of Nature Series, McGraw-Hill, 1966.

Ranwell, D. S. *Ecology of Salt Marshes and Sand Dunes*. London: Chapman & Hall, 1972.

Remane, A., and C. Schlieper. *Biology of Brackish Water*. New York: John Wiley & Sons, 1971.

Roberts, M. F. *Tidal Marshes of Connecticut*. New London, Conn.: The Connecticut Arboretum, Connecticut College, 1971.

Schubel, J. R. *The Living Chesapeake*. Baltimore, Md.: Johns Hopkins University Press, 1981.

Silberhon, G. M. *Common Plants of the Mid-Atlantic Coast*. Baltimore, Md.: Johns Hopkins University Press, 1982.

Teal, John, and Mildred Teal. *The Life and Death of the Salt Marsh*. New York: Ballantine, 1969.

the Barrier Beach and Island

D. W. BENNETT

The eastern shoreline of the United States from Long Island to Georgia is edged by a string of sandy islands no more than a few miles wide (if that) and ranging in length from 5 to 25 miles. They are known as barrier islands because they form a soft, mobile buffer between the open ocean and the true mainland.

Cape Hatteras, North Carolina, is such a barrier island: it is 50 miles long, narrow except at Buxton, and relatively unspoiled. Atlantic City sits on a barrier island, but it is so urbanized that it is hard to think of it as kin to Hatteras. Within a short drive from Philadelphia, however, are several barrier islands with relatively unaltered geology and biology. One is

Cape Henlopen, Delaware, on the shore of Delaware Bay. In New Jersey, Island Beach State Park is a beauty, with some 9 miles of natural sand. Holgate, the southernmost mile of Long Beach Island, is another good example, as is Stone Harbor Point, the southernmost mile of Seven Mile Beach, and our destination for this excursion.

The typical barrier island is made up of the following parts, beginning from the ocean: first, the wet beach of gently sloping sand between low and high tide, followed by a stretch of dry flat beach. Next we see the beginnings of beach vegetation, usually sparse stands of beach grass, and behind this come sand dunes, sometimes in one line, sometimes in several. The dunes end with a slope to the water on the bay side; this part of the island is usually fringed by salt marsh.

Barrier islands are relatively inhospitable environments for living things. They are sandy; thus they drain rapidly and do not support a wealth of vegetation. Temperatures in summer can reach beyond 120° F on the beach and dune surface. Not only are the islands misted by salt spray during much of the year and by salt water overwash during storms, but there is little shelter from the winds. Waves churn the beach sands at the surf line. During cold winters the backsides of barrier beaches in New Jersey are ice-rimmed and the ice tears at marsh plants. Except for mountaintops and true deserts, it is hard to imagine a system less conducive to wildlife, and yet wildlife abounds.

STONE HARBOR POINT

Seven Mile Beach is an excellent place to examine a barrier island habitat, particularly at Stone Harbor Point, on its southern end. Although a visit is worthwhile year round, certain times are better than others. This part of New Jersey is enormously busy during the summer season, especially on weekends when the population swells to about 75,000—from the quiet winter low of about 2,000. Hot weekends between Memorial Day and Labor Day are most crowded. When possible, avoid these times, and if you plan a summer visit, go during midweek. The very best times are from mid-September through Thanksgiving, and in April and May.

Seven Mile Beach also offers a good example of a barrier island modified by development, one that has been partially stabilized by man-made structures in an effort to protect homes and keep the beach where it is. A word about the formation and natural history of barrier islands will contribute to your understanding of their importance.

Barrier beaches in the mid-Atlantic region are geologically young, made up of sediments washed down from more elevated regions of the north and west. They are also relatively short-lived, because they are constantly exposed to the forces of the sea. Left to their own devices, barrier beaches appear to be eroding landward and southward until they join the mainland as the back bays fill in. Then the ocean will attack the "new" mainland and lay out new barrier beaches.

Seven Mile Beach is a thin band of unconsolidated sediments, mostly fine-grained quartz sand deposited by wave action. When it was first formed (3,000 to 5,000 years ago) this strip of island was located about 5 miles east of the mainland and separated from it by a broad featureless bay. While the newly formed barrier beach bore the brunt of the sea, the still water behind it began collecting sediments washed from the mainland and in through the inlets at either end. In time, these sediments filled in parts of the bay until vegetation could catch hold and grow. These plants, in turn, caught more sediments and contributed their own particulate matter. As you drive to Seven Mile Beach from the mainland, the old "bay" is now salt marsh, interlaced by tidal cuts. These cuts are still silting in. If left undredged, they would finally close entirely and the barrier island would be connected to the mainland, a process that would take many hundreds of years.

Barrier islands are subject to the forces of tides, currents, waves, winds, and rain, all at work to move the island. In southern New Jersey, the net movement of water along the beach is from north to south. (This is called littoral drift or longshore current and is the result of a complicated set of forces and configurations: the Gulf Stream, prevailing winds, flow of Hudson and Delaware River water, and the shoreline's orientation.) The effect of this north-to-south longshore current is that a typical grain of sand at Avalon (at the northern end of Seven Mile Beach) will move south in a series of loops—up the beach on a wave, back down in the backwash, and then up again. Each trip moves the grain a bit toward Stone Harbor at the island's southern end. There it may drift into the inlet, sometimes into the bay, and sometimes into the ocean at the inlet entrance. Other grains of sand are picked up by waves and deposited offshore. Still others are blown offshore or back across the island and into the bay, or washed across the island during severe storms. The net result is that Seven Mile Beach loses much of its existing sand while gaining little from elsewhere. In a typical year as much as 100,000 cubic yards of sand might be expected to move along the beach to Hereford Inlet at the southern tip of this barrier island.

Left to itself, Seven Mile Beach would move south and slightly west (due in part to a rise in sea level)—about an inch every 10 years. To protect homes on the island, an effort has been made to stabilize the beach with rock. One result is that the beaches of Seven Mile Beach are narrowing and must be replenished with new sand mined from an outside source. Another is the shape of the island, blunt at the north end, where the heavy seas hit, and tapered at the southern end, where newly arriving sand tails off.

Stone Harbor Point is deeply set back or indented from the rest of the island because it is starved for sand by the pile of rocks jutting into the water just to its north. This is a good place to see the dramatic movement of barrier islands and to look at a cross section of beach habitat. There is a large parking lot at the south end of Stone Harbor at 123rd Street on the oceanfront. From this lot, Stone Harbor Point stretches about a mile southwest. About five blocks to the south a wooden bulkhead extends out to sea, ending at a large stone jetty. Beyond this is Stone Harbor Point. It is evident right away that the beach south of the jetty is heavily eroded. This is because it is in the "shadow" or downstream of the jetty, which robs the rest of the Point of sand.

Stone jetties themselves create microhabitats worth mentioning. Barnacles can settle and grow on rocks close to the

SAND MOVEMENT OR LITTORAL DRIFT ALONG SHORELINE

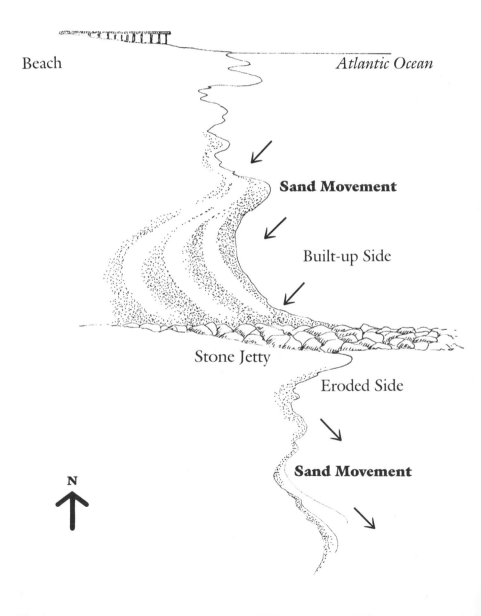

Beach

Atlantic Ocean

Sand Movement

Built-up Side

Sand Movement

Stone Jetty

Eroded Side

Sand Movement

N

water, and near the waterline there are sometimes thick sets of small Blue Mussels. Currents scour little potholes near the jetty's tip, a good place to look for juvenile fish. And on the jetties themselves, shorebirds, usually Ruddy Turnstones in the fall, will be seen picking up food. In midwinter, these jetties are good places to scan with field glasses for Purple Sandpipers.

The northern side of this jetty also serves as a gathering place for small baitfish, especially during fall migrations. I have seen considerable predatory activity around this jetty: bigger gamefish, Bluefish and Weakfish (Sea Trout), feeding on bait while gulls hover overhead to pick up the pieces.

The shore south of the jetty attracts shorebirds during the spring and (especially) fall migrations, particularly when the tide is low. Most common are Sanderlings, Dunlin, as well as Semipalmated Sandpipers, often in flocks of several hundred. They will be mixed with Ring-billed, Herring, and Great Black-backed Gulls, plus hordes of Laughing Gulls. Least (Little) and Common Terns dive for fish near the beach; in the fall these are joined by Royal (and occasionally Caspian) Terns.

In the summer, Least and Common Terns, Piping Plovers, and Black Skimmers use the Point for nesting, one of the few remaining suitable spots in New Jersey. The two tern species have specific nesting needs: open or lightly vegetated flat sand,

Least Tern

above high tide but not in or near dunes. They usually stake out their nesting colonies in May and have completed the rearing duties by mid-August. The nests (just depressions in the sand), the eggs, and the chicks are well camouflaged and easy to trample, so you should stay clear of the nesting sites when they are occupied. The terns will let you know when you are intruding by screaming at, diving toward, and defecating on you. Usually, the nesting sites, which can change each year, are toward the tip of the Point. The best course is simply to avoid the area during nesting.

Black Skimmers often nest later than terns and higher up the beach. Again, they should be left alone. Piping Plover nests are few and scattered. In all cases, stay clear and walk with care.

The high tide line is a good place to browse for driftwood, seaweed, shells, and such. Among the common finds: "mermaids' purses," which are like thick, black plastic envelopes, one by two inches, with stringy black spines at each corner (these are egg cases from fish called skates, shark-like creatures with "wings"); necklaces of yellow disks the size of thick quarters strung together (these are egg cases of whelks, the shells you put to your ear to listen for ocean sounds); jellyfish, especially the ones that look like bottoms of old-fashioned, round milk bottles; and the shells of crabs, scallops, clams, and mussels.

The wet sand area between high and low tide is home for beach or sand fleas—amphipods—little shrimplike creatures that often jump against your legs as you walk. You can also shake them out of wet seaweed. At and in the surf line there may be Mole Crabs, which look like one-inch pinkish-brown piglets without feet. They scurry or swim in with the waves and then rush back as the water recedes.

On summer and fall evenings, Ghost Crabs leave their burrows above the high tide line and move toward the water to forage. Their burrows are holes with mounds of sand nearby; usually you can detect their footprints leaving the burrow. At night try picking them up in the beam of a good flashlight; their ability to move and change directions quickly will impress you.

Above the high tide line is dry softer sand with little apparent life. There is some life in and below the surface sand grains,

Stone Harbor
Point
Nature Walk

STONE HARBOR
AND AVALON ↑

BEACH

2nd Ave. (Dune Dr.)

122nd St.

HOMES

123rd St.

PARKING
LOT

ROCK JETTY

Path

DUNES

WOODEN BULKHEAD

NUMMY ISLAND

SETBACK EROSION AREA

ROCK JETTY

SALT MARSH

DUNES

SANDBAR

(often exposed at low tide)

OVERWASH
AREAS

MARSHY
AREA

BAY

BEACH

ATLANTIC OCEAN

BEACH

GENERAL TERN,
SKIMMER,
SHOREBIRD
NESTING AREA

POINT   *Hereford
Inlet*

N

•••••• = **Walk Along Beach**

but much of it is microscopic and hard to classify. Farther up the beach toward the dunes you will see the first signs of vegetation, usually American Beach or Dune Grass, and sometimes Sea-rocket, Seaside Spurge, Dusty Miller, Beach Pea, Seaside Sandwort, and Russian Thistle. Most of these "pioneer" plants are perennial (Sea-rocket is an annual), and they usually populate the dry sand by shooting stems underground rather than by seeding. American Beach Grass is a good example, sending noded shoots out from the main plant. Some of the nodes develop lateral buds which pop up above the sand's surface to form blades, stems, and small flowers. You will sometimes see a series of plants every foot or so along the shoot for up to 20 feet. American Beach (Dune) Grass, by the way, is the grass whose blades describe circles in the dry sand on breezy days.

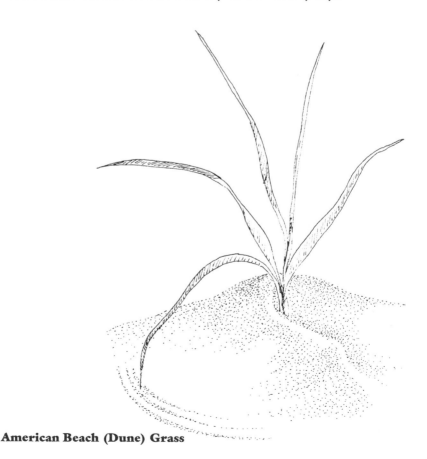

American Beach (Dune) Grass

American Beach Grass builds dunes by catching wind-blown sand, and the grass grows with the dune. It is not uncommon to find grass blades near the top, although the original root system lies some 5 to 25 feet below, where the dune started building. Snow fencing is sometimes placed on beaches to serve as artificial grass to trap sand. Snow fences work but, unlike beach grass, cannot grow with the dune. Grass, then, is the dune's better friend. The dunes, in turn, serve as the beach's reservoir of sand during storms. On your visits, keep out of dunes, so they and their nurturing grasses can grow undisturbed.

Seaside Goldenrod and Monarch Butterflies

Beach Pea and Dusty Miller also inhabit this flat sand area. Both have prostrate creeping stems, but they are right on the surface, with relatively shallow root systems. Beach Pea has a purple or violet flower and blooms throughout the summer; Dusty Miller, covered with small furry hairs to reflect the strong sun, has tiny yellow blooms from July into September.

Other beach plants adapt to the harsh dry heat by having waxy or leathery stems and leaves. Seaside Sandwort is a fleshy succulent that stores water in its thick leaves. Sea-rocket, an annual, seeds early and can produce a second generation before the summer is out. It has pale lavender flowers (July to September), and its seed pods are rocket-shaped.

Near the tops of the dunes you begin to find the more "permanent" plants, including Poison-ivy, Beach Plum, Northern Bayberry, Common and Stinking Groundsels, Winged Pigweed (Lamb's-quarters), Beach Pinweed, and wormwood. Mixed with them might be Dusty Miller, Beach Pea, Seaside Goldenrod, Poverty Grass, Beach (Wooly or False) Heather, and also spurges, whose stems turn a red-orange as fall approaches. All these plants thrive in this less-than-fertile landscape, a shore environment that combines extreme temperatures, lack of moisture, and lots of wind, sand, and salt. They thrive by reaching deep for water, storing water in their fleshy leaves, hugging the ground or clustering in the lee of a dune, and developing resistance to the scalding of salt spray. Moreover, the dry hot surface is misleading. Just inches below the hot summer sand the temperature drops, and moisture is available to plants that can send roots down. Yet their hardiness is also a limitation. If you transplant them to fertile, well-watered areas, they fare badly.

Other living things survive in the dunes. Be watchful for insects like Digger Wasps, Velvet Ants, Tiger Beetles, Beach Spiders, and grasshoppers. It is interesting that most species seen on beaches have closely related but different colored relatives living inland. In sandy habitats, the insects almost always come in shades of gray-brown. The best way to spot them is to find a comfortable spot and quietly wait; insects will not move a great deal in the heat of a summer day, but watch in low spots between dunes.

In the fall Monarch butterflies move through here on their journey to Mexico, where they winter. Monarchs head for goldenrod (I once saw a Praying Mantis camped on a stalk of goldenrod, eating a Monarch it had ambushed). The Monarch migration is a thing of beauty and wonder. The migrants you see will not return as far north the following spring, but their offspring will. Along with Monarchs are lesser numbers of Painted Ladies, Buckeyes, Red Admirals, and various species of sulphurs and swallowtails; you may also see dragonflies, some of which have flown across the New York Bight from Long Island.

At Stone Harbor Point the dunes are migrating landward, pushing across former wetland areas and toward the bay. In several locations one can see overwashes where high tides have punched through the dunes and washed a delta of sand westward. If the overwash reaches the bay it will pour into the water and form the basis for new salt marshes.

If you continue across the island, past the dunes and the overwashes, you will see the first wetland plants. The high shrub is Marsh-elder; it looks like Northern Bayberry with a toothed leaf. There are also rushes, the biggest of which is *Phragmites* or Common Reed Grass. Also known as Plume Grass, it can grow to more than 10 feet and has a full tassel in summer and fall. Sea-lavender blooms in fall, and the bunchy succulents Slender and Woody Glassworts, which grow in areas of high salt soil, turn a lovely red-orange in the fall.

At and near the wetland edge are three wetland grasses: Spike (Salt) Grass, Salt Hay or Saltmeadow Cordgrass, and Saltmarsh Cordgrass. The latter two are the most common. Salt Hay is about a foot high and blows over in swirling "cowlicks." It is cultivated for mulch on New Jersey's Delaware Bay side. Saltmarsh Cordgrass grows closer to the water, reaches a height of 3 to 6 feet, and is an important food and habitat for many fish and animals of the salt marsh.

Finally, the transect (or at least the dry transect) ends at the edge of the marsh. Here at the Point, the view to the west from the backside of the barrier island is across Great Channel to Nummy Island, a rectangular marshy island bisected by Ocean Drive. We'll talk about Nummy and other nearby islands later.

There are birds at Stone Harbor Point twelve months of the year. Some, such as the gulls, don't migrate. But most move south through the Point in late August through early November, and begin passing north again in March. The sea ducks, which have bobbed in the winter surf off Hereford Inlet—Common Goldeneye, Oldsquaw, Bufflehead, Greater Scaup, Horned Grebe, and Red-breasted Merganser—leave in March and April, about the same time the first northbound flights of shorebirds, raptors, and swallows begin to pass over. The warblers follow behind in early May. But in truth, fall is a better time to see migrations in southern New Jersey, and other areas concentrate birds even better than Stone Harbor Point. It is the summer population that makes the Point especially interesting.

The nesting of Least and Common Terns here is cause for celebration. In most years Black Skimmers nest here too, and usually a few pairs of Piping Plovers. Terns are superb flyers, quick and darting. They need to be, for they feed on quick darting prey, the small baitfish that swim in schools along the beach and in the back bays. These birds can hover over the water, spot a fish, and dive quickly into the water to grab their catch.

Piping Plovers have short, stubby bills adapted for feeding along the water and in wet sand. They are almost the exact color of dry sand and can be peeping near you and yet be almost impossible to see. One tip: their shadows on the beach are sometimes more visible than the birds themselves.

Black Skimmers are bigger than Common Terns and more colorful; they are black on top with long, thick red bills. Their lower mandible is longer than the upper and they feed by skimming along the water surface with the lower mandible cutting a shallow groove. When they strike their prey, the head jerks back, they snap up the meal and fly away. Because of this adaptation, they seldom feed in the surf, preferring the still waters of the back bays. Evening is the best time for seeing this activity.

These four species—the two terns, Black Skimmer, and Piping Plover—are threatened or endangered in New Jersey, and indeed much of the United States, primarily because broad undisturbed beaches where they nest are in such short supply. They begin choosing nesting territories in May, hatch eggs in June and July, and feed the young through the rest of the summer. If the first nesting is disturbed (by tides, people, or animals), they can try a second time, and Black Skimmers can nest late in summer. For these reasons nesting areas between the dunes and the high tide line at the south end of the Point should be avoided, especially mid-May through early August. The best way to "visit" them is from afar with spotting scopes or field glasses, with the sun at your back.

Red-winged Blackbirds nest in the shrubs and tall grasses behind the dunes, and sometimes a few Gray Catbirds and Common Yellowthroats too. On the marsh side look for Marsh (Long-billed Marsh) Wrens, Clapper Rails, and American Black Ducks. American Kestrels (Sparrow Hawks) and Northern Harriers (Marsh Hawks) hover or swoop to hunt through the winter season. Wading birds will feed on the marsh side during the warmer months. The beach is dominated by gulls, including Herring, Great Black-backed, and Ring-billed. These are joined by huge numbers of Laughing Gulls which nest in profusion on some of the islands in the bay and fly over to the beach to roost and feed.

A handful of landbirds spend winter on the beaches and in the dunes. Most numerous are Yellow-rumped (Myrtle) Warblers, in dull winter garb. More striking are Snow Buntings, usually in groups of a dozen or more, often with Horned Larks among them, as well as Eastern Meadowlarks and Song Sparrows.

In the fall, the migration south is impressive: overhead fly Snow Geese and Canada Geese, Double-crested Cormorants, Brant, and Tree Swallows (huge swarms line the telephone wires to the north and sometimes settle down on the edge of the dunes after wild flights through nearby bayberry groves). Offshore and low on the horizon will be strings of all three species of scoters (black sea ducks) and scattered Common and Red-throated Loons in their winter plumage. At night, overhead, listen for the sounds of warblers and shorebirds, and all day long behold great sprinklings of shorebirds on the beaches and bay mudflats, feeding, running, and leapfrogging south. It is possible to see almost every North American shorebird here in a season.

One shorebird, the American Oystercatcher, deserves special mention, for this uncommon, large, and showy shorebird can often be seen at Stone Harbor Point, perhaps on a sandbar here or inside Hereford Inlet. With its black and white body and heavy bright red bill, it tends to be off by itself, apart from the smaller, more common shorebirds, as if establishing itself as the guardian of the outer beach. It is a splendid bird to see.

Raptors accompany this flood of moveable lunch. Buteos are usually farther inland, but falcons, harriers, and accipiters often hug the shoreline. We see only a few at a time here, but as they move down the peninsula they eventually rendezvous at Cape May Point. More about this later.

Fish also migrate in the fall. Schools of White and Striped Mullet come out of the inlets with each tide, and especially on rough days pour south along the beach, usually right in the breaker zone. You will see beach seiners and cast netters catching mullet for bait along Stone Harbor beaches from late summer on. Mullet (and the Atlantic Menhaden, which are farther offshore) attract Weakfish, Striped Bass, and Bluefish, all of which can drive a school of the smaller fish into the surf as they feed in a frenzy of swirling water, leaping fish, and darting terns and gulls.

Mammals, reptiles, and amphibians are not well represented at Stone Harbor Point. Common species can be named in a breath—Eastern Cottontail (Rabbit), several species of mice, Norway Rat, a misplaced Raccoon or two, Eastern Box Turtle, Northern Diamondback Terrapin (the estuarine turtle), and a Fowler's Toad here and there. Because of the dense human population and the use of pesticides (in a vain attempt to control mosquitos and Greenhead Flies), plus destruction of habitat, these species fight a last stand at Stone Harbor Point. In my youth, Eastern Hognose Snakes were common; I haven't seen one for years.

The Point demonstrates the way the entire coast of New Jersey used to look, minus a few species and minus the large dunes that should be here, if they hadn't been destroyed to make way for a few more houses. There are several other areas near the

Point worth a visit; these too represent ecosystems largely lost:

Big Sand Dunes: Drive north paralleling the ocean from Stone Harbor Point. Follow the directions in "The Salt-Water Marsh." From 57th Street to 45th Street in Avalon, there is a stretch of high, handsome dunes. You can park along the shoulder of the road and walk one of three paths that take you through the dunes to the beach. Here is a much more impressive array of dune vegetation—small trees and shrubs, husky Poison-ivy, Northern Bayberry, and Virginia Creeper, all providing enough cover for songbirds to feed and even nest (Gray Catbird, for one). Closer to the beach are good stands of Seaside Goldenrod and lots of healthy Dune Grass. The dunes here have been stabilized, fertilized, and protected, so the plants are profuse. Their leaves are beginning to accumulate and produce traces of fertile soil. In the past, all of this beach was heavily duned, high and broad, full of mice, rabbits, toads, and snakes.

Salt Marsh: The four miles of salt marsh between Stone Harbor and the mainland can be scanned from the roads coming onto the barrier island from the Garden State Parkway. Herons and egrets dot the marsh during feeding hours all summer long. Northern Harriers haunt the marshes, and Ospreys nest on cedar trees and platforms, especially in Avalon on Cedar Island, west of the waterway and usually visible from the dock at the west end of 8th Street.

Stone Harbor Bird Sanctuary: This refuge for roosting herons and egrets is located on the Ocean Highway at 114th Street. It is at its very best in the late afternoon, when hundreds of waders, including Snowy Egrets, Great (Common) Egrets, Glossy Ibis, Great Blue and Little Blue Herons, and Tricolored (Louisiana) Herons come to roost from their day's fishing in the marshes, dropping from the sky to the overburdened trees of the sanctuary. (The trees here are Black Cherry, Red Cedar [Eastern], and American Holly, all of which thrived when Seven Mile Beach was pristine.) As these herons arrive, others depart; Black-crowned Night-Herons, for instance, leave the sanctuary to take over the feeding habitat during dark hours. It's a treat for the eye and ear, one of the few places where people can see quantities of wading birds without disturbing them. The rookery is occupied from late April until early October.

Ring Island: Just west of Nummy Island, this island hosts the largest collection of nesting Laughing Gulls in New Jersey. You can view it by going south on Ocean Drive from Stone Harbor toward Wildwood. A high bridge crosses Great Channel; park off the road on the shoulder at the foot of the bridge. Ring Island lies to the northwest. In June and July it is a cloud of birds, and if the wind is blowing your way, a blare of noise carries as some 40,000 pairs of gulls cater to the care and feeding of 80,000 youngsters.

Wetlands Institute: Located on the causeway that connects Stone Harbor to the mainland, this refuge is the subject of another chapter in this book.

Cape May Point: A trip to South Jersey, including Stone Harbor Point, should be accompanied by a visit to Cape May Point, especially in September and October. This is the best time to see concentrations of migrating raptors which have moved down the coast until "trapped" as land runs out. Many raptors dislike crossing water, and faced with the flight across Delaware Bay, hesitate, sit down, feed, or head back up the bay looking for more land. Any of these choices makes the birds available for longer observation.

The very best time to visit Cape May Point is on a fall weekday during or directly after a strong west or northwest wind. Start at Cape May Point State Park. Spend a few minutes on the Cape May Bird Observatory platform to find out what's flying; then strike out on your own to avoid the crowd and see the birds. Several good nature trails fan out from the park, and a helpful map is available at the information center.

Once again, if you want to see a barrier island in action (instead of people), go off-season and off-hours.

Directions to Stone Harbor, New Jersey (Wetlands Institute and Stone Harbor Point)

From the City Line Avenue entrance onto the Schuylkill Expressway (I-76 East) travel 10.4 miles following the signs for New Jersey to the toll booth at the Walt Whitman Bridge. After paying the toll (75 cents in 1985), cross the bridge and follow the signs for the North-South Freeway and Atlantic City. Drive 4.4 miles from the toll booth to Route 42 South. Drive 7.8 miles along Route 42 South and bear left on the Atlantic City Expressway. Travel 26.4 miles on the expressway to the Great Egg Harbor toll booth ($1.00 in 1985). From here travel another 9.9 miles along the expressway to the Garden State Parkway South (Exit 7 South for Ocean City and Cape May). Bear right on the Garden State Parkway South and drive 27.1 miles to the Stone Harbor Exit (Exit 10B). Along the way you will pass two toll booths each requiring 25 cents in 1985. At the light for the Stone Harbor Exit turn left on Stone Harbor Boulevard (Route 29) and drive 2.8 miles east to the Wetlands Institute on your right. The parking lot, museum, observation tower, and start of the nature trail welcome you almost immediately. A one-way trip from Philadelphia takes approximately one hour and forty-five minutes.

To reach Stone Harbor Point, the southern mile of the barrier island of Seven Mile Beach, leave the Wetlands Institute parking lot and turn right on Stone Harbor Boulevard (Route 29). Drive 0.7 miles east, crossing the bridge over the Intracoastal Waterway, to the first light in the town of Stone Harbor. Here make a right on Ocean Drive (3rd Avenue) and drive 1 mile to the parking lot of the Stone Harbor Bird Sanctuary (on your left) at 114th Street. The Sanctuary stretches from 111th to 117th Street and is between 2nd and 3rd Avenues.

After stopping at this famous heronry, turn left (south) on Ocean Drive (3rd Avenue) and at the first left 0.2 miles further turn on 117th Street (here one can also continue along Ocean

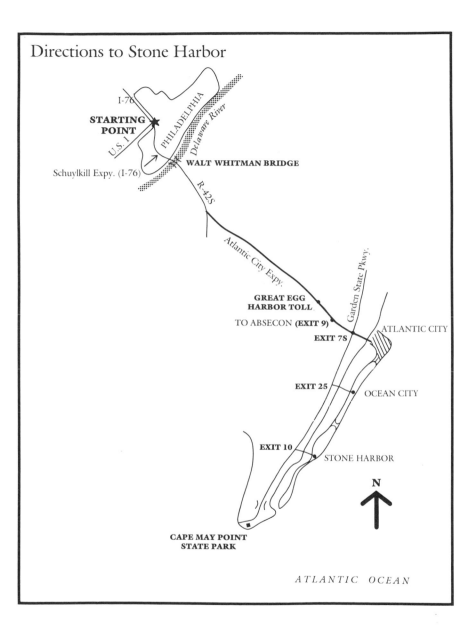

Directions to Stone Harbor

I-76

STARTING POINT

U.S. 1

PHILADELPHIA

Delaware River

Schuylkill Expy. (I-76)

WALT WHITMAN BRIDGE

R-42S

Atlantic City Expy.

Garden State Pkwy.

GREAT EGG HARBOR TOLL

TO ABSECON **(EXIT 9)**

EXIT 7S

ATLANTIC CITY

EXIT 25

OCEAN CITY

EXIT 10

STONE HARBOR

N

CAPE MAY POINT STATE PARK

ATLANTIC OCEAN

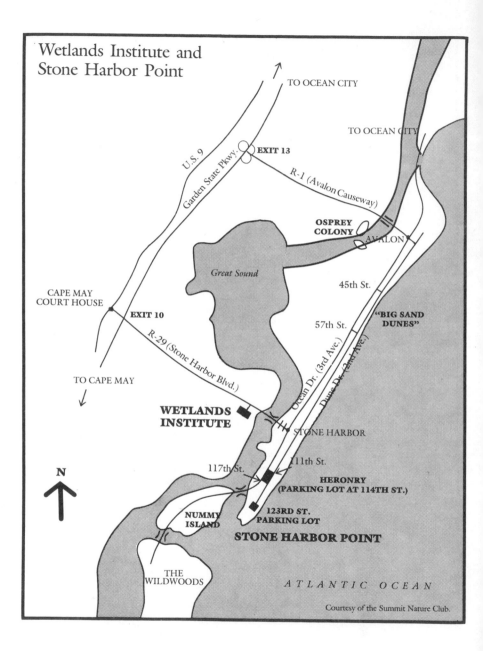

Wetlands Institute and Stone Harbor Point

TO OCEAN CITY

TO OCEAN CITY

U.S. 9

Garden State Pkwy.

EXIT 13

R-1 (Avalon Causeway)

OSPREY COLONY

AVALON

Great Sound

45th St.

CAPE MAY COURT HOUSE

EXIT 10

"BIG SAND DUNES"

57th St.

R-29 (Stone Harbor Blvd.)

Ocean Dr. (3rd Ave.)

Dune Dr. (2nd Ave.)

TO CAPE MAY

WETLANDS INSTITUTE

STONE HARBOR

N

117th St.

111th St.

HERONRY (PARKING LOT AT 114TH ST.)

NUMMY ISLAND

123RD ST. PARKING LOT

STONE HARBOR POINT

THE WILDWOODS

ATLANTIC OCEAN

Courtesy of the Summit Nature Club.

Drive for another 0.5 miles to the bridge for Nummy Island and its vast salt marshes). Drive 0.1 miles on 117th Street to the stop sign and make a right on 2nd Avenue. Travel south 0.3 miles along 2nd Avenue to the large parking lot at 123rd Street on the oceanfront. South of here is Stone Harbor Point and the beginning of the nature walk (about a ten-minute drive from the Wetlands Institute).

To reach the "Big Sand Dunes" in Avalon return to the Stone Harbor Bird Sanctuary. From here backtrack north on Ocean Drive (3rd Avenue) for 1 mile to Stone Harbor Boulevard. Continue north on Ocean Drive past this intersection and drive 2.0 miles to 57th Street in Avalon. Turn right on 57th Street, drive 0.1 miles and at the stop sign turn left on 2nd Avenue (Dune Drive). The dunes are on the right stretching from 57th to 45th Street in Avalon (about 0.7 miles). From 45th Street continue 0.8 miles north on 2nd Avenue to the second light in town. Turn left here and drive 3.3 miles west on the Avalon Causeway. Cross over the Intracoastal Waterway to the entrance for the Garden State Parkway North and Philadelphia.

Barrier Beaches and Islands of the Delaware Valley Region

Below is a listing of some barrier beaches and islands in the Delaware Valley area similar to Stone Harbor Point.

NEW JERSEY

Except for Island Beach State Park, most of the following areas possess only some features of a typical barrier beach; few, for example, have appreciable sand dunes. From north to south, here are some suggestions:

Shark River Inlet, Monmouth County, between Avon and Belmar, New Jersey, off Route 35. The inlet itself has narrow but interesting beaches; inland, near the railroad tracks and the Belmar Basin are some good bays for gulls and wintering waterfowl, including the Barrow's Goldeneye (for the past decade). Like all Jersey shore towns, it is hectic during the summer months.

Manasquan Inlet, Ocean County, between Manasquan and Pt. Pleasant Beach, New Jersey, off Routes 34 and 35. The rock jetties here collect invertebrates and the mudflats behind are habitat for shorebirds and waterfowl in season.

Island Beach State Park, Ocean County, near the towns of Toms River and Seaside Heights, New Jersey, off Route 37 (occupies southern 10 miles of Island Beach). There is a fee, usually $4 per car in the summer season, $1 per car other times. Very crowded on summer weekends. Nature trails, wide open beaches, superb dunes, and good birding. Nature center. Phone: (201) 793-0506.

Holgate Division of the Edwin B. Forsythe National Wildlife Refuge, Ocean County, near the towns of Beach Haven and Manahawkin, New Jersey, off Route 72 (southern tip of Long Beach Island). Proceed south as far as you can drive along Bay Avenue on Long Beach Island, then start walking. It's about a mile to the tip of this barrier island. Good tidal flats for birds, some nice pools for fish sampling. Good for wintering waterfowl. Phone: (609) 652-1665.

North Brigantine Natural Area, Atlantic County, near Atlantic City and the town of Brigantine, New Jersey, off Route 87 (on Brigantine Island). From Atlantic City follow the signs to Harrah's Casino and drive over the bridge and into the town of Brigantine, heading north on Route 87 as far as you can go. From the north end of town it is a nice 2-mile walk to the inlet. Wild beach, nice dunes, good birding. Phone (c/o Wharton State Forest): (609) 561-0024. A small sample of barrier beach with a large stone jetty still exists on the extreme southern tip of Brigantine Island, but has been decimated by summer housing construction.

Corson's Inlet State Park, Cape May County, between Ocean City and Strathmere, New Jersey, off Ocean Drive. This is a wild, unstabilized inlet with constant shifting sands and to date without major human interventions such as jetties, seawalls, or groins. On the Ocean City side of the inlet is a classic barrier beach (formerly called Ocean Crest State Park), while on the Strathmere side are extensive sand flats (Whale Beach). Phone (c/o Belleplain State Forest): (609) 861-2404.

Cape May Point, Cape May County, New Jersey, including Cape May Point State Park and Higbee Beach Wildlife Management Area. See Fresh-Water Marshes listing and the section in this present chapter.

DELAWARE

For a state with a short ocean coastline, Delaware has two good barrier beach areas. Both are off Route 1 (14), approximately an hour-and-a-half drive south of Wilmington, and also easily accessible from the Delaware side of the Cape May–Lewes Ferry.

Cape Henlopen State Park, Sussex County, near Lewes, Delaware, off Route 1 (14) and U.S. 9. Good off-season spot for long hikes; sand flats, tidal pools, dune vegetation, and good birding. Home of the "walking dunes," which move several feet southward every year, and also home of one of the highest sand dunes (the "Great Dune") along the Atlantic seaboard. Entrance fee. Nature center. Phone: (302) 645-8983.

Indian River Inlet, Delaware Seashore State Park, Sussex County, between Rehoboth Beach and Bethany Beach, Delaware, off Route 1 (14) about 8 miles south of Cape Henlopen State Park. Best approach is from the south side of the inlet. Waterfowl in the back bay, inlet jetties with rocky habitat, plus extensive beaches along the ocean. Visitor center.

Mermaid's Purse

Suggested Readings on Barrier Beaches and Islands

Many of the following books will contain pertinent sections on both the salt-water marsh and the ocean as they border the barrier beach and island on either side.

Amos, William H. *The Life of the Seashore*. New York: Our Living World of Nature Series, McGraw-Hill, 1966.

Arnold, Augusta Foote. *The Sea-Beach at Ebb-Tide*. 1940. Reprint. New York: Dover Publications, 1968.

Bascom, Willard. *Waves and Beaches: The Dynamics of the Ocean Surface*. Garden City, N.Y.: Doubleday, Anchor Press, 1964.

Bennett, D. W. *New Jersey Coastwalks*. Highlands, N.J.: American Littoral Society, 1981.

Berrill, Norman J. *The Living Tide*. New York: Dodd, Mead, 1951.

_____ and Jacquelyn Berrill. *1001 Questions Answered About the Seashore*. New York: Dover Publications, 1976.

Burton, Robert. *The Seashore and Its Wildlife*. New York: G. P. Putnam & Sons, 1977.

Carson, Rachel. *The Edge of the Sea*. Boston: Houghton Mifflin, 1955.

Crowder, William. *Seashore Life Between the Tides*. New York: Dover Publications, 1975.

Eltringham, S. K. *Life in Mud and Sand*. New York: Crane, Russak, 1971.

Fox, William T. *At the Sea's Edge*. Englewood Cliffs, N.J.: Prentice-Hall, 1983.

Galli, Joan, and Joseph L. Lomax. "Higbee Beach—Pond Creek Meadow, A Very Special Place." *New Jersey Outdoors* 4 (1977): 6–7, 30–31.

Gosner, Kenneth. *Field Guide to the Atlantic Seashore*. Boston, Mass.: Houghton Mifflin, 1978.

Kaufman, W., and Orrin Pilkey. *The Beaches Are Moving*. Durham, N.C.: Duke University Press, 1983.

Kopper, Philip. *The Wild Edge*. New York: Times Books, 1979.

Leatherman, Stephen P. *Barrier Island Handbook*. Washington, D.C.: National Park Service, 1979.

Lomax, Joseph, Anne Galli, and Joan Galli. *The Wildlife of Cape May County, New Jersey*. Pomona, N.J.: Center for Environmental Research, Stockton State College, 1980.

MacGinitie, George E., and Nettie MacGinitie. *Natural History of Marine Animals*. 2nd ed. New York: McGraw-Hill, 1968.

Martin, E. William. "An Unspoiled Bit of Atlantic Coast." *Natural History*, August 1960. (Reprint available from New Jersey State Museum, Bulletin no. 11, February 1970.)

Miner, Roy Waldo. *Field Book of Seashore Life*. New York: G. P. Putnam & Sons, 1950.

Moore, Hilary B. *Marine Ecology*. New York: John Wiley & Sons, 1958.

Nordstrom, Carl. *Living with the New Jersey Shore*. Durham, N.C.: Duke University Press. In press.

Petry, Loren, and Marcia Norman. *A Beachcomber's Botany*. Chatham, Mass.: Chatham Conservation Foundation, 1968.

Reiger, George. *Wanderer on My Native Shore*. New York: Simon and Schuster, 1983.

Ricciuti, Edward R. *The Beachwalker's Guide*. Garden City, N.Y.: Doubleday, 1982.

Rudloe, J. *The Erotic Ocean: Handbook for Beachcombers*. New York: Harcourt Brace Jovanovich, 1971.

Shannon, Howard J. *The Book of the Seashore*. Garden City, N.Y.: Doubleday, Doran, 1935.

Silverberg, R. *The World Within the Tide-pool*. New York: Weybright and Talley, 1972.

Southward, A. J. *Life on the Seashore*. Cambridge, Mass.: Harvard University Press, 1976.

the Atlantic Ocean

ALAN BRADY

It's **eight o'clock** at night and the boat *Miss Barnegat Light* lies at her berth. She awaits the arrival of some eighty birders who intend to take her approximately 100 miles off the coast of New Jersey in search of seabirds and other marine life. People begin to straggle aboard, staking out their sleeping spots. Some will stay in the spacious cabin-lounge, but if the weather appears favorable, many will roll out their pads and sleeping bags on the upper deck. Although it's the end of May, the temperatures in the North Atlantic can be quite cool, making the open deck a cold place to sleep. There is much "bird talk" as people move off in small groups to discuss the possibilities for the next day. Field guides lie open to the seabird sections and identification points are studied. There is also the weather forecast to consider, and the departure time; some people wonder whether two 50-pound cakes of frozen fish chum will be sufficient to attract birds throughout the journey.

The engines, which have been humming all along, are revved up at last, signalling the captain's arrival on board. The usual one or two late arrivals hurry aboard. Many birders have come a long way, and if they cut their time too close, or develop car trouble, they will miss the whole trip. The boat finally leaves the dock and we're off to what we hope will be another successful pelagic expedition.

HUDSON CANYON

The trip out of Barnegat Light, New Jersey, is now regularly scheduled for birders and whale watchers off the coast of New Jersey. It is jointly sponsored by the Delaware Valley Ornithological Club located in Philadelphia and the Urner Club of northern New Jersey, but is open to any interested persons who wish to embark. The trip was spawned in 1975, one year after the boat *Miss Barnegat Light* made her arrival in New Jersey. The boat itself is unusually well-suited for observation. It is a catamaran, about 100 feet long, with twin diesel engines. The decks are broad, and because of the two hulls she's incredibly stable, especially when the engines are shut down. This stability can be a tremendous aid when trying to pick up minute field marks on a fast-moving bird.

Prior to 1975 some early adventurers had been to Hudson Canyon on commercial fishing boats and discovered the richness of sea life there. At that time the major purpose of the boats was catching Tilefish—delectable but difficult to catch because they live at great depths. The fuel costs for so distant a trip, however, plus the fact that Tilefish have apparently decreased in both size and numbers since those days have limited the Hudson Canyon trips to chartered boats. The cost is prohibitive for a small group of birders and whale watchers, while the boats available for shorter ocean trips are too small for this distance.

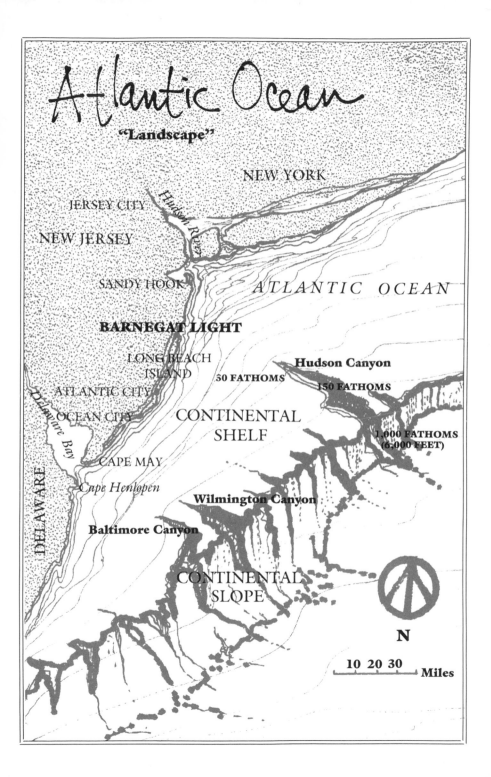

Our first offshore sea trips were on a variety of boats embarking from Atlantic City, Absecon, Brigantine, Cape May, and Beach Haven, New Jersey. We went from 10 to 25 miles offshore and occasionally had some excellent sightings. More often, however, we were limited to one or two Wilson's Storm-Petrels. Some trips actually reported no truly oceanic species at all, an indication that the birds were farther out. Gradually we discovered that there is a minor area for pelagic species probably 5 to 20 miles from shore, followed by a large stretch of ocean almost devoid of life until the 60-mile mark. From there the sea life becomes more abundant. When the depth increases suddenly, as it does over the Hudson Canyon 85 miles from shore, the aquatic life can be spectacular.

WILSON'S STORM-PETREL FEEDING BEHAVIOR

The Hudson Canyon is the extension of what used to be the Hudson River. During the Ice Age, the continental shelf, now under water, was the shoreline of North America. The river made a steep sudden cut as it flowed to the continental shelf, dropping the ocean floor there from 150 fathoms to over 500 fathoms. As the glaciers melted and ran off into the ocean, the water rose and the shoreline receded. Well-preserved Mastodon bones and other land fossils are occasionally dredged up by boats dragging for scallops along the ocean floor of the continental shelf, indicating that it was once part of the North American land mass. Now the underwater canyon produces an upwelling effect in the ocean, bringing nutrients to the surface that attract birds, fish, and mammals seldom seen elsewhere.

The first birds likely to be sighted, even before the sun is up, are Wilson's Storm-Petrels, fluttering over the surface like large black butterflies. It's exciting to find the first ones, but as visibility increases and these petrels (usually) become abundant,

one realizes that they are one of the commonest birds of the world. To a person on his first trip, the abundance of some pelagic species can be staggering. Estimates on different trips have run from five thousand to as high as seventy-five thousand Wilson's Storm-Petrels sighted. They are attracted to fish oil-chum slicks where in good light you can occasionally see the yellow webbing between their toes—a special observational challenge for the pelagic birder. These little birds hover over the water and dangle their feet, stirring the surface in search of food. They appear to be walking on water; hence the name "Petrel" for St. Peter who, it is told, walked on water.

Northern Fulmars, seldom seen close to shore, usually feed actively at dawn. They are the sturdiest of flyers and become more active as the ocean becomes rougher. With a few flaps and a stiff glide they are masters of the worst weather, only alighting to surface-feed on some scraps from the boat. Their habit of sweeping high above the waves before gliding down over the surface makes them visible at a great distance. Since Northern Fulmars nest in the Northern Hemisphere, they are seen in decreasing numbers by the end of May, as most of the birds are already on their breeding grounds. Most of the other large oceanic species sighted are South Atlantic nesters who "winter" in the North Atlantic.

Greater Shearwaters, probably the commonest shearwater off our coast, have been recorded in large numbers—as many as 10,000—during their migration period in late May. Later in the summer, they will have traveled farther north. Sometimes they are so plentiful and hungry that they dive after baited hooks; fishing boats have been known to leave an area when many are around. They have a striking black and white pattern and sail with ease close to the ocean's surface. On occasion, while banking, a wing tip will slice the water's surface leaving a trailing "V" pattern, a characteristic that has given them the name "shearwater."

An associate of the Greater Shearwater is the Sooty Shearwater, a bird of similar size, habits, and flight. Often seen near shore in smaller numbers, they become more common farther out at sea. They appear more buoyant in flight than the Greaters and often swing high in the air as they propel themselves

Greater Shearwater

effortlessly over the ocean. Their silvery underwing, which contrasts with their dark body and upper wing, identifies them at a great distance.

Cory's Shearwaters, which prefer warmer water than most other birds, arrive in small numbers and become more abundant later in summer. Their larger size, yellow bill, and languid flight distinguishes them from the other shearwaters.

Manx and Audubon's Shearwaters are similar in appearance, but fortunately for identification purposes are seldom seen in the same area at the same time. The Manx is a cold water bird, nesting in the North Atlantic, and seldom appears in our area in any numbers. One or two individuals on each trip is all we can expect. Audubon's reaches its northern limit off Cape May in the summer, when the water temperature is excessively high. Do not expect to see this bird unless the temperature of the water is over 75° F.

With luck we will see one of the great whales. An especially good area is about 15 or 20 miles from shore. While scanning the horizon we might sight a "blow," the exhaling of air and water from a whale as it surfaces. The commonest whale of these waters is the Finback (Fin), which is gray above and lighter below with a long slender body. They migrate northward off the New Jersey coast April through May. In recent years they have become more numerous, probably because they are protected by the International Whaling Commission. We still await a sighting of the only larger animal inhabiting our area, the Blue Whale, which was hunted in the Atlantic almost to extinction. It has been protected since 1967, perhaps not too late for a recovery.

Suddenly a skua dashes in from above, looks us over, and continues on its way. It's seldom that we have more than a brief look at this powerful bird. The golden hackles and the paler underparts of the South Polar Skua separate this species from the Great Skua, a slightly larger bird. These two species, so similar in appearance, nest at opposite ends of the earth. The South Polar Skua's breeding ground lies in the Antarctic and the Great Skua's centers in Iceland. On only one occasion in early May were these two birds seen together from our boat. Each also nests at opposite times of the year, so while the most opportune time to see a South Polar Skua is from April through November, you will probably sight the Great Skua from December through early May.

A close relative of the skuas is the Pomarine Jaeger, another strong flyer usually found at great distances from shore, although occasionally seen along beaches. When commercial fishing boats were more plentiful in the canyon area, seventy-five to one hundred Pomarine Jaegers could be seen on one trip. They prey on gulls that follow the ships, forcing the slower gulls to disgorge the contents of their stomachs on the water's surface. On rare occasions, a splendid dark-phase jaeger will veer close to inspect us and we can observe its rich, dark brown plumage.

Meeting the Long-tailed Jaeger is an unforgettable experience. No other seabird is so beautifully graceful. These birds stand out in a crowd with their long thin wings, long streamer tails, and narrow shafts of white flashing in their primaries. They make other jaegers seem sluggish by comparison. They are the ultimate in aerodynamic form and their flight style matches their appearance.

The midsized Jaeger, the Parasitic, usually inhabits shallower waters closer to shore where there are plenty of terns to harass. In the fall, when many young jaegers migrate south, it takes much skill to separate the immature Pomarine from the Parasitic, since they have not yet developed the elongated tail feathers that readily separate the adults.

Two other birds that present a challenge are the sea-going Phalaropes, the Red-necked (Northern) and the Red. In the fall, when both are present, the Red shows a lighter back than the Red-necked. Spring plumage presents no problem, however. The Red is dark brick red underneath while the Red-necked is white. Our most amazing flight of Red Phalaropes occurred on a November trip when we estimated 10,000 scattered over a large area.

In the deep waters of Hudson Canyon we usually find Risso's (Grampus) Dolphin, a fifteen-foot-long gray mammal that travels in groups and is quickly identified by its long, curved dorsal fin. Their bodies are covered with scratches, the cause of which is not known. These large dolphins turn lighter with age and we frequently spot an all-white individual with the group. Pilot Whales with their jet black color and melon-shaped heads are sometimes present in the same area.

Most of our trips are planned for the warmer months, but winter trips are necessary to view some species. This is the time to find alcids off the coast, although a good captain and some extra fortitude are also necessary. Members of the alcid family are seabirds related to the now extinct Great Auk. Razorbills can be found from 5 to 20 miles off the beach, and a group of eighty Dovekies were discovered at the 20-mile marker out of Cape May in early December (1983) on a Cape May Bird Observatory trip. Dovekies are one of the most rarely seen of the alcids, coming close to shore only after storms. This discovery may stimulate an annual trip to see if they repeat their presence in future years. Atlantic (Common) Puffins, also a very rare sight, are only found at much greater distances from shore.

From early November through April the first birds to meet the boats are Black-legged Kittiwakes, which pick us up several miles out and follow in our wake all day long. As the boats near land they drop off and veer out to sea. Northern Gannets also follow alongside as the boats plough out, the striking black and white plumage of the adults a spectacular sight. The mixture of gannets and gulls on these winter trips can be exciting, for as the gannets dive into the water the assorted gulls hover about the boat in great numbers. Great Black-backed, Herring, and Ring-billed Gulls are most common, but this is the time and place to find Iceland and Glaucous as well as an occasional rarity such as a Thayer's, Sabine's, or Lesser Black-backed Gull. These are birds that ocean birders travel far and endure much to see, often for only a split-second, barely enough for a good identification. One must be well-briefed to know what to look for, because instant recognition of field characteristics is crucial for correct identification. For instance, if a Leach's Storm-Petrel appears with a Wilson's, its nighthawklike flight, forked tail, short legs, brownish appearance, and smaller, divided white rump patch all help to distinguish it from a Wilson's. There may only be one or two seconds to observe all this.

Although these trips have always been planned with oceanic birds in mind, the possibility of seeing mammals is ever present. Even the very rare Right Whale was once found as we were returning from Hudson Canyon. We spotted her at sunset close to our boat as she lay on the surface with her calf, her enormous head and distinctively marked flukes showing above the surface. In the seventeenth century Right Whales were prolific in this area, but the heavy hunting in Delaware Bay and adjacent areas almost eliminated them. Since their protection in 1937 a gradual increase has been noted, and we hope for

more sightings in the future. The Right Whale was given its
unfortunate name by whalers as it was the "right" whale to kill
because it remained afloat afterwards.

The famous Hump-backed Whale, widely distributed in
both Atlantic and Pacific Oceans, is surprisingly rare off the
coast of New Jersey. We have had only a few sightings, including one from shore at Cape May Point as the whale rounded
the Point from Delaware Bay and headed out to sea. It is probable that the main northern migration of Humpbacks takes
place beyond our limits since they are regularly seen near
Bermuda in April and May and then appear in New England
waters shortly after. The Humpback's centrally located dorsal
fin, long flippers, and distinctive habit of raising its great tail
flukes before sounding are its trademarks.

On several occasions a smaller whale has been seen leaping
clear out of the water. Once this action was repeated six or
seven times; the observers were being treated to a spectacular
view of a Minke Whale. These whales have been seen scattered
throughout the area as they follow the fishing and scallop
fleets. The smaller size and white underparts help distinguish
them from the Sei Whale, also found here in small numbers.
Sei Whales often associate with other larger whales, are dark
blue-black in color, and look much like a small version of the
Blue Whale. Fortunately, most whales give us a longer time to
identify them than do the seabirds.

If you have been to the shore in spring or summer you may
have seen Atlantic Bottle-nosed (Bottlenose) Dolphins playing
beyond the surf. These dolphins have followed the mackerel
northward in April, and many remain on their calving grounds
off New Jersey during the summer months. Schools of fifty to
one hundred dolphins follow the fish from the coastline to at
least 100 miles at sea. Encounters with other species of dolphins are rare. The Harbor Porpoise and Common and Striped
Dolphins have been seen on occasion and there are records of
stranded Spotted and Short-snouted Spinner Dolphins as well
as the Atlantic White-sided Dolphin.

Since the enforcing of the 200-mile restriction for foreign
fishing in 1977, we have not encountered any large fishing op-

Atlantic Bottle-nosed Dolphin

erations. Until that time foreign fishing fleets, complete with factory ships for processing the catch, roamed these waters and devastated the great schools of fish that had once been present. Now the fishing is steadily improving, with various kinds of codfish and whiting in the winter and a tremendous movement of mackerel in the spring. Bluefish arrive in numbers early in June and stay for the summer. Out on the brink of Hudson Canyon, sport fishermen troll for White and Blue Marlins and Common Swordfish, and lately sharks have been the target of some fishing boats. The largest common sharks out here are the Hammerhead and the Basking Shark, often ten feet in length. The Ocean Sunfish is a curiosity that lies on the surface with a protruding fin and appears to the uninitiated to be a giant shark.

We stop for sea turtles because we only see them rarely. Both the Atlantic Leatherback and the Atlantic Loggerhead might turn up, and on one occasion an Atlantic Hawksbill floated alongside the boat. Under heavy pressure from the tortoise-shell trade, the Atlantic Hawksbill has become quite rare even in the Caribbean where it nests. All these sea turtles nest much further south, but disperse over the ocean until they return again to their original nesting beaches.

An observer can venture into the North Atlantic a great many times and always find new life there. The enigma of the ocean will prove difficult to solve because observers on a single boat can only sample a tiny fraction of ocean life. One day the ocean will be alive with birds; the next day all life will have disappeared—apparently off to another feeding area. Yet there's always the chance of finding the rare species, often after storms blow them off course. Bridled and Sooty Terns are occasionally in our waters after late summer and fall storms. Arctic Terns cross our waters on their spring northern migration route across the Atlantic. Even the Yellow-nosed and Black-browed Albatrosses have been recorded off New Jersey shores. The possibility of sighting one lures many pelagic birders back to the sea. It seems that the more often one goes, the more fascinating the sea becomes. Certainly it has that effect on me. The ocean is truly the last remaining ornithological frontier and it is a challenge to be a part of it.

Persons interested in participating in one of these adventures, whether for simple enjoyment or for the study of bird and marine life (or both), should contact the Delaware Valley Ornithological Club at the Academy of Natural Sciences, 19th and the Parkway, Philadelphia, Pennsylvania 19103; call (215) 299-1181. Or contact the Urner Club, Newark Museum, Newark, New Jersey; call (201) 733-6600—or the Cape May Bird Observatory, Box 3, Cape May Point, New Jersey 08212; call (609) 884-2736. Occasional pelagic trips are sponsored by each organization. The Thursday issue of the *Philadelphia Daily News* will give fishing and boating advertisements and one can occasionally discover an advertised trip to Hudson Canyon or to an area far enough from shore for good pelagic birding. Birders are often permitted on the upper decks, away from the fishermen, and often charged less. Ask the captain.

**Atlantic
Leatherback Turtle**

Directions to Barnegat Light, Long Beach Island, New Jersey

To reach Barnegat Light Yacht Basin, Long Beach Island, New Jersey, from Philadelphia, proceed from the intersection of U.S. 1 (City Line Avenue) and the Schuylkill Expressway (I-76 East). Enter the Schuylkill Expressway and drive 0.7 miles along the ramp, then bear left on U.S. 1 North (Roosevelt Boulevard). Drive 7.2 miles to Robbins Avenue, following the signs for the Tacony-Palmyra Bridge. Make a right on

Directions to Long Beach Island

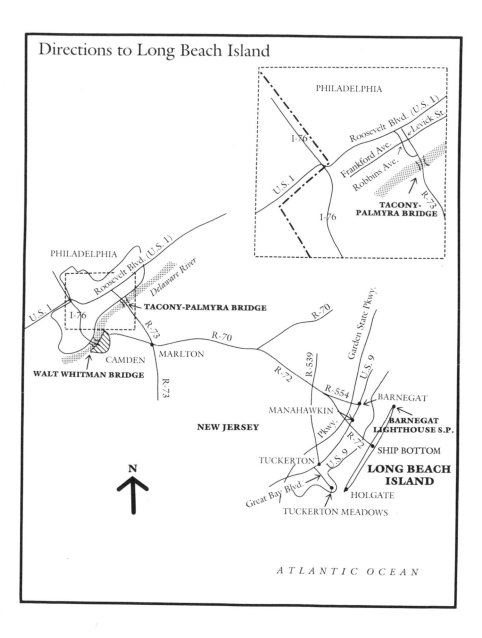

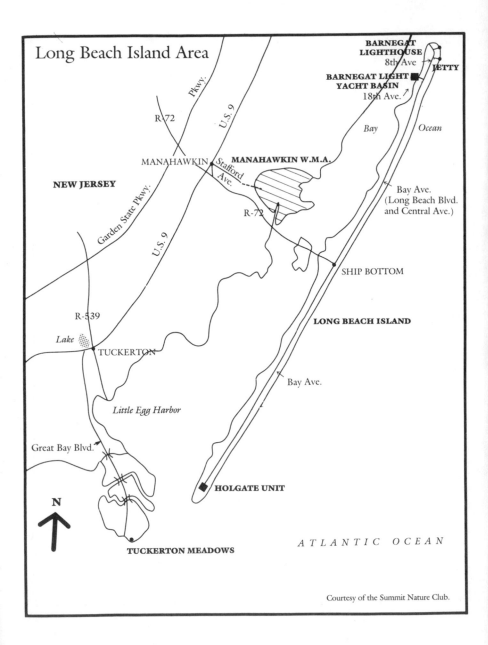

Long Beach Island Area

BARNEGAT
LIGHTHOUSE
8th Ave
JETTY

BARNEGAT LIGHT ■
YACHT BASIN
18th Ave.

Bay

Ocean

Pkwy.

R-72

U.S. 9

MANAHAWKIN **MANAHAWKIN W.M.A.**
Stafford
Ave.

NEW JERSEY

Bay Ave.
(Long Beach Blvd.
and Central Ave.)

R-72

Garden State Pkwy.

U.S. 9

SHIP BOTTOM

R-539

LONG BEACH ISLAND

Lake

TUCKERTON

Bay Ave.

Little Egg Harbor

Great Bay Blvd.

N

■ **HOLGATE UNIT**

A T L A N T I C   O C E A N

TUCKERTON MEADOWS

Courtesy of the Summit Nature Club.

Robbins Avenue (U.S. 13 North) and travel 1.6 miles; bear left for the bridge at the light. Cross the bridge and pay 25 cents (1985) toll. This is now Route 73 South. Drive 9.9 miles until reaching a circle. Go three-quarters of the way around the circle and follow the signs for Lakehurst and Route 70 East. Travel 17.8 miles on Route 70 East, passing two circles (at 5.5 and 10.2 miles) to a third circle, where you should follow the signs for Long Beach Island and Route 72 East (one-quarter of the way around the circle). (The entrance to Lebanon State Forest, an outstanding example of Pine Barrens habitat, is to the left 0.9 miles along Route 72 East.) Drive 26.1 miles to the bridge for Long Beach Island. Cross the bridge and travel another 2.4 miles to Long Beach Boulevard (Bay Avenue), which is located at the yield sign after two traffic lights in the town of Ship Bottom. Turn left on Long Beach Boulevard, following the signs for Surf City and Barnegat Lighthouse. Drive 7.7 miles, passing the towns of Harvey Cedars and Loveladies, to 18th Street in the town of Barnegat Light (Long Beach Boulevard turns into Central Avenue here). Turn left on 18th Street, drive 0.1 miles to the stop sign, then carefully cross Bay Avenue to the large parking lot at the Barnegat Light Yacht Basin, from which the pelagic boat trip departs.

The 8th Avenue jetty, famous for its wintering sea ducks, is 0.6 miles further along Long Beach Boulevard (Central Avenue) from 18th Street. Make a right on 8th Avenue and drive another 0.2 miles to the dunes. Walk twenty yards up through the dunes until you see the jetty a little to the right. You can reach the famous lighthouse by walking several hundred yards along the beach to the left. The lighthouse can also be reached by driving 0.4 miles further on Long Beach Boulevard past the intersection with 8th Avenue. Make a right at the stop sign, and the entrance to Barnegat Lighthouse State Park is 0.1 miles further. Park your car in the lot provided and walk forty yards to the bluff overlooking the bay and jetties. A one-way trip from Philadelphia to the Barnegat Light area takes approximately two hours.

An alternative way to reach Barnegat Light is to take the Vine Street Exit off I-76 East (Schuylkill Expressway) and cross the Ben Franklin Bridge (toll of 75 cents in 1985). Take

U.S. 30 East, and following the signs for Routes 70 and 38 East, pick up Route 70 East to Marlton, New Jersey, where it intersects with Route 73 South. Stay on Route 70 East and proceed as outlined before.

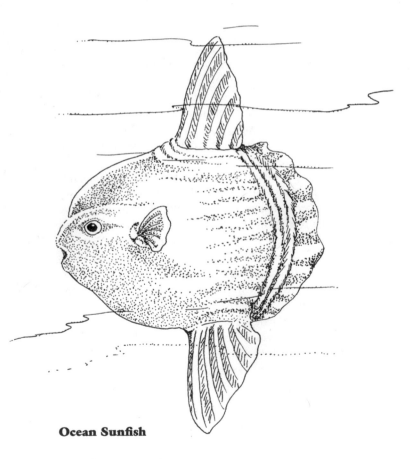

Ocean Sunfish

Suggested Readings on the Atlantic Ocean

The Wetlands Institute (see "The Salt-Water Marsh") has an excellent marine library where some of the following books may be studied. In this listing, field identification guides will be included for the specialized pelagic birds, fish, mammals, and other wildlife that sometimes receive cursory treatment in the standard field guides.

Babcock, Harold L. *Turtles of the Northeastern United States*. New York: Dover Publications, 1971.

Behrman, Daniel. *The New World of the Oceans: Men and Oceanography*. Boston: Little, Brown, 1969.

Berrill, Norman J. *The Life of the Ocean*. New York: World Book Encyclopedia, McGraw-Hill, 1966.

Burton, Robert. *The Life and Death of Whales*. New York: Universe Books, 1973.

Carr, Archie F. *The Windward Road: Adventures of a Naturalist on Remote Caribbean Shores*. New York: Alfred A. Knopf, 1955.

Carson, Rachel. *The Sea Around Us*. New York: Oxford University Press, 1961.

Coker, R. E. *This Great and Wide Sea*. Chapel Hill, N.C.: University of North Carolina Press, 1947.

Cousteau, Jacques Y. *The Silent World*. New York: Harper & Row, 1953.

Cushing, D. H., and J. T. Walsh. *The Ecology of the Seas*. Philadelphia: W. B. Saunders, 1977.

Dawson, Elmer Yale. *Marine Botany: An Introduction*. New York: Holt, Rinehart and Winston, 1966.

Ellis, Richard. *Dolphins and Porpoises*. New York: Alfred A. Knopf, distributed by Random House, 1982.

———. *The Book of Sharks*. New York: Grosset & Dunlop, 1976.

———. *The Book of Whales*. New York: Alfred A. Knopf, 1980.

Engel, Leonard, and The Editors of Time-Life Books. *The Sea*.
    New York: Life Nature Library, Time-Life Books, 1961.
Fichter, George S., and Edward C. Migdalski. *The Fresh and
    Salt Water Fishes of the World*. New York: Alfred A.
    Knopf, distributed by Random House, 1976.
Gross, Meredith Grant. *Oceanography*. 2nd ed. Columbus,
    Ohio: Charles E. Merrill, 1971.
Hardy, Alister. *The Open Sea: Its Natural History*. Boston:
    Houghton Mifflin, 1971.
Harrison, Peter. *Seabirds: An Identification Guide*. Boston:
    Houghton Mifflin, 1983.
Heintzelman, Donald S. *A World Guide to Whales, Dolphins,
    and Porpoises*. New York: Winchester Press, 1981.
Hill, Maurice N., ed. *The Sea: Ideas and Observations on Progress
    in the Study of the Seas*. 3 vols. New York: Interscience
    Publishers, 1962–64.
Hood, Donald W., ed. *Impingement of Man on the Oceans*. New
    York: Wiley-Interscience, 1971.
Katona, Stephen, and David Richardson. *A Field Guide to the
    Whales, Porpoises, and Seals of the Gulf of Maine and Eastern
    Canada: Cape Cod to Labrador*. New York: Charles Scrib-
    ner & Sons, 1983.
Leatherwood, Stephen, and R. R. Reeves. *The Sierra Club
    Handbook of Whales and Dolphins*. San Francisco: Sierra
    Club Books, 1983.
McClane, Albert J., ed. *McClane's Field Guide to Saltwater
    Fishes of North America*. New York: Holt, Rinehart and
    Winston, 1978.
McNally, Robert. *So Remorseless a Havoc: Of Dolphins, Whales
    & Men*. Boston: Little, Brown, 1981.
Marx, Wesley. *The Oceans: The Last Resource*. San Francisco:
    Sierra Club Books, 1981.
Maxwell, Arthur E. *The Sea*. New York: John Wiley & Sons,
    1970.
Nelson, Byron. *Seabirds: Their Biology and Ecology*. New York:
    A. W. Publishers, 1979.
Pritchard, Peter C. H. *Living Turtles of the World*. Neptune
    City, N.J.: T. F. H. Publications, distributed by Crown
    Publishers, 1967.

Riley, John P. *Chemical Oceanography*. New York: Academic Press, 1975.

Russell, Frederick S., and Maurice Yonge. *The Seas: An Introduction to the Study of Life in the Sea*. 4th ed. New York: F. Warne, 1975.

Scheffer, Victor B. *A Natural History of Marine Mammals*. New York: Charles Scribner & Sons, 1976.

Schlee, Susan. *The Edge of an Unfamiliar World: A History of Oceanography*. New York: E. P. Dutton, 1973.

Tait, Ronald V., and R. S. De Santo. *Elements of Marine Ecology: An Introductory Course*. New York: Springer-Verlag, 1972.

Tuck, Gerald, and Hermann Heinzel. *A Field Guide to the Seabirds of Britain and the World*. London: Collins, 1978.

Watson, Lyall. *Sea Guide to Whales of the World*. New York: Elsevier-Dutton, 1981.

Weyl, Peter K. *Oceanography: An Introduction to the Marine Environment*. New York: John Wiley & Sons, 1970.

INDEX

Absecon Wildlife Management Area, 186
Academy of Natural Sciences of Philadelphia, xiv, 233
Accipiter(s), 207. *See also* Hawk(s); Raptor(s)
Acid mine runoff, 99
Acid rain, 90
Adder's-tongue. *See* Lily, Trout-
Admiral, Red, 21, 204
Ailanthus, 18, 87, 143
Alapocas Woods, 43, 45
Albatross:
  Black-browed, 233
  Yellow-nosed, 233
Alcid(s), 229–30
Alder:
  Common. *See* Alder, Hazel
  European, 55
  Hazel, 10, 97
  Seaside, 78
  Smooth. *See* Alder, Hazel
Alga(ae), 101, 169, 171, 175, 176
  Brown. *See* Rockweed
Allegheny River, 99
Amphibian(s), 20, 100, 138, 178
Amphipod(s). *See* Flea, sand
Andorra Natural Area, 41
Anemone:
  Rue-, 16
  Tall. *See* Thimbleweed
  Wood, 13, 28
Angle Wings family. *See* Question Mark; Comma
Ant, Velvet, 203
Aphid(s), 28, 65, 104
Aphid Lion. *See* Lacewing, Green
Appalachian Plateau (Physiographic Province), xiii, 83, 85, 86, 90–92, 111, 118, 126. *See also* Mountains, Poconos
Appalachian Trail, 92, 106, 112
Apple:
  American. *See* Apple, Sweet Crab
  Sweet Crab, 19
Apple Pie Hill (and fire tower), 138, 153
Appoquinimink Wildlife Area, 189
Arbutus, Trailing, 111
Arrow Arum, 65, 67
Arrowhead, Broad-leaved, 65, 67, 142, 144
Ash:
  Green, 10, 12, 18, 54, 56
  White, 12, 18, 19, 88
Aspen(s), 87, 89, 99
  Bigtooth, 68, 88, 91, 110, 144
  Quaking, 88, 90–91
Assunpink Wildlife Management Area, 41
Aster(s), 23, 28
  Barren's, 31
  Blue Wood, 96
  purple, 23
  Sickle-leaved Golden-, 144
  white, 23
  White Wood, 96
Atlantic City, 186, 193
Atlantic Coastal Plain (Physiographic Province), xi, xii, 11, 38, 41, 42, 43, 74, 125
Atlantic County Park, 41, 186
Atlantic Flyway, 74
Atlantic Hawksbill, 233
Atlantic Leatherback, 232–33
Atlantic Loggerhead, 232–33

Atlantic Ocean, xi, xii, 41, 50, 74, 86, 126, 157, 159, 160, 185, 194, 195, 196, 205, 207, 213, 215, 216, 221–41
Atsion Recreation Area, 137, 140, 151
  Atsion Mansion, 151
  Lake, 149, 151
  Ranger's Station, 140, 149, 150, 151
Audubon Wildlife Sanctuary, 37
Augustine Wildlife Area, 189
Auk, Great, 229
Autumn foliage, 11, 110
Avalon, 185, 196, 208, 213
  Cedar Island, 208. *See also* Osprey
Avens, White, 110
Azalea, Pink, 27, 88

Bake Oven Knob, 118
Bald Eagle Reintroduction Program, 113
Baldcypress, 25
Baltimore (butterfly), 25
Barnacle(s), 175–76, 196–98. *See also* Crustacean(s)
Barnegat Division of Edwin B. Forsythe National Wildlife Refuge, 186
Barnegat Light, 222, 234, 237
  8th Avenue jetty, 237
  Yacht Basin, 234, 237
Barnegat Lighthouse State Park (and Lighthouse), 237. *See also* Barnegat Light
Barrier beaches and islands, xi, xiv, 42, 75, 157, 159, 160, 169, 170, 177, 182, 185, 190, 193–218
  formation, 195–96
  jetty effects, 195, 196
  protective function, 159, 193
  topography, 194
  vegetation. *See* Beach plants
Bass:
  Black Sea, 164

Striped, 207
White, 60
Bass River State Forest, 152
  Lake Absegami, 152
  Ranger's station, 152
Basswood, American, 88
Bat(s), 98–99
  Big Brown, 99
  feeding adaptations, 98–99
  Hoary, 99
  Little Brown. *See* Myotis, Little Brown
  Red, 99
  Silver-haired, 99
Batona Hiking Club, 140, 153
Batona Trail, 140, 142, 143, 153
  Evans Bridge, 140, 153
  Ongs Hat, 140, 153
Batsto River, 142, 143, 144, 145, 146, 153
Batsto Village, 126–27, 133, 149, 150, 151
  Batsto Forge, 127
  Iron Master's Mansion, 151
  local history, 126–27
Bayberry, Northern, 52, 133, 143, 161, 168, 170, 179, 203, 204, 206, 208
Beach plants, 201, 203, 208, 215
  adaptations, 201, 203
  "permanent," 203. *See also* Succession, primary
  "pioneer," 201. *See also* Succession, primary
Bean, Wild, 169
Bear, Black, 103, 107–8, 118, 120
  behavior, 107–8
Beaver, 77, 99, 107, 120, 136
Bedstraw(s), 103, 142
Bee(s), 20, 56, 105
  Honeybee, 23
Beech:
  American, 10, 12, 18, 27, 28, 88, 89, 91
  Blue. *See* Hornbeam, American
Beechdrops, 27
Beetle(s), 23, 24, 179

Blister, 104
Ladybird, 104
Long-horn, 102
Soldier, 23
Tiger, 139, 203
Belleplain State Forest, 186, 215
Bellevue State Park, 43
Beltzville State Park, 118
Bergamot, Wild, 103
Big Pocono State Park, 118
"Big Sand Dunes" (Avalon), 185, 208, 213
Binoculars, xiii
Biocides, 104
Birch(es), 87, 89, 99, 103
  Black. *See* Birch, Sweet
  Gray, 88, 90, 91, 143
  River, 10, 25
  Sweet, 88, 89, 91, 103
  Yellow, 89
Bittercress, Pennsylvania, 51
Bittern:
  American, 62, 63
  Least, 51, 62, 63
Bitternut, 88
Bittersweet, American, 68
Bivalve(s). *See* Mollusk(s)
Blackberry(ies), 28, 51
Blackbird, Red-winged, 52, 58, 62, 63, 66, 167, 206
  behavior, 58
Blackbird Creek, 77, 189
Blackbird State Forest, 43
Black-eyed Susan, 23
Bladderwort(s), 130
Bleeding-heart family. *See* Dutchman's-breeches
Blenny, Crested, 164
Blockhead Mountain, 100, 113
Bloodroot, 13, 24
Blue(s) (butterflies), 22
  Eastern Tailed, 20
Blueberry(ies), 91, 107, 130, 133, 152
  Highbush, 106, 142, 143
  low-growing, 91
Bluebird, Eastern, 19, 20, 27, 32, 59

Bluefish, 198, 207, 232
Bobcat, 111
Bobolink, 52, 66
Bog iron, 125, 130
"Bog thief." *See* Redroot
Bombay Hook National Wildlife Refuge, 77, 78, 189
  Allee House, 189
  Bear Swamp Pool, 77
  dikes (auto tour), 189
  Finis Pool, 77
  Raymond Pool, 77
  Shearness Pool, 77
Boneset, 24
Borer:
  Locust, 23
  Wood-, 102
Bouncing Bet, 68
Bowman's Hill State Wildflower Preserve, 37, 40
Brackish water habitats, 43, 60, 74, 76, 77, 78, 79, 170, 177, 178, 180, 189, 190
Brambles, 143
Brandywine Battlefield State Park, 37
Brandywine Creek State Park, 43–44, 77
  Tuliptree Trail, 43–44
Brandywine River (Creek), 37, 43, 45
Brandywine River Museum, 37, 73
Brandywine River (Creek) Watershed, 73
Brant, 166, 206
Brier(s). *See* Greenbrier(s)
Brigantine Division of Edwin B. Forsythe National Wildlife Refuge, 74–75, 76, 77, 186, 187
  dikes (auto tour), 75, 186
  Doughty Creek, 75
  East and West Pools, 75
  Leeds Eco-Trail, 186
Brigantine Island, 186, 214
"British Soldiers." *See* Lichen, Match Stick
Brodhead, William A., 100
Brodhead, William (L. W.), 97, 111

Bruce Lake State Forest Natural Area, 118–19, 120
Bryozoan(s) (moss-animals), 176
Buckeye, 204
Bufflehead, 64, 205
Bug(s), 179
   Ambush, 103–4
   Tarnished Plant, 23
Bullfrog, 58
Bullhead, Brown, 60, 98
Bull's Island, 41
Bulrush:
   Great, 65
   River, 65
Bunting:
   Indigo, 19, 27
   Snow, 206
Burdock, Common, 21
Bur-reed(s), 144
   Great, 58, 65
Buteo(s), 207. *See also* Hawk(s); Raptor(s)
Butter-and-eggs, 22
Buttercup(s), 22
   Common, 20
Butterfly(ies), 20–22, 51, 68, 75, 179
   Cabbage, 22
   caterpillar, 20–22, 179
   European. *See* Butterfly, Cabbage
   larva(ae). *See* Butterfly(ies), caterpillar
   relationship to flowers, 20–22. *See also* Mutualism
Butterflyfish, Spotfin, 164
Butterfly-weed, 21–22
Butternut, 31
Buttonbush, Common, 66, 97, 142

Cabbage, Skunk, 15
Cabomba. See Fanwort
Camouflage, 108–9, 166, 168, 174, 199, 203, 205
Camphorweed, 169
Canadian Life Zone, 88
Canary Creek and Old Mill Creek Marshes, 189
Cancer-root, One-flowered, 27

Canvasback, 64
Cape Hatteras (North Carolina), 193
Cape Henlopen State Park, 194, 215
   "walking dunes," 215
Cape May Bird Observatory, 230, 233
Cape May Canal, 42
Cape May County Park, 41–42
Cape May–Lewes Ferry, 215
Cape May Point, 42, 207, 209, 215, 228, 230, 231
Cape May Point State Park, 42, 75, 209, 215
   Cape May Bird Observatory platform, 209. *See also* Hawk-watching lookouts
Cardinal, Northern, 19, 27, 167
Carnivorous (insectivorous) plants' adaptation, 132, 134
"Carolina Bays," 43
Carolinian Life Zone, 88
Carp, 60, 62
Carrot, Wild. *See* Queen Anne's Lace
Catalpa:
   Common. *See* Catalpa, Northern
   Northern, 16
Catamount. *See* Lion, Mountain
Catbird, Gray, 19, 27, 137, 206, 208
Catfish, Channel, 60
Catskill Mountains, 108
Cattail(s), 52, 56, 58, 62, 63, 65, 66, 76
   Broad-leaved. *See* Cattail, Common
   Common, 63
   Narrow-leaved, 63
   uses, 63
Cedar:
   Atlantic White, 130, 133, 134, 140–42, 143, 144, 145
   Eastern Red, 18, 87, 88, 168, 208
   Southern White. *See* Cedar, Atlantic White
Cedar bog(s), 125, 137, 140, 145
Cedar-of-Lebanon, 25
Celandine, 9
   Lesser, 51, 56
Charles Rogers Sanctuary, 42, 75

Chat, Yellow-breasted, 19
Chatsworth, 152
Checkerberry. *See* Wintergreen
Checkerspot. *See* Baltimore (butterfly)
Cherry, Black, 18, 22, 88, 169, 208
Chesapeake Bay, 112
Chesapeake-Delaware Canal, 44, 78, 189
Chestnut:
  American, 3, 31, 87, 88
  Chinese, 31
Chestnut blight, 3, 31, 87
Chickadee:
  Black-capped, 94, 102
  Carolina, 14, 136
Chickweed:
  Common, 20
  Field, 31
  Field, Hairy, 39
Chicory, 22–23
Chigger, 139
Chipmunk, Eastern, 9
Chum, 222, 226
Churchman's Marsh, 77–78
Churchville Nature Center, 37
Cicely, Sweet, 96
Cinquefoil, Common, 20, 22
Clam(s), 162, 164, 174, 199
Climax community, 4, 17, 18, 88, 90, 91
Cloak, Mourning, 15, 51, 104, 139
Clover:
  bush-, 143
  Red, 20
  White, 20
  White Sweet, 23
  Yellow Sweet, 23
Clubmoss(es). *See* Moss(es), club
Cobia, 164
Codfish, 232
Coffeetree, Kentucky, 32
Cohansey Formation (aquifer), 126
Cohosh, Blue, 29
Coltsfoot, 110
Columbine, Wild, 102, 110
Comma, 21
Commensalism, 65

Composite family. *See* Daisy family
Compound leaves, 55–56, 64, 65
Concerned Area Residents for the Preservation of Tinicum Marsh (CARP), 55
Coneflower, Thin-leaved, 23
Conifer(s), 9, 11, 18, 32, 89, 95, 101, 109, 110, 120
  adaptation to environment, 89
  cuticle, 89
Consumers, 4
Continental plates of North America and Africa, 30, 85, 126
Continental shelf (North America), 225
Coot, American, 64
Copper family (butterflies), 22
Copperhead, Northern, 39, 104–5
Cordgrass(es) (Marsh Grass[es]), 157, 159, 168, 169, 175
  Saltmarsh, 159–60, 204
  Saltmeadow. *See* Salt Hay
Cormorant, Double-crested, 206
Corson's Inlet State Park, 186, 215
Cottontail, Eastern, 19, 51, 106, 207, 208
Cottonwood:
  Common. *See* Cottonwood, Eastern
  Eastern, 10, 68
Cougar. *See* Lion, Mountain
Cowbird, Brown-headed, 9, 96
Cowslip. *See* Marsh-marigold
Cow-wheat, 133, 142
Coyote:
  Eastern, 88, 111
  Western, 111
Crab(s), 175, 199
  Blue, 60, 175
  Fiddler, 174
  Ghost, 199
  Hermit, 174–75
  Horseshoe, 176
  Mole, 199
Cranberry, Large, 130, 142, 144
Cranberry–Black Spruce–Tamarack bog, 92
Cranberry bog(s), 125, 130, 152

Crappie:
  Black, 60
  White, 60
Creeper, Virginia, 17, 30, 169, 208
Cricket(s), 179
  Field, 139
Crossbill:
  Red, 101
  White-winged, 101
Crow:
  American, 19, 170
  Common. *See* Crow, American
  Fish, 68, 167, 170
Crowberry, 133
Crum Creek Valley, 40, 73
Crustacean(s), 175
Cuckoo, Yellow-billed, 105, 137
Cucumber-root, Indian, 13
Cutgrass, Rice, 108

Daisy:
  Field. *See* Daisy, Ox-eye
  Ox-eye, 20, 23
Daisy family, 23
Damselfly(ies), 51, 58–59, 139
  behavior, 58–59
  Black-winged, 98
  Bluet, 98
  nymph(s), 59, 98
Dandelion, Common, 20
Dangleberry. *See* Huckleberry, Tall
Decomposers, 4, 13–14, 98
Deer, White-tailed, 13, 15, 30, 94, 106, 108, 136, 180
Delaware and Raritan Canal State Park. *See* Bull's Island
Delaware Bay, xi, 41, 42, 43, 74, 157, 166, 171, 176, 180, 186, 187, 188, 189, 190, 194, 209, 230, 231
Delaware Canal, 37–38
Delaware-Chesapeake Canal. *See* Chesapeake-Delaware Canal
Delaware River, xii, 38, 39, 41, 43, 52, 74, 83, 84, 85, 86, 87, 88, 90, 100, 104, 112, 113, 114, 121, 195

Delaware Seashore State Park. *See* Indian River Inlet
Delaware Valley Ornithological Club (Philadelphia), 222, 233
Delaware Water Gap, 84, 86, 87, 91, 92, 99, 100, 108, 111, 112, 114, 118
Delaware Water Gap (town or borough), 92, 94, 113
Delaware Water Gap National Recreation Area, xiii, 83–118, 119, 120, 121
  Headquarters (Bushkill), 84, 113, 117
Delaware Wildlands, Inc., 77
Delmont Boy Scout Reservation, 15
Den tree(s) (deadwood), 14, 25, 54, 102–3
Dennis Creek Wildlife Management Area, 186
Devil's Hole (State Game Land no. 221), 119
Devil's-bit, 31
Dingmans Falls and Visitor Center, 84, 117, 119, 121
  Dingmans Waterfall, 119
  Silver Thread Waterfall, 119
Dividing Creek. *See* Egg Island–Berrytown Wildlife Management Area
Dix Wildlife Management Area, 186
Dogbane, Intermediate, 28
Dogwood, Flowering, 12, 18, 28, 88
Dolphin(s), 231
  Atlantic Bottlenose. *See* Dolphin, Atlantic Bottle-nosed
  Atlantic Bottle-nosed, 231
  Atlantic White-sided, 231
  Common, 231
  Grampus. *See* Dolphin, Risso's
  Risso's, 229
  Short-snouted Spinner, 231
  Spotted, 231
  Striped, 231
Dove, Mourning, 19
Dovekie, 229–30
Dover Publications, xv

Dowitcher, Short-billed, 166
Dragon Run Marsh, 78
Dragonfly(ies), 51, 58–59, 139, 179, 204
  behavior, 58–59, 98
  nymph(s), 59, 98
Duck, American Black, 52, 62, 64, 166, 206
  Ring-necked, 64
  Ruddy, 64
  Wood, 54, 59, 75, 103, 120
Duck Potato. *See* Arrowhead, Broad-leaved
Dunlin, 166, 198
Dusty Miller, 201, 203
Dutchman's-breeches, 7, 10, 12, 24
Dwarf Forest. *See* Pygmy Forest

Eagle:
  Bald, 111, 112–13
  Golden, 111
Earth Star, 131
Earwig(s), 102, 174
Eastern Hemlock–Native Rhodo-dendron–Fern community, 90, 97, 101, 105
  adaptations, 90
Echo-location. *See* Bat(s), feeding adaptations
Ecotone, 27
Eel, American, 60, 163
Eft, Red. *See* Newt, Red-spotted
Egg Island–Berrytown Wildlife Management Area, 187
Egret(s), 62, 68, 166, 175, 176, 180, 181, 188, 208, 209
  Cattle, 166
  Common. *See* Egret, Great
  Great, 62, 66, 161–62, 166, 208
  Snowy, 62, 66, 161–62, 166, 208
Elder:
  Box, 10, 30, 32, 65, 88
  Marsh-, 170, 204
Elfin family, 139
Elm, American, 10, 18, 88, 94
Endangered (or threatened) species,

14, 56, 57, 58, 111, 112, 137, 138, 169, 170, 177, 205–6
Estuary(ies), 74, 157, 177, 185, 187, 190, 207. *See also* Brackish water habitats
Evansburg State Park, 38
Evening-primrose, Common, 22, 169
Evergreen(s). *See* Conifer(s)
Everlasting, Pearly, 179
Extirpation, 112

Fairmount Park, 38, 40
Falcon(s), 207. *See also* Hawk(s); Raptor(s)
"Fall line," xii
Fanwort, 98
Federal Clean Water Act, 160–61
Fern(s), 11, 13, 24, 101, 110
  Bracken, 132
  Christmas, 110
  Cinnamon, 144
  Common Polypody, 101, 144
  Curly Grass, 140
  Cut-leaf Grape-, 110
  Fragile, 101–2
  Hay-scented, 110
  Leathery Grape-. *See* Grape-fern, Cut-leaf
  Maidenhair, 13
  Maidenhair, Aleutian, 39
  Marginal Shield, 104
  Royal, 108
  sorus(ii) (spores), 104
  Spinulose Shield, 104
Filefish, Orange, 164
Finback, 228
Finch(es), 32, 101
  House, 167
Fir(s), 11
Five-Mile Woods Preserve, 38
Flea:
  beach. *See* Flea, sand
  sand, 199
Fleabane, Daisy, 23
Flicker:
  Northern, 19, 54, 102, 136, 168

Flicker (*cont.*)
  Yellow-shafted. *See* Flicker,
    Northern
Flounder:
  Summer, 164
  Winter, 164
Fly(ies), xiv
  Deer, 139
  Greenhead, 179, 207
  Spanish, 104
Flycatcher:
  Acadian, 10, 27, 41
  Alder, 73
  Great Crested, 14, 137
  Traill's. *See* Flycatcher, Alder; Fly-
    catcher, Willow
  Willow, 19, 64
Folcroft Landfill, 63. *See also* Tinicum
  National Environmental Center
Folded Appalachians. *See* Ridge and
  Valley (Physiographic Province)
Foliage, autumn. *See* Autumn foli-
  age
Food chains, 4, 179
Forest(s), 86–87, 159, 160, 185,
  189
  Boreal. *See* Forest, Canadian-zone
  Canadian-zone, xi, xiii, 73, 119,
    120, 121. *See also* Forest, North-
    ern Mixed Hardwood–Conifer-
    ous
  Eastern Deciduous, xi, xii, 3–47,
    50, 72, 73, 74, 75, 76, 77, 88,
    89, 105, 106, 125, 136, 186;
    adaptation to environment, 11,
    89; oak-hickory, 11, 41, 42
  Hardwood, 18, 88, 89, 109. *See
    also* Forest, Eastern Deciduous
  Mixed Deciduous-Coniferous, 9,
    87, 88, 89, 90–91, 92–96,
    118, 120
  Northern Hardwood, 88, 91
  Northern Mixed Hardwood–
    Coniferous, 96
  Pine-Oak, 75, 76, 125, 133, 136–
    37, 142, 143, 152, 186. *See
    also* Pine Barrens

Forest soil types:
  acidic, 90, 106, 109
  calcium deficiency effects, 30, 109
  hydric (wet), 10, 24, 29, 38, 43,
    45, 50, 55, 68, 106, 108–10,
    142
  mesic (well-drained), 10, 14–15,
    24, 38, 45
  xeric (dry), 10–11, 32, 38, 41
Forest vegetation layers:
  canopy, 4, 7, 11, 12, 32, 96, 131
  herbaceous layer, 11, 12, 132
  shrub layer, 11, 12, 27, 143, 145.
    See also Forest vegetation layers,
    understory
  subcanopy, 11, 12, 18, 27. *See also*
    Forest vegetation layers, under-
    story
  understory, 11, 12, 18, 27, 88, 91,
    95, 104, 105, 106, 131, 143
Fortescue Wildlife Management
  Area, 187
Fossils, 44, 120, 225
Four-wheel drive, 127, 140, 142,
  149, 153
Fox:
  Gray, 136
  Red, 19, 136
Franklintree, 25
French Creek State Park, 15, 38
Fresh-water habitats (other), 4, 37,
  38, 39, 40, 41, 42, 43, 44, 45, 49,
  50, 56, 69, 72–79, 92, 94, 96,
  106, 107, 118, 119, 120, 125,
  130, 131–32, 134, 136, 138, 139,
  140, 142, 144, 146, 177, 178,
  186, 187. *See individual rivers,
  streams, lakes, ponds, etc.*
Fresh-water marshes, xi, 37, 38, 39,
  40, 41, 42, 43, 49–81, 177, 185,
  189, 190
  formation, 49
Fritillary:
  Greater, 22
  Lesser, 22
Frog:
  Carpenter, 138

Green, 9, 58
New Jersey Chorus, 138
Pickerel, 9, 58, 100
Southern Leopard, 58, 138
Wood, 25, 51, 58
Frostweed, 133
Fruitfly, Mediterranean, 23
Fulmar, Northern, 226
Fungus(i), 4, 14, 27, 31, 101, 131

Gadwall, 64
Gall(s), 23, 28, 51, 65
Blackberry Knot, 51
Cone, 28
formation, 23, 28, 65
Goldenrod Ball, 51
Goldenrod Bunch, 51
Hackberry Nipple, 65
Horned Oak, 51
Spiny, 28
Gallfly(ies), 65
Goldenrod, 23
Gallinule:
Common. *See* Moorhen, Common
Purple, 78
Gallwasp(s), 65
Gambusia, 60
Gannet, Northern, 230
Geological history, xii, xiii, 4, 30, 49,
84–86, 126, 195, 225
George W. Childs State Park,
117–18, 119
Geranium, Wild, 12, 16, 29
Geranium family. *See* Geranium,
Wild; Herb-Robert
Ginger, Wild, 12–13, 24, 29
Ginseng, Dwarf, 24, 29
Glacier (and glaciation), xiii, 72, 75,
83, 86, 87, 91–92, 106, 126, 225
glacial lakes, 72, 75, 91–92, 120
glacial till, 86, 92
Wisconsin, 75, 126
Glassboro Wildlife Management
Area, 42
Glassboro Woods. *See* Glassboro
Wildlife Management Area

Glasswort:
Dwarf, 160, 173
Slender, 160, 173, 204
Woody, 173, 204
Glen Providence Park, 38
Gnatcatcher, Blue-gray, 14, 167
Gneiss, 32
Goat Hill Serpentine Barrens, 39
Golden Club, 144
Golden Field Guide Series, xiii
Goldencrest, 134
Goldeneye:
Barrow's, 214
Common, 205
Goldenrod(s), 23, 28, 111, 178, 204
Blue-stemmed, 110
Broad-leaved. *See* Goldenrod,
Zigzag
Early, 110
Seaside, 178–79, 203, 208
Sweet, 146
Zigzag, 96, 110
Goldenseal, 29
Goldfinch, American, 9, 19, 21, 52
Goldfish, 98
Goose:
Canada, 9, 62, 64, 206
Snow, 166, 187, 206
Goshawk, Northern, 109
Gouldsboro State Park, 121
Grand Canyon (Pennsylvania), 99
Grape(s), Wild, 17, 32, 87, 169
Grass(es), 18, 19, 111, 131, 132,
144
American Beach, 194, 201–2, 208
American Dune. *See* Grass, Ameri-
can Beach
Cane. *See* Grass, Common Reed
Common Reed, 62–63, 164, 171,
204
Little Bluestem prairie, 111
Plume. *See* Grass, Common Reed
Poverty, 203
Salt. *See* Grass, Spike
Spike, 171, 204
western prairie, 39
Grasshopper(s), 179, 203

Great Bay Boulevard Wildlife Management Area. *See* Tuckerton Meadows
Great Channel, 204, 209. *See also* Stone Harbor Point; Seven Mile Beach
"Great Dune," 215. *See also* Cape Henlopen State Park
Great Swamp National Wildlife Refuge, 75–76
  Lake Passaic (Glacial), 75
Grebe:
  Horned, 205
  Pied-billed, 64
Greenbrier(s), 18, 31, 131, 142, 143
  Common, 88, 91, 106
Grosbeak:
  Evening, 101
  Pine, 101
  Rose-breasted, 167
Ground Pine, 109
Groundhog. *See* Woodchuck
Groundsel:
  Common, 203
  Stinking, 203
Groundsel-tree, 170
Grouse, Ruffed, 106, 108–9, 120, 136
Gull(s), 68, 175, 198, 205, 206, 207, 214, 230
  Glaucous, 230
  Great Black-backed, 198, 206, 230
  Herring, 162, 170, 174, 198, 206, 230
  Iceland, 230
  Laughing, 176–77, 198, 206, 209
  Lesser Black-backed, 230
  Ring-billed, 198, 206, 230
  Sabine's, 230
  Thayer's, 230
Gum:
  Black. *See* Gum, Sour-
  Sour-, 10, 12, 27, 132, 142, 143

Hackberry, 10, 65
Hackensack Meadowlands Environment Center, 187
  Bergen County Landfill, 187
  Hackensack River Estuary, 187
  Kingsland Creek Marsh, 187
Hairstreak family, 22
Hake:
  Red, 164
  Spotted, 164
Hammerhead. *See* Shark, Hammerhead
Hare, Snowshoe, 88, 106, 111, 120
Harrier, Northern, 51, 168, 206
Hawk(s), 19, 51, 52
  Broad-winged, 109, 111
  Cooper's, 111
  Fish. *See* Osprey
  Marsh. *See* Harrier, Northern
  Red-shouldered, 109
  Red-tailed, 51, 52, 105, 111
  Rough-legged, 51
  Sharp-shinned, 111
  Sparrow. *See* Kestrel, American
Hawk (raptor) migration, 111–12, 119, 121, 207, 209
Hawk Mountain Sanctuary, xiii, 106, 112, 118, 119, 121
  River of Rocks, 119
Hawk-watching lookouts, 75, 111, 112, 118, 119, 121, 209
Hawkweed(s), 20, 22
Hay Creek, 38
Hayfever, 23
Hazel, American, 31
Heather:
  Beach, 203
  False. *See* Heather, Beach
  Golden-, 130, 131, 134, 142, 143
  Wooly. *See* Heather, Beach
Heislerville Wildlife Management Area, 187
  East Point Light (lighthouse), 187
Hellebore, False, 29
Hemlock, Eastern, 11, 87, 88, 89, 90, 91, 94, 95, 106, 108, 110
Hemp, Indian, 28. *See also* Dogbane, Intermediate

Hepatica, Round-lobed, 106
Herb-Robert, 110
Hercules-club, 64
Heron(s), 62, 68, 166, 175, 176, 180, 181, 188, 208, 209
  Great Blue, 62, 66, 166, 189, 208
  Green. *See* Heron, Green-backed
  Green-backed, 62
  Little Blue, 51, 166, 208
  Louisiana. *See* Heron, Tricolored
  Night-. *See* Night-Heron
  Tricolored, 51, 166, 208
Herrontown Woods, 42
Hickory(ies), 18
  Mockernut, 11-12
  Pignut, 11-12
  Shagbark, 10, 11, 88
Hickory Run State Park, 119
  Boulder Field, 119
Higbee Beach Wildlife Management Area, 42, 76, 215
  Pond Creek Meadow, 42
Highlands. *See* New England Uplands
Holgate Division of Edwin B. Forsythe National Wildlife Refuge, 188, 194, 214
Holly:
  American, 143, 208
  Largeleaf. *See* Winterberry, Mountain
  Low Gallberry. *See* Inkberry
Honeysuckle:
  Japanese, 17, 32
  Swamp, 140
Hopewell Village National Historic Site, 38
Hophornbeam, Eastern, 12, 88
Hopper(s), Leaf, 103, 179
Hornbeam, American, 10, 12
Horse Shoe Trail, 38, 40
Horsetail(s), 110
Huckleberry(ies), 109, 130, 131, 132, 133, 134, 142, 143
  Black, 91
  Low-growing, 142
  Tall, 132, 142, 143

Hudson Canyon, 222-33
  effects on food supply, 225
Hudson River, 195, 225
Hudsonia. *See* Heather, Golden-
Hummingbird, Ruby-throated, 7
Humpback. *See* Whale, Humpbacked
Hydroid(s). *See* "Snail Fur"

Ibis, Glossy, 166, 208
Indian-pipes, 13-14, 27
Indian River Inlet, 215
Inkberry, 130, 133, 142, 143
International Whaling Commission, 228
Introduced species, 22, 54, 56, 60, 62-63, 87, 100, 109, 164
Ipecac, American, 133
Iris, Yellow, 58
Iron Hill Hardwoods, 44
Ironweed(s), 22
Ironwood. *See* Hophornbeam, Eastern
Island Beach State Park, 194, 213, 214

Jack:
  Common, 164
  Crevalle. *See* Jack, Common
Jack-in-the-pulpit, 13, 24, 29
Jacobs, Joseph, 169-70
Jacob's-ladder, 24, 29
Jaeger(s), 229
  feeding habits, 228-29
  Long-tailed, 229
  Parasitic, 229
  Pomarine, 228-29
Jay, Blue, 94, 136
Jellyfish, 199
Jetty(ies), 195, 196-98, 214, 215, 237. *See also* Barrier beaches and islands, jetty effects
Jewelweed. *See* Touch-me-not
Joe-Pye-weed(s), 22, 24
  legend of Joe Pye, 24
  Spotted, 24

Junco:
    Dark-eyed, 168
    Slate-colored. *See* Junco, Dark-
        eyed
Juniper, Common, 104, 111

Kestrel, American, 51, 206
Killcohook National Wildlife Ref-
    uge, 187
Killdeer, 68
Killifish. *See* Mummichog
    Banded, 60
Kingbird, Eastern, 19, 137
Kingfish, Northern, 164
Kingfisher, Belted, 10, 52, 98, 170
Kinglet:
    Golden-crowned, 101
    Ruby-crowned, 101
Kingsnake, Eastern, 137
Kittatinny Point Information Station
    and Visitor Center, 84, 113, 121
Kittiwake, Black-legged, 230
Knapweed, Spotted, 91, 103
Knotweed(s), 65

Lacawac Sanctuary, 119–20
Lacewing, Green, 104
Lackawanna State Park, 120
Ladies'-tresses, Slender, 31
Lady's-slipper, Pink, 133, 145
    white variety, 133
Lake Lacawac, 92, 120
Lamb's-quarters. *See* Pigweed,
    Winged
Larch, European, 87
Lark, Horned, 206
Laurel:
    Mountain, 91, 106, 131, 143;
        food value, 106
    Sheep, 130, 131, 143
League of Women Voters, 55
Leatherleaf, 130, 142–43, 144
Lebanon State Forest, 140, 151–52,
    153, 237
    Ranger's station, 140, 151, 152,
        153
Legume(s). *See* Pea family

Lehigh River, 100
Lenape Indians, 87, 104
Lester G. MacNamara Wildlife Man-
    agement Area, 76, 188
Lettuce, Sea, 176. *See also* Sea
    Lettuce
Lichen(s), 17, 91, 101, 131
    Goblet. *See* Lichen, Pixie-cup
    Match Stick, 101, 131
    Pale Shield, 101
    Pixie-cup, 101
    Red Crest. *See* Lichen, Match Stick
    Reindeer, 101
Lily:
    Bullhead-, 130, 144
    Fragrant Water-, 98, 130, 142,
        144
    Trout-, 10, 13, 29
    White Water-. *See* Lily, Fragrant
        Water-
    Wood, 31
    Yellow Pond-, 62. *See also* Spatter-
        dock
Linden, American. *See* Basswood,
    American
Ling. *See* Hake, Red
Lion, Mountain, 111
Little Creek Wildlife Area, 78, 189
    observation tower, 78
    Pickering Beach, 78
    Port Mahon Road, 78
Littoral drift, 195–96. *See also* Bar-
    rier beaches and islands, formation
Lizard, Northern Fence, 138
Lobelia, Pale-spike, 31
Localization effect, 87–88
Locust:
    Black, 18, 19
    Honey, 10, 55–56
Long Beach Island, 186, 188, 194,
    214, 234, 237
Long Pond, 73
Longshore current. *See* Littoral drift
Longwood Gardens, 37, 45
Loon:
    Common, 206
    Red-throated, 206

Loosestrife:
  Fringed, 24
  Purple, 56, 58, 60, 66, 87
  Spiked. *See* Loosestrife, Purple
  Yellow, 130
Lord Stirling Park, 75
Lotus, American, 76
Lower Forge Wilderness Area, 140–46. *See also* Wharton State Forest
  Mannis Duck Pond, 144
  Quaker Bridge, 140–42, 143, 149
Lums Pond State Park, 44

Mackerel, 231, 232
Mad Horse Creek Wildlife Management Area, 188
Magnolia:
  Swamp. *See* Magnolia, Sweetbay
  Sweetbay, 140, 143
  Yulan, 25
Maleberry, 133
Mallard, 62, 64, 166
Mallow, Marsh, 169
Manahawkin Wildlife Management Area, 76, 186, 188
Manasquan Inlet, 214
Mannington Meadows, 76
Mantis, Praying, 204
Maple(s), 12, 88, 89, 91
  Ashleaf. *See* Elder, Box
  Norway, 12
  Red, 10, 12, 18, 25, 27, 65, 88, 89, 90, 94, 108, 130, 131, 133, 134, 142, 143, 144
  Silver, 10
  Striped, 88, 91, 104
  Sugar, 12, 88, 89, 94
Marlin:
  Blue, 232
  White, 232
Marsh Creek State Park, 73
Marsh-marigold, 56
Martin, Purple, 54, 62, 64
Mast, 109
Mastodon, 225
May-apple, 13, 24, 29

Meadow-beauty, Virginia, 130, 143
Meadowlark, Eastern, 206
Meadow-rue:
  Early, 98
  Tall, 24
Meesing Nature Center, 121. *See also* Tannersville Cranberry Bog Preserve
Menhaden, Atlantic, 207
Merganser:
  Common, 64–65
  Hooded, 65
  Red-breasted, 205
"Mermaids' Purses," 199. *See also* Skate(s)
Middle Creek Wildlife Management Area, 73
Midge(s), 98
  Biting, 179
Migration. *See specific wildlife groups or species*
Milkweed, Common, 21–22, 179
Mill Grove. *See* Audubon Wildlife Sanctuary
Millbrook, 84
Mills, Herbert, 158
Mimicry, 22
Mink, 66, 107
Minnow(s) ("Minnies"). *See* Mummichog
  Sheepshead, 174
"Miss Barnegat Light" (boat), 221, 222
Mite, Marsh, 171
Moccasin-flower. *See* Lady's-slipper, Pink
Mockingbird, Northern, 19, 88, 167
Mole:
  Common. *See* Mole, Eastern
  Eastern, 136
  Star-nosed, 110
Mollusk(s), 164, 174
Monarch, 22, 52, 75, 104, 179, 204
  migration, 204
Moorhen, Common, 56, 58, 62, 63
Morning-glory, Pickering's, 144
Morris Arboretum, 40–41

Morristown National Historical Park, 75
Mosquito(es), xiv, 59, 60, 69, 207
Salt Marsh, 179
Mosquito Fish. *See Gambusia*
Moss(es), 17, 101, 110
Carpet, 101
club, 109–10, 130, 134. *See also* Ground Pine
Fern, 101
Giant Club, 101, 111
Rose, 110
Sphagnum, 108, 130, 142, 143, 144
Moth(s), 23, 98
caterpillar, 63, 179
Cattail, 63
Cecropia, 179
cocoon. *See* Moth, pupa(ae)
Gypsy, 4, 31, 32, 105–6
larva(ae). *See* Moth, caterpillar
pupa(ae), 179
Silk, 105
Mt. Minsi, 92–113, 117, 121
Caldeno Creek, 97, 99, 100, 101, 110
Hunter's Spring, 101
Indian Shelter, 104, 105
Kittatinny House, 92, 97, 100, 101
Lake Lenape, 92, 97–100, 101, 103
Resort Point Overlook (Gap Overlook 1), 92, 100
Sphagnum Moss swamp, 106–8, 110
Table Rock, 92, 101, 104, 110–11
Water Gap House, 97
Mt. Tammany, 92, 121
Mountain(s), xi, xii, xiii, 10, 37, 41, 72, 83–123
Appalachians. *See* Mountain(s), Kittatinny Ridge; Mountain(s), Poconos
formation, 84–86

Kittatinny Ridge, xiii, 83–84, 85, 86, 92, 111–12, 118, 121, 122–23
Poconos, xi, xiii, xiv, 73, 83, 84, 85, 86, 87, 88, 89, 92, 95, 98, 100, 106, 107, 109, 111, 113, 114, 118, 119, 122–23
Mountain-mint, Narrow-leaved, 31
Mouse (Mice), 207, 208
White-footed, 110
Mudbar formation, 56, 60, 62
Mulberry:
Red, 51, 65
White, 51, 65
Mullein:
Common, 22, 142, 169
Moth, 23, 142
Mullet:
Striped, 207
White, 164, 207
Mullica River, 127, 130, 131, 132, 133, 153, 188
Sleeper Branch, 130, 131, 132, 133–34
Mummichog, 60, 164, 174
Mushroom(s), 131
Muskrat, 52, 56, 63, 66–67, 68, 77, 78, 99, 107, 136, 180
adaptations and behavior, 66–67, 180
Mussel(s), 162, 174, 199
Blue, 198
Ribbed, 175
Mustard, Garlic, 51
Mutualism, 20, 101
Myotis, Little Brown, 98, 99, 136. *See also* Bat(s), Little Brown

National Audubon Society, xv, 112
National Marine Fisheries Service, 161
National Park Service, 84, 117
Nature Conservancy (The), 120, 121
Nelumbo. See Lotus, American
Neshaminy Creek, 39, 40
Neshaminy State Park, 38–39, 73

Nettle:
  Stinging, 21, 54, 62
  Wood, 62
New England Uplands (Physiographic Province), xiii
New Hope, 38, 40
New Jersey Green Acres Program, 158
New Jersey Wetlands Act, 160
Newt, Red-spotted, 99–100
Nighthawk, Common, 137
Night-Heron:
  Black-crowned, 52, 62, 66, 166, 174, 209
  Yellow-crowned, 166, 174
Nightshade, Enchanter's, 13
Nockamixon State Park, 39
Nolde Forest State Park, 39
Norman G. Wilder Wildlife Area, 44
North Brigantine Natural Area, 214
Nottingham Park, 39
Nummy Island, 159, 181, 182–85, 188, 204, 209, 210–13
Nuthatch, White-breasted, 14, 94, 136

Oak(s), 4, 12, 18, 30, 31, 32, 87, 88, 89, 91, 94, 96, 97, 104, 105, 106, 130, 131, 143
  Bear. *See* Oak, Scrub
  Black, 12, 13, 31, 88, 90, 142
  Black (Red) group, 12
  Blackjack, 31, 131, 142, 143
  Chestnut, 11, 12, 88, 90, 104, 142
  Chinkapin, 142
  Northern Red, 12, 27, 88, 89, 104, 132
  Pin, 10
  Post, 133
  Scarlet, 12, 31, 88, 90
  Scrub, 91, 111, 131, 142, 143
  Swamp White, 10, 94
  White, 12, 27, 32, 66, 88, 90, 94, 142, 143
  White group, 12

Ocean Crest State Park. *See* Corson's Inlet State Park
Oceanic bird(s). *See* Pelagic bird(s)
Octoraro Area, 39, 73
Odonata. See Damselfly(ies); Dragonfly(ies)
Oldsquaw, 205
Opossum, 15, 88, 109, 136
Orchid family, 13, 29, 130, 133
Orchis, Showy, 13, 16, 29
Orioles:
  Baltimore. *See* Northern
  Northern, 7, 105, 167
Osprey, 111, 112, 113, 167, 169–70
  nesting behavior, 169–70
Osprey Reintroduction Program (East Stroudsburg University), 112
Otter Reintroduction Program (East Stroudsburg University), 99
Otter, River, 77, 78, 99, 107, 180
  habits and status, 99
Ovenbird, 14, 27, 95, 105, 137
Overwash, 204. *See also* Barrier beaches and islands; Sand dune(s), formation
Owl(s), 19, 42
  Barred, 39, 75, 103, 110
  Eastern Screech-, 25, 102, 110
  Great Horned, 25, 30, 103
  Short-eared, 51, 168
Oyster(s), 164
Oystercatcher, American, 162, 181, 207

Painted Lady, 21, 204
  American, 21, 179
Painter Arboretum. *See* Tyler Arboretum
Pakim Pond Recreation Area, 151
Panther. *See* Lion, Mountain
Parasitism, 9, 23, 27, 96
Parsley family. *See* Cicely, Sweet; Queen Anne's Lace
Partridgeberry, 110

Parvin State Park, 42
Pea, Beach, 201, 203
Pea family, 20, 55
Peace Valley County Park. *See* Peace Valley Nature Center
Peace Valley Nature Center, 39, 74
Peaslee Wildlife Management Area, 76
Pedricktown Marsh, 76
  Oldman's Creek, 76
"Peep." *See* Sandpiper(s)
Peeper, Northern Spring, 10, 15, 51, 58, 99, 138
Pelagic (oceanic) bird(s), 221, 224, 226, 229, 230, 231, 233, 239
  nesting grounds and distribution, 226, 228
Pelagic trip information, 233
Penn Forest Reservoir, 118
Penn State Forest, 152
  Lake Oswego, 152
Pennsbury Manor State Park, 74
  Manor Lake, 74
  Money Island, 74
  Van Sciver Lakes (Upper and Lower), 74
Pennsylvania Game Commission, 107, 112, 113
Pennsylvania State Game Land no. 180, 120
Pennypack Creek, 39
Pennypack Park and Environmental Center, 39
Pepperbush:
  Coast, 130, 142
  Sweet. *See* Pepperbush, Coast
Perch, Yellow, 60
Persimmon, Common, 88
Pesticides, 32, 105–6, 169, 170, 207
  DDT, 105
  organophosphate(s), 105
  Sevin, 105
Peters Valley, 84
Peterson Field Guide Series, xiii
Pewee, Eastern Wood. *See* Wood-Pewee, Eastern
pH, 90

Phalarope:
  Northern. *See* Phalarope, Red-necked
  Red, 229
  Red-necked, 229
Pheasant, Ring-necked, 19, 51, 68, 109
Philadelphia Conservationists, 55
Phlox, Moss. *See* Pink, Moss-
Phoebe, Eastern, 15, 19, 137
Photosynthesis, 4, 11, 13–14, 89, 175
  chlorophyll, 11, 13, 14, 89
Phragmites. See Grass, Common Reed
Physiography and Physiographic Provinces, xii, xiii
Pickerelweed, 62, 65, 67
Piedmont (Physiographic Province), xii–xiii, 4, 10, 37, 41, 42, 43, 72, 126
Pigweed, Winged, 203
Pine(s), 11, 142, 143
  Eastern White, 7, 11, 15, 17, 87, 88, 89, 90, 102
  Pitch, 39, 91, 111, 127, 130, 131, 133, 134, 142, 143; adaptation to fire, 127–30
  Red, 90
  Scrub. *See* Pine, Virginia
  Shortleaf, 143
  Virginia, 18, 31
Pine Barren rivers, 132, 137, 153
Pine Barrens, xi, xii, xiv, 31, 42, 125–55, 188, 237
  ghost towns, 126
  wildlife, 136–39
Pink:
  Deptford, 22
  Moss-, 31
  Rose-, 31
  Slender Marsh-, 132
Pintail, Northern, 52, 64
Pinweed, Beach, 203
Pinxter-flower. *See* Azalea, Pink
Pipefish, Northern, 163
Pipewort(s), 130, 144

Pipsissewa, 133
Pitcher-plant, 121, 134
Plains (The). *See* Pygmy Forest
Plantains, 169
Pleasant Mills, 127
Pleasant Mills–Batsto, 127–34, 149.
    See also Wharton State Forest
    Constable Bridge, 131, 132, 133
    fire-cut, 131–32
    "moon-scape," 130–31, 132,
        134
    nature trails, 134
    Nescochague Creek, 127
    "New Pond," 133
    Pleasant Mills United Methodist
        Church, 127, 149, 150
Plover(s), 176, 181
    Black-bellied, 68, 166
    Piping, 198, 199, 205, 206
    Semipalmated, 68, 166
Plum, Beach, 203
Pocono Environmental Education
    Center (PEEC), 84, 117, 120
Pocono Lake, 120
Pogonia, Rose, 130, 134
Poison-ivy, xiv, 18, 96, 167, 203,
    208
Pokeweed, 169
Pollination, 20, 24, 105
Pollution (effects and control), 63,
    67–68, 69, 89–90, 99, 100, 160
Poppy family. *See* Celandine
Porcupine, 109
Porpoise, Harbor, 231
Port Mahon (Road), 189. *See also*
    Little Creek Wildlife Area
Port Republic Wildlife Management
    Area, 188
Predator(s), 19, 20, 22, 25, 59, 66,
    103–4, 105, 175, 177, 198, 204,
    207
Prickly-pear (cactus), 91
Prime Hook National Wildlife Ref-
    uge, 78, 189
    Petersfield Ditch, 78
    Prime Hook Creek, 78
Princeton Institute Woods, 42, 75

Princeton Wildlife Refuge. *See*
    Charles Rogers Sanctuary
Producers, 4
Promised Land State Park, 120
Psshing. *See* Squeaking
Puffer, Northern, 164
Puffin:
    Atlantic, 230
    Common. *See* Puffin, Atlantic
Puma. *See* Lion, Mountain
Purple, Red-spotted (butterfly), 22,
    104
Pussytoes, Field, 20
Puttyroot, 29
Pygmy Forest, 152

Quakertown Marsh, 74
Queen Anne's Lace, 20, 22, 103,
    169, 179
Question Mark, 21

Rabbit. *See* Cottontail, Eastern
    Marsh. *See* Muskrat
    Snowshoe. *See* Hare, Snowshoe
Raccoon, 15, 66, 103, 136, 177,
    180, 207
Raccoon Ridge, 121
Racer, Northern Black, 19–20, 57,
    137, 177
Ragweed(s), 23
    Common, 169
    Great, 169
Ragwort, Small's, 31
Rail(s), 73
    Black, 76, 78
    Clapper, 162, 174, 206
    Virginia, 58, 63, 68
Rancocas State Park and Nature Cen-
    ter, xv, 42, 76
Raptor(s), 111, 112, 205, 207, 209.
    See also Eagle(s); Falcon(s); Har-
    rier; Hawk(s); Osprey
Raritan Canal, 41
Raspberry(ies), 28
Rat(s), 177
    Marsh Rice, 180
    Norway, 180, 207

Rattlesnake, Timber, 104–5, 137
Ray(s), 162
Razorbill, 229
Reading Prong, xiii
Redpoll, Common, 101
Redroot, 130
Red-spotted Purple. *See* Purple, Red-spotted (butterfly)
Redstart, American, 14, 95, 96, 98, 137, 167
Reeves Bogs, 152
Rhododendron:
    Great. *See* Rhododendron, Native
    Native, 90, 97–98, 108
    relationship with Eastern Hemlock, 90
    relationship with Red Maple, 108
    Rosebay. *See* Rhododendron, Native
Rice, Wild, 51–52, 65–66, 68, 76
Ricketts Glen State Park Natural Area, 120
Ridge and Valley (Physiographic Province), xiii, 83–84, 85, 86, 118. *See also* Mountain(s), Kittatinny Ridge
Ridley Creek State Park, xii, 4–24, 33, 34, 40
    Colonial Pennsylvania Plantation, 6, 30
    Headquarters. *See* Ridley Creek State Park, Jeffords' Hunting Hill Mansion
    Jeffords' Hunting Hill Mansion, 6, 34
    Picnic area 16, 21
    Picnic area 17, 17, 18, 19, 21, 34
    Ridley Creek, 6, 7, 9, 10, 14, 15, 22, 23–24
    Ridley Creek Historic District, 7–8
    Sycamore Mills, 7
    Youth Hostel, 24
Ring Island, 176–77, 209
Roach, Wood, 102
Robin, American, 14, 27
Rock Cress(es), 91
    Lyre-leaved, 31

Rock plant community, 101–2, 110
Rockford Park, 45
Rockweed, 175
Roebling Memorial Park. *See* Trenton Marsh
Rose, Multiflora, 17, 28, 32
Route 9 (Delaware), 189–90
Ruff, 76
Rush(es), 56, 132, 204
    Path, 133
Rutgers University Marine Field Station. *See* Tuckerton Meadows

St. Johnswort:
    Canadian, 144
    Common, 23, 132, 144
    Coppery, 132
Salamander(s), 100
    Four-toed, 100
    Lead-backed. *See* Salamander, Red-backed
    Marbled, 100
    Northern Dusky, 15, 32
    Northern Red, 15, 100
    Northern Two-lined, 15, 100
    Red-backed, 14, 100
    Spotted, 14, 100
    Spring, 100
Salt Hay, 160, 171, 187, 204
Salt-water habitats (other), 157, 159, 160–61, 162, 164, 169, 175, 176, 177, 181, 188, 194, 196, 205, 206, 207, 213–14, 215, 237. *See also individual bays, estuaries, inlets, tidal creeks, etc.*
Salt-water marsh(es), xi, xii, 42, 43, 74, 75, 76, 77, 78, 79, 150, 157–91, 194, 206, 208, 213, 216
    dredge spoil island(s), 161
    factors affecting vegetation, 159, 161, 170, 171, 173–74
    formation, 159, 195
    function, 160
    salt panne, 170, 171, 173, 174, 175, 177; formation, 173
Saltwort(s). *See* Glasswort
Samphire. *See* Glasswort, Dwarf
Sand dune(s), 75, 194, 199, 201,

202, 203, 204, 206, 207–8, 214, 215, 237
formation, 202, 204
Sanderling, 198
Sandmyrtle, 131
Sandpiper(s), 164, 166, 176, 181
Least, 62, 68, 166
Pectoral, 68, 166
Purple, 198
Semipalmated, 68, 166, 198
Solitary, 62, 68
Spotted, 166
Stilt, 166
Western, 166
White-rumped, 166
Sandwort:
Pine-barren, 130, 131, 134, 142, 143
Seaside, 201, 203
Saprophyte, 13–14
Sassafras, 88, 133, 143
Satyr, Little Wood, 22
Scallop(s), 199, 225, 231
Scaup:
Greater, 64, 205
Lesser, 64
Schuylkill River (Valley), 38, 40, 55
Schuylkill Valley Nature Center, xv, 40
Scoter(s), 206
Sea Lettuce, 176
Sea Robin:
Common. *See* Sea Robin, Northern
Northern, 164
Sea-blite, 171
Seahorse, Lined, 162–63
Sea-lavender, 171, 204
Sea-rocket, 201, 203
Sedge(s), 56, 108, 132
Tussock, 131
Seed dispersal, 9, 21, 22, 28
Serpentine Barrens, 30–31, 39
Seven Mile Beach, 159, 182, 194, 195, 196, 208, 210
Shad, Gizzard, 60
Shale Barrens, 91
Shark(s), 162, 232

Basking, 232
Dogfish, 162
Hammerhead, 232
Sand. *See* Shark, Dogfish
Shark River Inlet, 213–14
Shawangunk Conglomerate, 85, 86
Shearwater(s), 226, 227
Audubon's, 227–28
Cory's, 227
flight characteristics, 226. *See also individual species*
Greater, 226
Manx, 227–28
Sooty, 226–27
Shohola Waterfowl Management Area. *See* Pennsylvania State Game Land no. 180
Shorebird(s), 51, 52, 60, 62, 64, 68, 69, 74, 76, 78, 164, 166, 168, 188, 198, 205, 206–7, 214
Shoveler, Northern, 64
Shrew(s), 180
Short-tailed, 110
Silver-rod, 31, 111
Silverside:
Atlantic, 164
Common. *See* Silverside, Atlantic
Siskin, Pine, 101
Skate(s), 199
Skimmer, Black (bird), 177, 198, 199, 205, 206
feeding habits, 205
nesting habits, 177, 199, 205–6
Skimmer, White-tailed (dragonfly), 98
Skink:
Five-lined, 138
Ground, 138
Skippack Creek, 38
Skipper(s), 22, 139
Broad-winged, 179
Salt Marsh, 179
Skua:
Great, 228
South Polar, 228
Skunk, Striped, 15, 19, 177, 180
Slipper Shell(s), 176
Smartweed(s), 65

Smedley Park, 40
Snail(s). *See* Mollusk(s)
  Mud, 174–75, 176
  Salt Marsh, 171
"Snail Fur," 174–75
Snake(s), 19, 51, 105, 177, 208
  Corn, 137
  DeKay's. *See* Snake, Northern
    Brown
  Eastern Garter, 14, 19, 57, 68
  Eastern Hognose, 207
  Eastern Milk, 19
  Eastern Ribbon, 57, 100
  Northern Brown, 15, 57
  Northern Pine, 137
  Northern Ringneck, 15
  Northern Water, 9, 57, 68, 100,
    137, 177
  Scarlet, 137
Snakeroot, White, 96
  adverse effects, 96
Snapdragon family, 22
Solomon's-seal, 13, 24
  False, 13, 24, 110
  "true." *See* Solomon's-seal
Solomon's Plume. *See* Solomon's-
  seal, False
Songbird(s), 10, 14, 28, 58, 68,
  105–6, 167, 208
Sora, 58, 63, 68
Sorrel:
  Common. *See* Sorrel, Sheep
  Sheep, 110
Sparrow(s), 27, 52, 168
  Chipping, 19, 105, 137
  Field, 19
  Savannah, 168
  Seaside, 168
  Sharp-tailed, 168
  Song, 19, 55, 168, 206
  Swamp, 56, 168
Spatterdock, 62, 65, 66, 67
Sphagnum Moss–Black Spruce–
  Tamarack bog(s), 87, 119, 120,
  121
Sphagnum Moss swamp(s), 92,
  106–8, 110

Spicebush, 12, 21, 27, 88, 96
Spider, Beach, 203
Spleenwort:
  Ebony, 101, 110
  Maidenhair, 104
Spot, 60
Spring-beauty, 10, 13, 24
Spring Azure (butterfly), 139
Springfield Trail, 40
Spruce(s), 11, 95
Spurge(s), 203
  Seaside, 201
Squeaking, 19
Squirrel(s), 94
  Gray, 12, 94, 102, 136
  Northern Flying, 102
  Red, 9, 94, 102, 136
  Southern Flying, 102
Staggerbush, 130, 131, 133, 143
Starling, European, 54, 59, 60
Star-thistle. *See* Knapweed, Spotted
Stickleback:
  Fourspine, 164
  Threespine, 164
Stilt, Black-necked, 78
Stinkpot, 56
Stokes State Forest, 121
  Tillman Ravine, 121
Stone Harbor, 41, 150, 158, 159,
  181, 182–85, 188, 196, 207, 208,
  209, 210
Stone Harbor Bird Sanctuary, 159,
  180, 182, 185, 188, 208–9, 210,
  213
Stone Harbor Point, 182–85,
  194–208, 209, 210, 213
  dunes. *See* Sand Dune(s)
  Hereford Inlet, 159, 196, 205,
    207
  jetty. *See* Jetty(ies); Barrier beaches
    and islands, jetty effects
  "overwash." *See* Overwash
Storm-Petrel:
  Leach's, 230
  Wilson's, 224, 225–6, 230
Strawberry(ies), Wild, 103
Succession, 4, 17, 30, 49, 68, 87, 88,

91, 101, 152, 161
Clement's Model, 17
herbaceous phase, 18
mature (final) phase. *See* Climax
 community
pioneer phase. *See* Succession,
 woody phase
primary, 17, 101–2, 110–11, 208
secondary, 17, 18, 27–28
woody phase, 18
Successional fields, xi, xii, 4, 17–24,
 27–28, 32, 42, 50, 54, 64, 68, 73,
 75, 77, 120, 168, 188
"Sugar sand," 142
Sugarberry(ies). *See* Hackberry
Sulphur(s), 204
 Clouded. *See* Sulphur, Common
 Common, 20
 Orange, 104
Sumac(s), 91
 Shining. *See* Sumac, Winged
 Smooth, 17, 32
 Staghorn, 17, 88, 111
 Winged, 146, 168
Summersweet. *See* Pepperbush,
 Coast
Sundew(s), 121, 132
 Spatulate-leaved, 130, 144
 Thread-leaved, 130, 134
Sundrops, 31
Sunfish, 98
 Ocean, 232
 Pumpkinseed, 60
Sunfish Pond, 92, 121
Sunflower, Common, 9, 24
Susquehanna River, 99
Swallow(s), 64, 205
 Bank, 64
 Barn, 19, 64
 Cliff, 41, 64
 Northern Rough-winged, 64
 Tree, 19, 59, 64, 161, 168, 170,
 206
Swallowtail(s), 204
 Black, 9, 21, 104, 139
 Eastern Tiger, 9, 22, 104, 139
 Spicebush, 9, 21

Swamp Candles. *See* Loosestrife,
 Yellow
Sweetbells, Swamp, 131, 142, 143,
 144
Sweetfern, 146
Sweetgum, 10, 132
Swift, Chimney, 7
Swordfish, Common, 232
Sycamore, American, 7, 10
Symbiosis, 101

Talus slope(s), 91, 105
Tamarack, 88
Tanager, Scarlet, 14, 105, 167
Tannersville Cranberry Bog Preserve,
 92, 120–21
Taylor's Bridge. *See* Blackbird Creek
Tea, New Jersey, 31
Teal:
 Blue-winged, 52, 62, 64
 Green-winged, 62, 64
Termite(s), 103
Tern(s), 64, 65, 175, 177, 205, 207
 Arctic, 233
 Black, 65
 Bridled, 233
 Caspian, 65, 198
 Common, 65, 177, 198–99, 205,
 206
 Forster's, 65, 177
 Least, 177, 198–99, 205, 206
 Little. *See* Tern, Least
 nesting behavior, 177, 198–99,
 205–6
 Royal, 198
 Sooty, 233
Terrapin, Northern Diamondback,
 177–78, 180, 207
Theodore Roosevelt State Park. *See*
 Delaware Canal
Thimbleweed, 103
Thistle(s), 21, 22
 Bull, 21
 Canada, 21
 Russian, 201
 Star-. *See* Knapweed, Spotted
Thousand Acre Marsh, 78

Thrasher, Brown, 19, 136
Thrush(es), 14
   Wood, 14, 27, 105
Tick(s), xiv, 18, 139
Tilefish, 222
Timber-Beaver Swamp, 76–77
   Clint Millpond, 76–77
Tinicum National Environmental
   Center, 50–72
   boardwalk, 58, 59, 60
   canoe launch, 52, 54
   Darby Creek, 50, 52, 54, 56, 60,
      62, 63, 64, 65, 68
   dike (dike trail), 50, 54, 55, 56,
      58, 60, 62, 64, 65, 66, 67, 68,
      70; history and function, 54
   "horseshoe area," 62
   impoundment, 54, 55, 56, 58, 60,
      62, 66, 68
   incinerator (smokestack), 60
   observation blind(s), 50, 68
   observation platform, 64, 65
   sewage treatment plant, 60
   Tinicum Marsh Wildlife Preserve,
      55
   Visitor Center, 50, 52, 68, 69, 70
   water control structure(s), 54, 64
Titmouse, Tufted, 14, 94, 102, 136
Toad(s), 208
   American, 10, 14–15, 20, 25, 58,
      100
   Fowler's, 58, 178, 207
Toadfish, Oyster, 164
Toadflax. *See* Butter-and-eggs
Tobyhanna State Park, 121
Tocks Island Dam Project, 84
Toothwort, Cut-leaved, 10, 13
Tortoise Shell (butterfly):
   Compton, 21
   Milbert's, 21
Touch-me-not:
   Pale, 9, 68
   Spotted, 9, 68, 96
Towhee, Rufous-sided, 19, 27, 137
Transpiration, 11
Trawling, 162, 225
Treefrog, Pine Barrens, 138

Tree-of-Heaven. *See* Ailanthus
Trenton Marsh, 77
Trillium, Nodding, 29
Trout, 99
   Brook ("Brookie"), 100
   Brown, 100
   Rainbow, 100
   Sea. *See* Weakfish
Troy Meadows, 75–76
Trumpet-creeper, 7
Tuckahoe–Corbin City Tract. *See*
   Lester G. MacNamara Wildlife
   Management Area
Tuckerton Meadows, 188
Tuliptree, 12, 18, 22, 27, 28, 32,
   43–44, 88
Tupelo, Black. *See* Gum, Sour-
Turkey, Wild, 94, 108–9
Turnstone, Ruddy, 198
Turtle(s), 51, 56, 177
   Bog, 43, 75
   Eastern Box, 14, 56, 110, 138,
      207
   Eastern Mud, 56–57, 177
   Eastern Painted, 9, 56, 100, 138,
      177
   Midland Painted, 56
   Musk. *See* Stinkpot
   Red-bellied, 56, 57, 138
   Red-eared, 56
   sea, 232, 233. *See also* Atlantic
      Hawksbill; Atlantic Leather-
      back; Atlantic Loggerhead
   Snapping, 56, 68, 177
   Spotted, 56, 138
   Wood, 15, 56, 110
Turtlehead, 25
Tyler Arboretum, xv, 6, 15, 16, 24–
   34, 39
   azalea plantings, 24, 25
   Dismal Run Stream (Valley), 28,
      29–30, 31, 32
   Dismal Run Trail, 30
   dogwood plantings, 6, 24
   East Woods, 10, 32
   Education Center (barn), 6, 15,
      24, 25, 27, 29, 30, 31, 32, 34

Giant Sequoia, 6, 32
history, 6
holly plantings, 6
Indian Rock and its lore, 28
Lachford Hall, 6
Middle Farm, 27
Painter Brothers Trail, 15
Pinetum, 20, 32
Pink Hill, 30–31
Pink Hill Trail, 30–32
ponds, 25, 27
rhododendron collection, 6, 24, 25
Rocky Run Stream, 16, 25, 28
Rocky Run Trail, 25, 28
Serpentine Barren. *See* Serpentine Barrens
Valley Cottage, 30
Tyler State Park, 40

U.S. Army Corps of Engineers, 161
U.S. Environmental Protection Service, 161
U.S. Fish and Wildlife Service, 50, 55, 161
National Wildlife Refuge Systems, 50, 74
University of Delaware Marine Studies Complex, 189
Urner Club (northern New Jersey), 222, 233

Valley Forge National Historic Park, 37, 40
Veery, 14, 27
Vervain, White, 110
Viburnum, Mapleleaf, 12, 27, 88, 102
Viceroy, 22
Violet(s), 29, 106
Common Blue, 13, 20, 22, 24
Lance-leaved, 132
Northern Downy, 31
Round-leaved Yellow, 31
Smooth Yellow, 13, 24
Vireo(s), 7, 96
Red-eyed, 14, 96

Solitary, 96
Warbling, 96
White-eyed, 27, 96
Yellow-throated, 96
Vole, Eastern Meadow, 19, 180
Vulture, Turkey, 109

Wading River, 153
Wallpack Valley Environmental Education Center, 84
Walnut, Black, 7, 10
Walter S. Carpenter, Jr. State Park, 45
Warbler(s), 7, 18, 51, 52, 54, 94, 96, 119, 167, 205, 206
Bay-breasted, 95
Black-and-white, 14, 95, 105, 137, 167
Blackburnian, 95
Black-throated Blue, 95, 98
Black-throated Green, 95
Blue-winged, 19, 95
Canada, 95, 98
Cape May, 95
Cerulean, 7, 41
Chestnut-sided, 95, 167
Connecticut, 95
Golden-winged, 95
Hooded, 137
Kentucky, 14
Magnolia, 95
Myrtle. *See* Warbler, Yellow-rumped
Nashville, 95
Orange-crowned, 94
Pine, 39, 136–37
Prairie, 19, 137
Prothonotary, 39, 41, 42, 137
Tennessee, 94
Worm-eating, 16, 39, 95
Yellow, 9, 55, 95, 96, 98, 167
Yellow-rumped, 52, 94, 167, 168, 206
Yellow-throated, 39, 41
Washington Crossing Historic Park (Pennsylvania), 37, 38, 40

Washington Crossing State Park (New Jersey), 43
Wasp(s), 23, 65, 139
  Digger, 203
  Polistes, 23
Waterfowl, 51, 52, 56, 62, 64, 66, 68, 74, 78, 205, 206, 214, 215, 237
Waterleaf, Virginia, 96
Waterthrush:
  Louisiana, 27
  Northern, 95
Waxmyrtle berries, 52. *See also* Bayberry, Northern
Waxwing, Cedar, 9
Weakfish, 198, 207
Weasel, Long-tailed, 19, 55, 177, 180
Weevil:
  Acorn, 94
  Boll, 94
Wells, Malcolm, 158
Wetlands Institute, 42, 158–82, 185, 209, 210, 213, 239
  museum, 158, 162, 182, 210
  nature trail (roadbed), 162, 164, 167, 168, 169, 170, 171, 177, 182, 210
  observation tower, 158, 159, 160, 161, 162, 171, 182, 210
  Osprey nesting platform (trail marker 4), 169, 170
  pumphouse, 175
  research laboratories (with Lehigh University), 159, 175
  Scotch Bonnet Creek, 161, 162, 164, 169, 170, 175, 176
  Tidepool Shop (bookstore), 158, 164, 180
Whale(s), 228, 231
  "blow," 228
  Blue, 228, 231
  Fin. *See* Finback
  Hump-backed, 231
  Minke, 231
  Pilot, 229
  Right, 230–31; hunting history, 230–31
  Sei, 231
Whale Beach, 215. *See also* Corson's Inlet State Park
Wharton, Joseph, 126, 151
Wharton State Forest, 126–51, 153, 214
  Batona Camp Site, 136, 138
  Caranza Memorial, 136
  Ranger's station and Visitor Center, 136, 140, 146, 149, 153. *See also* Batsto Village
Wharton Tract. *See* Wharton State Forest
Whelk(s), 199
Whimbrel, 174
Whip-poor-will, 39, 137
White Clay Creek Valley, 45
Whitesbog, 152
Whiting, 232
Wigeon, American, 64
Wild Creek Reservoir, 118
Wildlife Management Areas, 74, 185
Willet, 168
Willow(s), 54, 55, 56, 62
  Black, 9, 10, 22, 55
  Sandbar, 55
Winterberry, Mountain, 108
Wintergreen, 133
  Spotted, 13
Winterthur Museum and Gardens, 45
Wissahickon Creek (Valley), 40–41
Witch-hazel, 12, 27, 28, 88, 103
Wolf, Gray, 111
Wood Nymph, Common, 22
Woodchuck, 19
Woodcock, American, 19, 68, 108–9
Woodland Beach Wildlife Area, 78–79, 190
  Taylor's Gut (impoundment and sluice), 78–79, 190
Woodpecker:
  Downey, 14, 23, 94, 102, 136

Hairy, 14, 102
Pileated, 102
Red-bellied, 14
Red-headed, 41
Wood-Pewee, Eastern, 14, 136
World Wildlife Fund, 158
Worm:
flat, 176
Plumed, 176. *See also* Worm, tube-dwelling
polychaete, 176
tube-dwelling, 176
Wormwood(s), 203
Worthington State Park, 121
"Wrack," 171, 176–77
Wren:
Carolina, 14
House, 19

Long-billed Marsh. *See* Wren, Marsh
Marsh, 62, 63, 66, 206; nesting behavior, 66
Sedge, 78
Short-billed Marsh. *See* Wren, Sedge

Yarding, 108. *See also* Deer, White-tailed
Yarrow, 21, 28, 169, 179
Yellowlegs:
Greater, 60, 62, 68, 164–66
Lesser, 60, 62, 68, 164–66
Yellow-poplar. *See* Tuliptree
Yellowthroat, Common, 18–19, 27, 55, 95, 137, 206

Design and maps by Liz Waite.

Composition by Eastern Graphics
in Merganthaler Linotron 202 Galliard.

Printing by the Maple-Vail Book Manufacturing Group
on Gladfelter Antique Cream.

Binding by Maple-Vail in Roxite B-53544 Linen Finish,
stamped in black foil.

Cover by Keith Press.